SAILING UPWIND

Praise for *Sailing Upwind*

"From TopGun to the top of military leadership, Admiral Sandy Winnefeld sailed to record heights of achievement—even for a Georgia Tech Yellow Jacket. Sandy gives us front-row insights into the critical thinking and innovative actions required to move a system slow to change in a different and positive direction. Much more than a memoir of Sandy's remarkable career, *Sailing Upwind* provides a valuable guide to living an inspirational life and providing impactful leadership."

—**Sam Nunn,** former U.S. Senator and Chair of
the Senate Armed Services Committee

"A vibrant exposition on leadership, risk, and innovation by an extraordinarily talented professional, interspaced with great sea stories! Highly recommended!"

—**Robert Work,** Former Deputy Secretary of Defense

"Sandy has not only written a really good book chock full of gripping stories of serving at every level in the military . . . he managed to weave into it an incredibly useful framework for understanding leadership, creativity, and problem solving. Any aspiring leader will benefit from picking it up . . . and I guarantee they won't be able to put it down."

—**Tim McGraw,** country music singer and actor

"Leadership, innovation, problem solving, and human connection make up the foundation of any successful profession, including the military, as I observed while traveling the world with Sandy on a USO tour. In *Sailing Upwind*, his engaging and unique voice captures the essence of a remarkable life and career."

—**Andrew Luck,** former National Football League quarterback

SAILING UPWIND

Leadership and Risk from TopGun to the Situation Room

Admiral Sandy Winnefeld

Naval Institute Press
Annapolis, Maryland

Naval Institute Press
291 Wood Road
Annapolis, MD 21402

Library of Congress Cataloging-in-Publication Data

Names: Winnefeld, James A., Jr., author.

Title: Sailing upwind : leadership, risk, and innovation from Topgun to the situation room / Adm. James A. Winnefeld Jr.

Description: Annapolis, Maryland : Naval Institute Press, [2023] | Includes index.

Identifiers: LCCN 2022044352 (print) | LCCN 2022044353 (ebook) | ISBN 9781682478745 (hardcover) | ISBN 9781682478905 (ebook)

Subjects: LCSH: Winnefeld, James A., Jr. | Admirals—United States—Biography. | Leadership. | United States. Navy—Officers—Biography. | BISAC: BIOGRAPHY & AUTOBIOGRAPHY / Military | BIOGRAPHY & AUTOBIOGRAPHY / Historical

Classification: LCC V63.W56 A3 2023 (print) | LCC V63.W56 (ebook) | DDC 359.0092 [B]—dc23/eng/20221123

LC record available at https://lccn.loc.gov/2022044352

LC ebook record available at https://lccn.loc.gov/2022044353

♾ Print editions meet the requirements of ANSI/NISO z39.48-1992 (Permanence of Paper).

Printed in the United States of America.

31 30 29 28 27 26 25 24 23   9 8 7 6 5 4 3 2 1

First printing

Contents

Preface

Why I Wrote *Sailing Upwind*

Racing a sailboat requires, among other things, steering it as closely as possible to the wind while not spilling the power generated by the sails and while remaining alert for shifts in wind direction and speed. Doing so accomplishes the counterintuitive feat of driving a machine against the direction of a prevailing energy field—namely, the wind.

As such, the title *Sailing Upwind* reflects my approach to my life's work: pushing as closely as possible to the edge of risk while remaining firmly under control and alert to change. I wrote this book because I wanted to pass along what I've learned about problem solving, risk management, and, above all, leadership through the lens of the diverse and exciting career through which I was privileged to sail.

Serving for thirty-seven years in the U.S. Navy—including nine extended overseas deployments—exposed me to the full spectrum of military operations and offered plenty of exposure to risks, both physical and mental. The journey began by operating some of the world-class equipment our nation provides to its military. It progressed into leading the young people who employ that equipment. It culminated by providing advice to the highest levels of government regarding whether and where force should be used at all.

My service overlapped diverse security issues across several generations, including the Cold War confrontation with the Soviet Union, conflicts with Iran and Iraq in the 1980s and '90s, the post-9/11 wars in Iraq and Afghanistan, and the globe's descent into a post-unipolar era of populism, nationalism, and counterglobalism. In jobs as diverse as instructing at the Navy Fighter Weapons School, or TopGun, commanding the nuclear-powered aircraft carrier *Enterprise*, and serving as the vice chairman of the Joint Chiefs of Staff, I enjoyed a front-row seat to some of the most important events and decisions of our times. I often felt like a juxtaposition of Winston Groom's character Forest Gump and Herman Wouk's Pug Henry.

But there's more to this book than simply telling my story. Somehow along the way, and probably from a slow start, I began to think critically, "sailing upwind" inside a system that can be reluctant to change. Time after time I enjoyed the adrenaline rush of helping push some long-standing process in a different and positive direction. In addition to the people with whom I was privileged to serve, this was the most fun part of my career. It was every bit as exhilarating as operating our nation's most complex fighting machines to the edges of their capability.

My late father, retired rear admiral Jim Winnefeld, picked up on this, telling me in an e-mail just a few months before he passed away that "the common characteristics of [your career] are problem-solving in a rigid institutional environment, and more recently in a fluid political environment. You need to collect your professional growth materials and interpret them in a lifelong context. This is not an ego trip. It is how you teach a new generation of problem solvers."

I was also blessed along the way to learn about leadership from extraordinary people. It quickly became apparent that leadership discriminates among excellent, mediocre, and failing organizations. It's true of every other profession, including the military, business, sports, and medicine. I always tried to figure out how good leaders perform well and why poor leaders come up short.

Few organizations other than the military devote many resources to developing the people who will one day be their leaders. There is no easy way—no single sound bite—that will magically transform someone into a virtuoso leader. Instead, it is a lifelong journey demanding three types of constant effort. First is personal study of leadership itself and of historical leaders, which implies lots of reading. Second is close, thoughtful, and critical observation of the leaders in one's own life. Third is the priceless experience gained in the crucible of one's leadership failures and successes. I know I'm not there yet, but I keep trying.

All of this is easier to learn when one has in mind a sound framework on which to attach accumulated knowledge. Based on personal study, observation, and experience at each (sometimes painful) step on my journey, I aligned my beliefs around five anchors, each of which has four essential links. They are pretty straightforward, but everything I continue to learn about leadership fits somewhere inside that framework. I very briefly describe these anchors and their links, along with a few quotes pertaining to each, in separate sections nestled between several chapters. These anchors have been helpful as I've evaluated my own performance and that of my subordinates, and perhaps they'll whet the reader's appetite to learn more.

That is why I wrote *Sailing Upwind*. I hope I've been able to pull it all off with humility and that the reader will find it both entertaining and valuable.

Finally, I'm grateful to the Naval Institute Press for granting an exception to conventional editing practices and permitting capitalization of the word "Sailor" when I refer to someone serving in the Navy. We do this for Marines, and it should be done for all men and women who serve our nation.

Sailing upwind with my sister, Lea, at the age of thirteen on an Olympic-class Flying Dutchman on San Diego Bay. *Winnefeld collection*

Foundations

True to an old saw, "I was born in a Navy hospital while my daddy was at sea." Thus, my entry into the military profession started via a fairly conventional route. Growing up in a Navy family, I experienced all the things military kids do: plenty of moves, long absences of a deployed parent, the challenge of always being the new kid in school, and the benefits of meeting lots of people and seeing many different places.

Even though I'm the great-grandson of an immigrant Prussian cavalryman, the sea service is in my blood. My grandfather was a rebellious youth who eloped in 1927 with the already-engaged daughter of a wealthy businessman. After they were married he served as a Navy enlisted man in World War II, including arduous duty as a mechanic on board a submarine tender in beautiful Perth, Australia. Perhaps some of my rebellious instincts are inherited from him.

My grandparents' tumultuous marriage only lasted long enough to produce two sons. My dad, James Alexander Winnefeld, born on the first day of 1929, was their eldest. As a teenager, he was inspired by a visit to a Navy destroyer and tales of submarine warfare during World War II. After a year at Drew University, he attended the Naval Academy to escape a turbulent post-divorce upbringing. He avoided inheriting his father's nature and was a rock of stability the entire time I knew him. He would later label the academy his surrogate parents. He eventually served as its commandant and loved the institution with all his heart until he died on Thanksgiving Day in 2015.

My mother, Fredda Mae Coupland Winnefeld, was the talented homecoming queen from the then-sleepy little town of Wildwood, a railroad crossroads in the central part of Florida. My dad managed a blind date with one of her roommates at Stetson University. When my mom saw him walking up the sidewalk wearing his Naval Academy midshipman's uniform, she told herself she would "someday marry that man." Somehow they met, and he fell for her.

My father, who was the "Color Company" commander during the spring of his senior year, selected her as the Class of 1951's "Color Girl." They kissed under all of the flags at the Naval Academy's final parade during graduation week. I have a wonderful photo of an iconic embrace between a beautiful southern girl in a white dress and floppy hat with long ribbons and a dashing young man in uniform. It was an event I would revisit in a moving way toward the end of my career. My parents were married less than a year after he graduated.

My dad wanted to be a submariner while he attended the academy but began his Navy career on board the old destroyer USS *Halsey Powell*. During the Korean War he directed naval gunfire from a motor whaleboat behind a hilly peninsula out of sight of his ship. Fired upon by the North Korean troops they were bombarding, he used the American flag in its most sacred role: placing a tourniquet on a wounded Sailor's leg.

He eventually attended flight school and ended up hunting submarines instead of driving them, flying the TBM Avenger and S-2 Tracker. He wanted to fly fighters but was the victim of bad timing during the week he received his Navy wings of gold. It is a testament to his talent and professionalism that he was one of the first officers in his naval aviation community to achieve flag rank. He retired as a two-star admiral. His enduring gifts to me—something both his and my contemporaries have often mentioned—were his towering example of integrity and his belief in service.

I was born in Coronado, California. When I was five years old my family moved to Naples, Italy, where my dad served as an admiral's aide. We lived in a small villa bathed in the fragrance of wisteria vines on a leafy hill called the Posillipo. With no American neighbors and my older sister, Lea, at school all day, there was not much to keep me occupied as a kid other than building mud models of the Neapolitan volcano Vesuvius, spewing its purple lava made of baking soda and vinegar mixed with red and blue food coloring.

Walter Isaacson points out how Jennifer Doudna, the pioneering researcher at the heart of his book *The Code Breaker*, resembles other creative people who grew up somewhat alienated from their surroundings. I believe my experience of being fairly disconnected from other kids at the critical ages of five and six years old, among other influences, profoundly shaped my willingness to be creative and think for myself.

To help fill my time, my mother gave her enduring gift: teaching me to read even before I entered kindergarten, a head start that helped immeasurably in my life and career. I'll never forget my first book: *Now We Are Six* (even though I was only five years old), by A. A. Milne, the creator of Winnie-the-Pooh. I eventually demanded to go to the NATO kindergarten in Naples, ending up in a classroom in the same building where one of my later commands, Striking and Support Forces NATO, would be located decades later. The steps up to the entrance of that building were much less intimidating as a grownup than they were as a child on my first-ever day of school.

After several more moves our family moved back to Coronado from Virginia at the end of my fifth-grade year—another disruption. I was immediately given a reading speed and comprehension test and achieved the highest score the teachers could remember. It would be convenient to think it was due to my mom teaching me to read at a young age. But it had more to do with the fact that the test was about the story of John Smith and Pocahontas, which I didn't even need to read due to my elementary school Virginia history education! I was lucky rather than good.

My physical progress arrived later, inspired by Mr. Bob Stites, my sixth-grade teacher at Crown Elementary School in Coronado, California. Stites was a short, wiry Texan who was tough as nails and ended up as the mayor of the city of Imperial Beach, on the border with Mexico. Every kid wanted to be in his class in sixth grade.

Unlike most elementary school teachers of the time, Stites forced us all into a physical fitness regimen rather than sending us out on the playground at recess and forgetting about us for an hour. He gave us all a physical fitness test and, based on the results, placed us in four "squads": Gold, Silver, Bronze, and Lead. To my profound embarrassment, I barely made the Silver Squad on my first try. Determined from that moment not to accept less than the Gold Squad, I gradually worked my way up against some pretty healthy California kids and vowed to stay in halfway decent shape for the rest of my life.

Learning to sail—and race against other kids—in small boats while living in Coronado paid dividends in many ways for me later as a naval officer. Being alone in a boat during a race on a cold and windy day, and managing to right it unaided after capsizing it, developed toughness and self-reliance. Handling a small boat developed fine instincts for the effects of wind, current, and tide that were priceless when I later commanded two ships. Managing the rigging required to make a boat sail faster than others was an excellent introductory lesson into mechanics. Making split-second tactical decisions to gain an edge over capable adversaries served me well in training for one-versus-one and many-versus-many fighter combat engagements. Finally, knowing the "rules of the game" of racing sailboats and how to exploit them to one's advantage during a race was helpful in many later bureaucratic battles.

But learning that—once equipped with a combination of knowledge and technology—one can successfully move a machine against the direction of a prevailing force was perhaps the most important lesson, thus the name for this book. And having the responsibility for launching, racing, and recovering an Olympic class Flying Dutchman at my local Navy Sailing Center at thirteen years old taught me about handling something much bigger than myself.

I believe that the character trait of challenging assumptions is not something that comes naturally; rather, it has to be learned. In that regard, my exposure to my father's brother, Carl Builder, was vital to my personal development. Carl dropped out of the Naval Academy after his second year because he felt he lacked the freedom to pursue his technical dreams. He went to UCLA and ended up as a rocket scientist and eventually a stalwart analyst at RAND Corporation. He and I had many conversations while I was in junior high school, and well beyond, that inspired me to consistently ask "why?" and "why not?" later in life rather than going with the flow.

Like many kids, I observed my father as he progressed through his career. It began while we lived near North Island Naval Air Station in Coronado, California. I was especially attracted as a young person to the glamour of Navy carrier aviation in World War II, which, viewed from the vantage point of the late 1960s, was not that far in the past. Hanging around the old buildings on that base, watching aircraft carriers getting under way, and seeing the propeller-driven aircraft flown by my dad evoked naval aviation history during the war. Through the distance of time, I could sense the then-newness of flying airplanes off ships, the clatter of piston engine–driven fighters, the heroism displayed in numerous battles, and the sunny, tropical romanticism of the Pacific.

Immediately after I was elected the president of my eighth-grade class in Coronado, my dad informed me he was being transferred to the Pentagon. I would once again be the isolated new kid, this time in Northern Virginia. I spent a lot of time at the console of a time-shared computer Fort Hunt High School installed in a closet—at about the same time Bill Gates was doing it in California. I didn't do nearly as well as he did, but working with the computer taught me lessons in the techniques and discipline of programming that were useful later on. I also convinced my parents to buy a Heathkit amplifier and radio tuner, which I built in my high school electronics class. It was a fascinating project that instilled a useful curiosity for electronics. These things, and playing football, were my primary interests.

Despite my attraction to naval aviation, when the Naval Academy accepted me, I turned it down in favor of a Navy Reserve Officers Training Corps scholarship to Georgia Tech. Like my grandfather, I was a bit of a rebel in high school. I studied hard in the courses, mainly mathematics and English, with exceptional teachers, but I hardly cared about the others. I really wanted to attend an Outward Bound course in Colorado and explore the western United States. I wasn't ready to fully commit to the U.S. Navy, partly because I resented the fact that my father was deployed during so much of my childhood.

I also knew that if I started the Naval Academy, I would never quit due to the embarrassment it would cause my father, and I didn't want to be stuck with unhappiness over my choice. Moreover, while I admired my father deeply, something told me that entering his profession should be done on my terms, on a different path, making my own way. NROTC seemed like a convenient middle ground: if I didn't like it, I could quit without feeling guilty.

Meanwhile, despite my average high school grades, I performed well enough on the PSATs and SATs to be selected as a National Merit Finalist. As such, I was one of the recipients of a letter Georgia Tech sent out each year to every finalist in the country. It was the only recruiting letter I received in an era when colleges didn't spend the same amount on marketing as they do today. Intrigued, I flew to Atlanta for a visit on a beautiful spring day.

Tech seemed like a great place to study, and it looked like a fun place to live, although I couldn't at the time understand why so many cars wore bumper stickers stating "To Hell With Georgia." Only later did I learn that the University of Georgia was Georgia Tech's archrival. So I accepted their offer of admission. The only thing I needed to give up in land-locked Atlanta was a promising opportunity to race sailboats in college.

Georgia Tech was a great choice. I received a fantastic aerospace engineering education, including the technical and problem-solving ability I use today. Tech's rowdy, irreverent, take-no-prisoners approach to engineering has served me well. In the mid-1970s, when ROTC was not exactly popular on most college campuses in the aftermath of the Vietnam War, it was no problem in relatively conservative Atlanta.

But I also love the Naval Academy and have always felt I couldn't have gone wrong at either institution. Indeed, of all the reasons people cite for having service academies, including "traditions" and the like, the one most people miss is their extraordinary value in attracting a diverse, well-rounded, and bright mass of young people into the military who would probably not otherwise join. I'm proud to have served on both the Georgia Tech Advisory Board and the Naval Academy Board of Visitors.

Our family moved from Washington, DC, to Virginia Beach the summer before I started college, when my dad took command of the amphibious ship USS *Trenton* (which would hold a bit of a twist later in my life). Nearby

Naval Air Station Oceana was the East Coast home of the brand-new F-14 Tomcat fighter.

I worked two jobs that summer, at a restaurant at night and as a carpenter by day. In the latter role, spending my days out in the open air, I could see these sexy-looking jets from a distance, flying gracefully around the landing pattern. So I demanded that my father take me to see one up close. It looked like it was going a thousand miles an hour just sitting in the hangar. For someone who didn't want to work at a desk and who loved taking risks, this was sheer adrenaline and love at first sight. I knew that day exactly what I wanted to do with any time I spent in the Navy.

Having the goal of becoming an aviator entrenched in my mind made it a lot easier to recover from a first quarter of burning the candle disproportionately at the wrong end with my newfound friends at Georgia Tech. Having something in mind that might be lost set me straight, and I studied harder after that.

While at Georgia Tech, I also took advantage of a Navy program that provided flying lessons to midshipmen as a cost-saving measure to weed out those not suited for naval aviation. As my first exposure to the other military branches' culture, I was also privileged to attend the Army's Airborne School in the sweltering summer heat at Fort Benning, Georgia. In both cases being in the air was not a problem for me—I loved it.

While a midshipman at Georgia Tech, I made my first attempt at writing for a real publication, the U.S. Naval Institute's *Proceedings* magazine. "NROTC Recruiting—Worm's Eye View of the Apple" was a modest effort as far as writing goes. Still, it was precious to my learning process as a thinker and a writer. I applaud the Naval Institute to this day for their tolerance of and willingness to help young authors. I came to understand that it is possible to think well but not write well, but that it is impossible to write well and not think well. Of course, it didn't hurt that a superb young editor named Fred Rainbow, with whom I remain friends to this day, helped tidy the article up.

I did much better academically in college than in high school in the end. When it came to "service selection," I was petrified that my reasonably good grades in Aerospace Engineering could result in my being drafted into the nuclear submarine community, which at the time was having trouble recruiting talent. It wasn't that I didn't want to be a submariner—it was actually intriguing, especially during the Cold War. Rather, I was far more motivated to fly aircraft off aircraft carriers. Luckily, I was selected for naval aviation.

Somehow, I "got out"—the Georgia Tech colloquial term for graduating—with the class of 1978 and earned a commission as an ensign in the U.S. Navy. My father, who was still on active duty at the time, spoke at my commissioning ceremony. His speech was titled "Newton's Three Laws of Leadership," a clever riff on Newtonian physics' laws of motion. He suggested that, in life as in the First Law, a body at rest will stay at rest, and a body in motion will remain in motion unless acted upon by some outside force. He carried the analogy further using Newton's other two laws. It was my first exposure to the notion of adding a special touch to any attempt at public speaking—something I have always endeavored to do. It was also an inspiration to never be in a position to be acted on by an outside force!

The morning after graduation, my hangover and I drove away from Georgia Tech. A bale of hay rode atop the ugly little olive-green Pinto station wagon my dad bought for me my senior year. The hay was left by my fraternity brothers, who tended to spend all-nighters cramming for exams, and to whom I always quoted my high school football coach's Thursday night speech: "The hay is in the barn; there's nothing more you can do."

The naval aviation training enterprise couldn't digest every graduating ensign at once in the early summer. After six months of arduous duty coaching sailing at the Naval Academy, young Ensign Sandy Winnefeld arrived in Pensacola, Florida, ready to trace the footsteps of the characters in naval aviation who preceded him.

TOP Flying a TA-4J Skyhawk in advanced jet training. *Winnefeld collection*

BOTTOM With RIO Lt. Cdr. Larry "Flash" Gordon (*left*) during carrier qualifications in the Tomcat. *Winnefeld collection*

Learning to Fly

The first task for any aspiring naval aviator is to complete ground school at Naval Air Station Pensacola. I thought it would be difficult. After all, the place produces the best pilots in the world. But it turned out to be pretty user-friendly due to the aerospace engineering education I received in Atlanta. I also quickly learned why physical examinations are the bane of any naval aviator; a single doctor or technician can end the entire process. While my distant vision was above average, I worried about astigmatism in one of my eyes (probably due to four years of college) and barely passed that part of the test. After that, some academics, a tough-but-do-able swimming syllabus, and some survival training filled out the course.

One of the first things I noticed after arriving on the base was a large group of Iranian student pilots. Because the Shah of Iran had purchased dozens of F-14s, they were attending the same curriculum we were, although their classes met separately. In my youthful foolishness, I swiped an Iranian Air Force officer's hat from the Pensacola Officer's Club. I still recall the name on the cap: Mehdi Bayat. Any guilt I felt about it at the time was erased as

I watched the revolution and the brutal hostage crisis that occurred, which reached its climax in early 1979 while I was still in Pensacola.

The revolution posed a real dilemma for those Iranian pilots, and I have no idea what happened to them or their families. I thought of them, including Mehdi, when I was older while reading V. S. Naipaul's *Among the Believers*. In one passage he writes that while waiting in an airliner on the ramp at Bandar Abbas airport, "we [watched] while American-made Phantoms of the Iranian Air Force took off. Later, I learned that two Phantoms had crashed, and the news was sickening: such trim and deadly aircraft, so vulnerable the inadequately trained men within." It would not be long before I would be face-to-face in the air with Iranian pilots—at least at a distance. Later, in a short story I wrote for *Proceedings* in 2020 named "Reunion," I used Bayat's name as a sympathetic Iranian pilot who escaped in a stolen Tomcat with an American pilot who was forced to eject from his F-14 and landed in Iran.

Once ground school was complete, the next step was primary flight training, which involved flying either the T-28 Trojan or the T-34 Turbo Mentor. The former was a big, old, radial-engine airplane that had a lot in common with World War II fighters other than its tricycle landing gear. It carried a reputation for being an absolute beast and a handful to fly. My father flew it when he was in flight training. On the other hand, the T-34 was a spiffy little turboprop that was easier to fly and thus more popular with student naval aviators, or SNAs, as we were known.

There was a large backlog between flight school's ground school and primary phases, so a couple of friends and I applied to attend the Navy's High Altitude/Low Opening parachute school, for which we were eligible, having earlier completed Army Airborne School. After all, there was only so much water skiing we could do on the bayous of Pensacola.

While on the way to parachute school in Lakehurst, New Jersey, I was delighted to receive a call asking whether I could start the following week in the T-28. I immediately said yes. Getting to fly the T-28—which resembled the World War II fighters I romanticized earlier in life—immediately rather than waiting to fly the T-34 was a win-win. After all, I'd be compared to other students flying the T-28, not those flying the T-34, so I wasn't worried about how hard the airplane was to fly. Others obviously made it through the T-28 program. So my disappointed friends and I turned around and drove back to Pensacola.

Flying the Trojan over the scrub palm-dotted rural Florida countryside and learning the basics of aerobatics, navigation, and handling a beefy radial-engine-powered airplane was pure joy, even as it was a strange and new environment. I'll never forget the sweet smell of 115/145 octane aviation fuel or one of my instructors urging me to land the airplane harder because "that's what carrier pilots do." Yes, it was intimidating, but was it ever cool!

My primary training included a few interesting moments, including a temporary engine failure in the landing pattern at Whiting Airfield, and nearly receiving a "down" due to a navigation error I made on one of my last flights before my solo check ride. Nonetheless, I made it through primary with good enough grades to be selected to fly jets.

Having been worried about hitting the same stretch of bad luck as my father many years earlier, I was elated to be selected for jets, along with several friends. It was one more leg on my ambition to fly the Tomcat. So I drove off to Kingsville, Texas, in the ugly Pinto for the next phases of my flight training, scavenging for gas in the middle of the night all along the way amid the oil crisis precipitated by none other than the Iranian revolution.

Flight school was my first real exposure to the importance of the three vital factors required to master any field—namely, natural ability, teaching, and motivation. In nearly any sport, or flying, the genuinely superior players are blessed with a potent combination of all three factors. But I also discovered that it's possible to do well with some measure of shortcoming in one. Quality instructors were a given. In my case, I possessed a modicum of natural situational awareness, eye–hand coordination, and good vision—but I knew many others who were better equipped. I knew I'd probably have to work harder than anyone else to do well, so that's what I did. As Samuel Goldwyn said, "The harder I work, the luckier I get." It's surprising how a little extra effort often makes an enormous difference, and doing so helped make up for most of my shortcomings.

The training was straightforward but continually increased in difficulty. Each of the latter two phases, known as intermediate and advanced training, involved landing an airplane—first a T-2 Buckeye and then a TA-4J

Skyhawk—on an aircraft carrier during the daytime. For most aspiring carrier pilots, this process is a one-shot deal because it takes a lot of expensive preparation to prepare for those first landings. That, plus the fact that most pilots either succeed the first time or not at all, means the program only rarely gives second chances.

The training for carrier qualification begins with the student performing day and night practice landings at an airfield, trying to put the airplane down in a simulated carrier landing, known as the "box," on the runway. The practice airfield is equipped with the type of special "lens" used at the carrier to assist pilots in landing in the small area on the flight deck required to catch an arresting gear cable. Each landing is graded and debriefed by instructors qualified as landing signal officers, or LSOs. Even though students at this stage only land on the carrier during the daytime, there is plenty of practice at night, with the box lit up and the rest of the runway lights extinguished to reduce depth perception.

If the LSOs feel a student is ready for "the boat" at the end of the field qualification period, the next step is to actually fly out solo to an aircraft carrier and attempt to qualify. That's right: even though one's first-ever landings on an aircraft carrier are done in a two-seat aircraft, they are always conducted alone. For one thing, there aren't enough instructors to have one in every student's back seat. But it also puts the onus of the landing entirely on the student. Nobody gets any help with the real thing. Nobody cares who you are when you're trying to land an airplane on a ship, and there is no bullshitting your way through it. When done successfully, it's a huge confidence-builder.

I don't even remember my first four landings in the Buckeye off the coast of Key West, which was required in the intermediate phase. It was over before I knew it. All I remember is a brief period of "hot refueling" aboard the ship, which was a great vantage point to view the dangerous but highly coordinated ballet of the flight deck. I was on a carrier flight deck—in the cockpit of an actual airplane, for heaven's sake—at sea!

It was a cacophony of activity: a whirl of windblown people in a rainbow of colored flotation gear and helmets (each color signifying a different job specialty), constant movement, the odor of jet fuel seeping into my cockpit, the crackle in my headset whenever the ship's radar swung by, the vibration and roar of airplanes landing and taking off right in front of me in an impossibly small space with so little tolerance for error, and the sheer exhilaration of having made it on board the ship. It's a special feeling I've never lost. It seemed so surreal—a breathtaking place reserved for a few people privileged to participate in such a unique human activity, including the hard-working flight deck crew. To this day, I've never gotten tired of watching it, and I wish every American could.

It was even more surreal because, for some reason, the Navy found it necessary to have a couple of Tomcats flying combat air patrol overhead while we did our landings just north of Cuba. We students were utterly intimidated by the sight of these fleet aircrews in the elevator of the same bachelor officers' quarters where we were temporarily housed. They were a subtle reminder that we would soon be entering the real world, assuming we made it through the rest of the curriculum. They were also a reminder that real people did this stuff, and there was no reason to be intimidated.

I was ecstatic to have qualified at "the boat" and called my dad immediately after landing ashore. After qualifying once again with six landings in the trickier Skyhawk at the end of the advanced phase, I made it through with solid enough grades to earn my gold naval aviator wings and land a spot in the F-14 community.

These precious billets were normally reserved for "plowback" instructors who remained in the training command for an extra year teaching students and gaining more experience. Bill "Whiskey" Bond and I felt blessed to be the first "nuggets" in a long time to go straight to the fleet to fly F-14s. Euphoric is probably a better word. We headed off to Miramar Naval Air Station in San Diego, California, to start our training at VF-124, the Fleet Replacement Squadron, otherwise known as the FRS.

At Miramar I rediscovered the beautiful, sparkling city of San Diego, the "cradle of naval aviation," where I was born and where I learned to sail.

The F-14 Tomcat was relatively new in the fleet at the time, and it was, of course, a much bigger and more complex machine than I had previously flown. I became familiar with its swing-wings, variable intake ramps, and retractable refueling probe. Its weapons systems included a new and more capable radar, an early-generation heads-up display, three types of missiles, and a gun. There was a lot to learn within a training process that only scratched the surface of the aircraft's technology.

I quickly learned that in the world of Navy fighter aviation, like so many other endeavors, the rich get richer—those who work a little harder rapidly accelerate. To be sure, I was surrounded by immensely talented peers, but working hard was, for me, not about being competitive per se. Instead, I merely wanted to perform as well as I could within my own space. So I was determined to let effort and curiosity reign over the temptation to coast through the program—and quickly earned the reputation for being a "sweat."

Several times while at the FRS I was privileged to fly with Cdr. Willy Driscoll in my back seat. Willy was a legendary ace from the Vietnam War and the smartest, hardest-working radar intercept officer, or RIO, in the business. He and his pilot, Randy Cunningham, shot down five MiGs. His extraordinary patience with those willing to do a little extra to learn was offset by little tolerance for those who showed up less than prepared for a flight. That probably derived from watching—and hearing—a MiG-21's bullets piercing his F-4 Phantom from the back seat while Cunningham chased a MiG from the front seat. He described it as sounding like a pencil being pushed through a piece of stretched aluminum foil. It was not a game for him.

At the time, the *Star Wars* movie was only a couple of years old, and I felt like a Jedi knight was in my back seat. Willie's fighter combat intellect was intimidating—and an inspiration to do everything in my power to excel and make a positive impression on the best in the profession. It reinforced my belief in the third pillar of achieving excellence: finding the right teachers.

Like the training command, the key phase of a young student's journey through the FRS was carrier qualifications. Except this time I would have to do it at night. Being thrown off a ship by a catapult and brought to a sudden stop by the arresting gear in the daytime was fun in its own right. But doing it at night, when it's pitch black at sea and there are zero peripheral cues for depth perception, is an entirely different experience.

The back of the ship is the great equalizer—as I mentioned earlier, it simply does not care what race or sex you are, how good-looking you are, or how smoothly you talk. One either learns to do it well and safely or one doesn't. Doing it at night—especially for the first time—requires extraordinary self-discipline, good vision, and eye–hand coordination. It demands an immense set of self-confidence to wrestle twenty-four tons of airplane and fuel through the darkness and onto that little spot on a moving flight deck. It's hard.

My qualification period occurred on the East Coast in the winter on board USS *Nimitz*, with a seriously pitching deck. Some said the sea state was out of limits for training landings, but deck time is precious, and they needed to get us through the program. That's what "waivers" are for, I supposed at the time. I was wearing a bulky, hot, itchy "poopy suit" that was supposed to keep me alive for a few minutes if I ended up in the water, which only made it more difficult to concentrate on landing the airplane.

Once again, I was working so hard I don't remember any of these landings, except perhaps during a day landing where I could swear the ship's propellers briefly protruded out of the water as the ship went through a large swell. My patient RIO, Lt. Cdr. "Flash" Gordon, coaxed me through enough successful day and night landings to qualify. To this day, I honestly don't know how I managed to execute that first landing at night. It's just so dark and different from any other challenge aviation has to offer.

My last hurdle before joining the fleet was to attend the Navy's three-week Survival, Evasion, Resistance, and Escape course, otherwise known as SERE School. Modeled after the Navy's experiences in Vietnam, the curriculum is intended to enable aviators who might find themselves behind enemy lines to cope with the challenges implied in the school's name. After two weeks of classes, the students are thrown into the field in rural Southern California to first survive with no food for several days, then run through an evasion course, and eventually be captured and exposed to what it's like to be a prisoner of war. By bending the rules and skirting the evasion exercise boundary, I managed to be one of two students to make it to "Freedom Village," where I was rewarded with a peanut butter and jelly sandwich. The other person who made it arrived an hour later, too exhausted to eat his sandwich, so he offered it to me.

If this was cheating, it seemed to be fair at the time. If I adhered to the rules imposed by an enemy, then I deserved the result. Bending a rule to achieve a higher objective foreshadowed a number of actions I took further down the line in my career. It was never about personal ambition; instead, it was about an insatiable urge to make something better.

One of the SERE School's staff was a former Navy enlisted man named Doug Hegdahl, who fell overboard from a ship and was captured by the North Vietnamese. He heroically memorized the names of every prisoner in Hanoi and feigned being mentally incompetent to be released. Doug was particularly adept at the soft side of interrogation, mimicking how the North Vietnamese would try to turn a prisoner of war against his own country. It was quite sobering.

During the "prison camp" portion of the course, many students were waterboarded. I somehow avoided this, perhaps because I made it to Freedom Village or because I didn't fall for any of the instructors' clever but somewhat sophomoric interrogation techniques. Other less fortunate captives found themselves strapped to the board. Candidly, that experience made many of us scratch our heads many years later amid the controversy over similar treatment of those who planned the attacks on our country on 9/11. But, to be clear, I join the ranks of those who believe torture in any form undermines the values of our nation.

Two weeks after the end of the SERE course I pulled a one-inch piece of cactus out of my back. But I had successfully finished the FRS and was headed to my first fleet squadron, the VF-24 "Fighting Renegades."

Welcome to the fleet, kid.

TOP The patch that every TopGun graduate wears *Jim Caiella*

MIDDLE A Russian TU-95 Bear Bomber *Official U.K. Ministry of Defence photo*

BOTTOM Every now and then you can enjoy Steel Beach on an aircraft carrier. *Winnefeld collection*

Life on Steel Beach

On September 2, 1983, the aircraft carrier USS *Ranger* was transiting westward across the Pacific west of Hawaii, on its way to the Arabian Gulf. The previous night, Maj. Gennadi Osipovich, flying in a Russian SU-15 fighter, had fired a missile that plummeted Korean Airlines Flight 007, a Boeing 747 flying from Anchorage, Alaska, to Seoul, Korea, into the Sea of Japan. All 269 people on board were killed.

No one in the West will probably ever know what Osipovich really saw in the flashing lights and dimly lit windows of the giant airliner, what he was told before he pulled the trigger, and whether this was a conscious act or a horrible mistake. But the world was outraged despite the Soviet Union's propaganda machine's statements that the airliner had purposefully flown into Russian airspace over Sakhalin island on a spy mission.

The Russians knew *Ranger* was somewhere in the vast Western Pacific. Because, in those days, aircraft carriers were assumed to carry nuclear weapons, the Russian military tried to localize them, sending their lumbering TU-95 Bear bombers out to do the job. In turn, carriers always launched alert fighters to intercept the Russian aircraft at a significant distance from these ships to demonstrate our ability to defend them. It was a dance that played out on every aircraft carrier deployment from the U.S. West Coast, including this, my second deployment with the Fighting Renegades of VF-24.

I had joined VF-24, which was commanded by a former Blue Angel named Bill Switzer, when the squadron was preparing to deploy on board USS *Constellation*. This is where I would learn the profession of being a carrier fighter pilot. I was anxious to challenge myself, a bit overconfident, and nervous about succeeding.

One of the first things a new pilot in a squadron has to do is find a call sign. Call signs are usually based on something someone has done (usually something embarrassing) or some kind of wordplay based on one's name. I had undeservingly received the call sign "Magic" in the training pipeline based on having luckily trimmed up my airplane well for a friend who was learning to fly formation on my wing. When I walked into VF-24's ready room, I was quickly informed that "Magic" wouldn't cut it for a new guy who couldn't possibly have done anything magic yet. Moreover, there was already a Magic in our squadron: Lt. Cdr. Larry Morris, a salty pilot who previously flew F-8 Crusaders and carried a wealth of sea stories in his hip pocket. I looked around and saw that a pilot named Chris Welty used his first two initials, "CJ." My initials spelled JAW, so I took on the call sign "Jaws."

Of course, a few rookie mistakes caused my new squadron-mates to try to hang a new call sign on me. But as long as one shows no sensitivity to an imposed call sign, it won't stick, and none of them did. It was only later that I learned people began to playfully spell out "Jaws" as "Just Admiral Winnefeld's Son." Never underestimate the creativity of a naval aviator, and humility is the most important element of leadership, so no worries.

My first "line period" occurred off the coast of San Diego immediately after I arrived in the squadron. The residual proficiency from recently qualifying in the FRS in choppy East Coast waters enabled me to perform well as a rookie in my first real exposure to the fleet. But landing on the deck of an aircraft carrier at night is a perishable skill, especially for those new to it. During subsequent line periods, I experienced my share of not-so-fun nights behind the back of the ship . . . including the humiliation of "bingoing" to the beach once my low fuel state precluded further landing attempts. There are those who have and those who will!

My first overseas deployment was a nonstop education: learning to fly the Tomcat around the ship, how a fighter squadron functions, and how to manage both the rigors and the drudgery of long periods at sea. Even though we ended up in the Indian Ocean, the first leg of a deployment was the long voyage across the Pacific Ocean during the Cold War. Port visits to the Philippines, Singapore, and Thailand were my first experiences with Asian culture. I experienced the stunning beauty of Western Pacific sunsets from both the flight deck and high above the ocean in a Tomcat. And I cut my teeth on what it's like to fly over the sea in bad weather when there is nowhere else to land but back on the ship.

Ranger maintained a good reputation for hiding from the Russians using a combination of deception and careful controls over its electronic emissions. Due to the planning time involved, the Bears' mission on the day after the KAL shootdown was likely scheduled well before the horrendous events of the previous evening. But this flight drew closer scrutiny from the U.S. intelligence structure that warned of such missions.

As usual, after topping off fuel from an A-6 Intruder tanker aircraft, we intercepted the Bears hundreds of miles away from the carrier. They seemed much smaller than I expected, flying a safe distance alongside them. One of the Russian pilots held up a crude sign in English asking, "Where is USS *Ranger*?" which we only answered with animated shrugs. And, yes, certain gestures appropriate to the previous evening's events were flashed back by certain aircrews. In yet another tense moment of the Cold War, the Bears never found *Ranger* that day.

The most challenging part of the flight was actually getting back to *Ranger* in the crappy Western Pacific weather. If she was hiding from the Russians, she was also hiding from us. Aircraft carriers move quickly and can cover quite a bit of water during a long flight—and we couldn't fly straight back to the ship lest the Bears try to follow. Aircraft remaining at altitude, above an undercast, to conserve fuel cannot find the ship visually. This was before the days of the Global Positioning System, and the F-14A was equipped with an older inertial navigation system that tended to drift after a jarring catapult shot and a long flight.

It's not a good feeling to have a limited amount of fuel in the middle of the ocean and not be sure where the only place on the planet to land safely is located. We used to joke that "the only time you have too much fuel is when you're on fire." We only knew where the ship started and the general direction it should have moved, and we could thus estimate where she might be later when we returned. We could also intermittently search for the carrier or the aircraft operating around it with our radars. Fortunately, after many tense minutes, we managed to locate *Ranger*, descend through the clouds, and land safely. Just another day in naval aviation.

We did well in these minor cat-and-mouse games during the Cold War. However, the threat from the slow Bear bombers was eclipsed by that of newer supersonic Backfire Bombers carrying long-range, high-speed antiship missiles. The theory was to try to shoot the archer rather than his arrows. Even though our systems and aircrews at the time were vastly superior to those used by the Russians, the Navy was trying to hammer out a set of tactics for "the outer-air battle" that would work against the Backfire. The problem was the solutions we used violated nearly every time-tested principle of war.

As a "nugget" aviator, I was full of questions and growing skepticism regarding the tactics of the day, which attempted to capitalize on the F-14's ability to track and shoot several targets at once. Under the prevailing method, fighters were dispersed in a grid on either side of the most likely threat axis. The grid was supposed to be maintained with little or no communications, with automatic movements by fighter aircrews to position their aircraft correctly. Tankers were sent to specific stations to find and refuel the fighters, or other fighters would launch to relieve those running low on gas. When threats appeared, the grid would respond accordingly, and alert fighters could be launched from the deck when necessary.

It was a scheme that worked well on paper but collapsed under its enormous complexity in execution. Radio frequencies were usually self-jammed by frustrated aircrews trying to straighten things out. After tense debriefings and encouragement to do better, the air wing would try to get it right during the next exercise—and more often than not would fail again. Worse, even when executed perfectly, it was not likely to intercept modern bombers before they launched their long-range weapons.

The community had fallen into an adage I later coined as "incredibly bright adults will work incredibly long hours perfecting fundamentally flawed concepts." While I had to wait until a subsequent tour to help improve these tactics, it was my first opportunity to appreciate having a questioning attitude about every aspect of my profession, even as a young person. If a concept is fundamentally flawed to begin with, no amount of tinkering will fix it. And someone has to point that out.

The most challenging task for a new carrier pilot is learning to safely and routinely land on board the ship on the first attempt, day and night. I needed to learn everything I could about how airplanes land on aircraft carriers to have any chance of succeeding. The best way to do that was to qualify as a landing signal officer, or LSO. My appetite to do so was amplified by the fact that my father was an LSO when he was a young aviator.

LSOs are trained and empowered to ensure the safety of pilots in carrier operations. It's a collateral duty above and beyond a pilot's normal billet in a squadron, so volunteering to do it indicates a willingness to put in a lot of extra work. In order to learn the technical aspects of their craft, aspiring LSOs attend a school whose motto is, appropriately enough, "Rectum non-Bustus."

The stakes are high—an accident of any kind is hazardous for the men and women working on the flight deck. A serious one can shut down a carrier's flight operations for hours, cause the expensive loss of aircraft or equipment, and inhibit a carrier's performance in combat. It can be catastrophic if it happens during "blue water ops," when there is nowhere else for fuel-starved aircraft to land.

LSOs develop a special camaraderie during many hours spent next to the runway during day and night field carrier landing practice. Their "office" during carrier operations is a special platform on the aft port side of the ship's flight deck. They often work under difficult conditions, with bad weather and a pitching deck at night. They're responsible for training a squadron's pilots in all aspects of operating around "the boat," as well as ensuring every approach is conducted safely, including providing verbal guidance over the radio regarding glideslope, airspeed, or lineup when a pilot needs it. They are colloquially referred to as "Paddles" based on the early days of naval aviation, when LSOs used a set of brightly colored paddles to indicate a pilot's position and any required corrections. I still own a set from those old days, handed down by my dad.

The other element I needed to master was being a lethal fighter pilot. I learned a lot from Willy Driscoll and others in the Fleet Replacement Squadron, but that merely scratched the surface. I count my lucky stars that I was assigned to then-lieutenant commander Marty "Streak" Chanik as his wingman.

Streak was a tall, affable former TopGun instructor with a bushy mustache and a telltale streak of gray in his otherwise pitch-black hair, from which his call sign was derived. He was all-in on our profession: a fighter pilot's fighter pilot and a colorful personality from whom I would learn a ton. Later in life, I would inherit USS *Enterprise* from his capable command.

Learning fighter stuff involved many different dimensions. It included properly executing a radar intercept; most effectively maneuvering one's airplane under high g-forces; keeping sight of a wingman in the middle of a complex, swirling, multiplane fight; properly operating the four different weapons carried by the Tomcat; and developing an elusive capability called "situational awareness." It also involved trying to remember everything that happened and, more importantly, why it happened, in a three-dimensional fight. Learning to be a good wingman was a prerequisite to becoming a good flight lead, and Streak—along with a few tolerant radar intercept officers—patiently showed me the way.

I'm sure that at this point in my progression I was overconfident. Former UCLA basketball coach John Wooden once said, "It's what you learn after you know it all that counts." But I also knew that further refining all these skills meant attending "TopGun," or what was then known as the Navy Fighter Weapons School and more recently as the Navy Strike Fighter Tactics Instructor program. Squadron commanders were generally allowed to send only one crew per squadron to the school during each interdeployment cycle, so we competed to be selected. It was not only recognition of effort, ability, and potential; it was the best five weeks of flying on the planet. I desperately wanted to go.

TopGun was an outgrowth of the Vietnam War, where U.S. fighter pilots started with an unacceptably poor kill ratio against North Vietnamese MiG-17, MiG-19, and MiG-21 fighters. These aircraft were technologically inferior to the F-8 Crusader and F-4 Phantom used by the U.S. Navy, but they were small and nimble, and their pilots punched above their weight. After the Navy assembled a team of highly proficient pilots and started a school designed from the ground up to "train the trainer," its kill ratio dramatically improved.

After my first overseas deployment, the Renegades' commander, Bill Switzer, selected me to attend the course along with Lt. Dave "Bio" Baranek. Dave, who would eventually be the best man in my wedding, had graduated from Georgia Tech a year behind me. We joined VF-24 simultaneously due to the shorter training pipeline for radar intercept officers. We felt lucky to have the opportunity to attend, along with our wingmen from sister squadron VF-211, Lt. John "Boomer" Stufflebeem and Lt. Steve "Jake" Jacobsmeyer. We soaked up every bit of high-tempo, graduate-level education and performed well in the class. If there really was a "TopGun Trophy," as depicted in the film of the same name, who knows, we might have won it. More importantly, we could now wear a TopGun patch on our flight suits.

During the mid-1980s Soviet fighter technology began to catch up to U.S. technology. Specifically, the MiG-23 Flogger's airborne radars and missile were finally good enough to shoot other aircraft in the forward quarter, rather than requiring a pilot to maneuver behind an opponent to aim at its hot tailpipe with a heat-seeking missile. This leveled the playing field somewhat between the Flogger and the Tomcat.

However, the Flogger could not use its radar when looking down toward the ground; its pulse radar could only see opposing aircraft when looking upward. The Tomcat's pulse doppler radar filtered out most of the ground clutter, which allowed it to "look down and shoot down" under most angles. While it was only a matter of time before the Russians would develop pulse doppler radar, a clever U.S. pilot would stay below his Russian opponent.

The fighter wing at NAS Miramar wanted to experiment with flying F-14s at especially low altitudes against simulated Floggers that might be themselves staying low to optimize their chances of looking up. So, Bio and I were chosen to fight for a couple of weeks against other F-14s simulating

MiG-23s over the Yuma, Arizona, desert. Loosened safety rules of engagement permitted full-blown fighting with essentially no hard or soft "deck." We were watched closely on an instrumented range and had to be extra careful close to the ground, but it was great fun. Talk about flying close to the edge!

Our ultimate destination during my first two overseas deployments was the Middle East due to the angry confrontation that began with the Iranian revolution. In those days carriers did not enter the Arabian Gulf, and there were no available ports in the region. So we spent most of our time right outside the Strait of Hormuz. Because we were concerned about hostilities with Iran, much of our flying involved holding on "combat air patrol" stations off the coast of Chahbahar in southeastern Iran, where there was an airfield capable of hosting fighter aircraft.

Because we were short of money for parts and fuel for our aircraft, we frequently endured no-fly days, steaming around in the hot sun, boring holes in the water with little to do. We would stand our fighter alerts, from which we could launch quickly to intercept any approaching Russian or Iranian aircraft, in stifling heat, often breathing the noxious gasses coming out of the conventionally powered *Ranger*'s exhaust stack.

If we didn't pull into port for forty-five days or more, we were entitled to two beers, which we enjoyed on "steel beach picnics" up on the flight deck. A really awful deployment was collectively known as a "six-pack cruise"—three consecutive forty-five-day line periods. It was ironic that, amid the ongoing tensions with Iran, the tasty melons and other produce delivered to the ship often arrived in wooden crates marked "Produce of Iran," probably by way of the United Arab Emirates.

During my first deployment in 1981 on board USS *Constellation*, the Navy had not yet implemented a zero-tolerance drug policy. One day Switzer landed on the ship, with Bio in his back seat, and caught a wire with an improper weight setting, dialed in by a Sailor apparently under the influence of an illegal drug. The Tomcat pulled the wire out of the arresting gear engine to the breaking point and trickled off the forward end of the landing area. Too slow to fly, even at full power, it landed in the water with a gigantic splash.

Dave pulled the ejection handle just in time—neither crew got more than one swing in his parachute before landing in the water. It was not long after that the

Navy implemented its no-drugs policy, and over time things got much better. But it imparted an early lesson that morale never rises when standards fall.

My second deployment on board USS *Ranger* was even rougher. On our first day the ship collided with an oiler. On our second day two expensive canopies from an EA-6B Prowler were accidentally blown off the aircraft in the hanger bay. On the third day we experienced the tragic loss of a Sailor who was blown overboard by jet blast on the flight deck. Then we discovered we would not be heading west after all.

Instead, we were diverted south to the coast of Nicaragua during tensions with that country. *Ranger* was old and tired, with poorly operating electrical power and air conditioning systems. Operating in humid, pitching deck conditions for a month or so led to some of the most challenging carrier landings I ever experienced. We were relieved to finally head west toward Hawaii.

We were expecting several port visits in the western Pacific during our deployment, which would be a welcome relief from the boring operations off Iran. However, as we pulled into Hawaii, we received the bad news that we would be heading once again straight to the North Arabian Sea. But I also got some welcome news from the commanding officer of TopGun: I would return to serve as an instructor.

In considering my future, I briefly pondered applying for the Navy's Test Pilot School, which could in turn lead to an application for the astronaut program. I would probably have been accepted by the former, but there was no guarantee of the latter. And even if selected, I was worried it would take too long to get a flight on the space shuttle. I was also concerned that, even though space flight would be the thrill of a lifetime, the flying in the astronaut program would be mundane: mostly cross-country flights in the T-38 jet trainer rather than dynamic, gut-wrenching, high g-force tactical chess matches or low-level flights through the California mountains. With memories of the hot, humid summers and cold, wet winters in south Texas from my experience in Kingsville, I didn't want to live in Houston. Finally, I wasn't ready to turn my back on ever returning to the fleet, which could be implied by entering NASA's program—if I ever even got there.

I also considered transferring to an adversary squadron, which was as good as any stepping-stone to apply for a position on the Blue Angels flight demonstration team. I have no idea whether the "Blues" would have selected me. They require a unique combination of flying skill, personality, and good looks I didn't possess.

No matter: I found the tactical aspects of being a fighter pilot tremendously rewarding intellectually and physically. I wanted to be the best in my profession, and I admired the culture of expertise so evident at TopGun, which I viewed as the pinnacle of the fighter business. Apparently Bio's and my performance as students was good enough to warrant us both being asked to return as instructors.

I still had several months of *Ranger*'s Indian Ocean deployment to finish, which included being on board during a tragic engine room fire that killed six Sailors and injured many others. But it was liberating to finally fly off the ship, through the beautiful little atoll of Diego Garcia in the Indian Ocean, on my way home to San Diego.

My first fleet tour was in the books.

TOP A pilot's view of landing on a carrier. Note the very slightly high "ball" on the Fresnel Lens to the left of the landing area. *Department of Defense photo by Lt. Robert Moore, U.S. Navy*

MIDDLE A Tomcat catching an arresting cable. Note the socket where the flight deck cross-deck pendant attaches to the purchase cable. *Official U.S. Navy photo by PHAN Kristopher Wilson*

BOTTOM Tomcat in tension on the catapult. Note the launch bar and holdback fitting on the nose wheel strut. *Official U.S. Navy photo by PH1 James Foehl*

Interlude

The Ultimate in Motor Sports

At this point the reader may be a bit curious about how this amazing machine called an aircraft carrier actually works. Operating high-performance aircraft in this environment requires a unique and special blend of airplanes, equipment, deck crews, and aircrews.

Let's start with the airplanes. Carrier-capable aircraft must be specially designed to tolerate operations at sea. They have strengthened landing gear and an internal structure able to handle hard landings—controlled crashes, really—as well as the stress of being thrown off the ship by a catapult. They need a strong, light, and reusable tailhook to snag an arresting cable on landing. Special high-pressure tires enable hard landings on non-skid-coated flight decks. Their nose landing gear must be able to mechanically accommodate hooking up to a catapult. They have to be able to fly slowly in order to not overstress a carrier's arresting gear or the airplane itself when catching a wire. And they have to handle the corrosive effects of salt air and water.

One of the unique advantages U.S. carriers have over many other nations' ships is their four catapults, which can accelerate aircraft from a standing start to flying speed in just a few seconds. This enables aircraft to launch with heavy combat and fuel loads, dramatically increasing their effectiveness. For traditional steam-powered catapults, two long cylinders, each with a heavy piston inside, are positioned just below long slots on the flight deck. Each cylinder has a similar slot running its entire length, which allows its piston to be attached to a shuttle that protrudes above the flight deck in the catapult track's opening. Special metal strips use the same steam that pushes the pistons forward to also seal the gaps in the cylinders behind the pistons as they are pushed forward, somewhat like a zipper. When fired, the catapult's piston pulls the shuttle and its attached aircraft down the track.

A water brake attached to the forward end of each cylinder spins water inside a horizontal conical tube, which is shaped to receive a similar shaped "spear" on the front of each piston. When the catapult fires and reaches the end of its cylinder, the spear slams into the water brake with a large thump, stopping the entire mechanism in only a foot or so. The aircraft releases from the shuttle, and off it goes.

The Navy's newest catapults are powered by a set of large electromagnets under the flight deck that pulls the shuttle forward. This method has enormous advantages as it eliminates the steam piping (along with the associated manpower and maintenance) required by traditional catapults and allows a more measured acceleration, which is easier on aircraft when they're launched.

Pilots are carefully and precisely directed into the proper position on a catapult by a highly trained Sailor known as a "yellow shirt." Because a jet aircraft is launched at nearly full power, a water-cooled ramp elevates to about forty-five degrees behind a plane after it taxis into position in order to divert the exhaust upward. A reusable "holdback" bar is then attached to the back side of the aircraft's nose gear. Meanwhile, the pilot hits a switch that lowers the aircraft's "launch bar," which is what connects the nose wheel to the catapult shuttle. The pilot taxis forward until the holdback catches in a slot on the flight deck and the launch bar is seated in the shuttle. Once the aircraft is connected to the catapult in this way, the yellow shirt simultaneously signals the pilot to set full power, with feet off the brakes, and for the catapult to be placed in "tension." This puts a little steam pressure in the cylinder, which, along with the aircraft's own power, pulls the aircraft forward against the holdback fitting. The pilot checks out the aircraft's engine and other instruments and "wipes out" the controls so troubleshooters can ensure that everything externally visible is working properly.

At this point a catapult officer—also known as a "shooter," who is one of several aircrews specially trained in catapult operations assigned to the ship—takes control of the launch. When the pilot is satisfied that the aircraft is ready to fly, he or she salutes the shooter in the daytime or turns on the airplane's lights at night. The catapult officer double checks the catapult setting, looks for a thumbs-up from troubleshooters stationed all around the aircraft, then touches the deck and points forward as a signal to launch the aircraft. A Sailor at the deck edge confirms thumbs-up all around, then hits the button that releases the full steam shot into the cylinder and launches the aircraft. The catapults are powerful enough that, should a pilot inadvertently leave the aircraft's parking brake on, it will still reach flying speed at the end of the stroke—albeit with two blown tires, two large black streaks running down each side of the catapult track, and a new call sign for its pilot.

Each catapult shot is different, with a carefully adjusted steam setting for each aircraft's type and weight, and for the temperature and wind speed over the flight deck. Trust is a vital element of this system. A pilot at full power on a catapult has to trust a nineteen-year-old Sailor to get the steam pressure calculations right. Another Sailor, who risks his or her life right below the powerful intakes of an aircraft at full power, must ensure the aircraft was correctly attached to the shuttle. And the troubleshooters must properly verify that everything is right with the aircraft—no hydraulic or fuel leaks.

When the catapult fires, it accelerates from 0 to around 140 knots in three seconds. Amusement parks try to recreate this feeling, but there's nothing like it in the world. It's great fun during the day but can be terrifying on a black, stormy night. And that's just the beginning—later, you have to come back and land. How does *that* work?

At the aft end of the flight deck, three or four arresting wires (depending on the class of ship) are stretched across the deck, held just off the deck by steel bows, to snag the tailhook of a landing aircraft. These exposed wires, called cross-deck pendants, are attached to longer purchase cables that wind through a complex pulley and damper system to the arresting-gear engines below the landing area. On most carriers, these engines consist of a huge horizontal hydraulic cylinder compressed by the arresting cables as they are pulled out by the aircraft using an eighteen-to-one pulley ratio.

The piston itself compresses at a rate unique to the type and weight of a landing aircraft, controlled by how a metering orifice opens that allows hydraulic fluid to escape from the cylinder. All of the aircraft's kinetic energy is converted into heat in the hydraulic oil during its three-hundred-foot stopping distance. After the wire is disengaged from the aircraft's tailhook, compressed air repositions the cylinder, which quickly retracts the wire back into its original taut location on the deck.

The landings are so violent and the tailhook engagement is so hard on the cross-deck pendants that they must be replaced after around a hundred landings, while the purchase cables are good for around a thousand landings. Our newest aircraft carriers have arresting engines powered by an electro-magnetic engine rather than a maintenance-intensive hydraulic system. It's taken time, ingenuity, and money to get both of these systems right, but they will pay big dividends in the long term.

One of the most complex pieces of gear used in the landing process is the system of lights—colloquially referred to as "the lens"—that helps guide a pilot down the glideslope to the small area on the deck where an aircraft's tailhook can engage an arresting cable. The goal is literally for the pilot's eyes to fly exactly the right path to enable the tailhook to land in exactly the right place.

This contraption, located on the left, or port, side of the landing area, has a set of horizontal green lights, known as datum lights, broken up in the center by a column of vertically arranged orange light cells. These cells, called Fresnel lenses, function the same way as traffic lights that can only be seen from a particular angle. Each cell points to a different portion of the glide slope so the pilot can only see one section of the cells at a time, depending on where the aircraft is relative to the optimal glideslope. If a pilot's eyes are perfectly on glideslope, a yellow-orange glow known as the "meatball" appears right in line with the horizontal row of datum lights. Correspondingly, if the airplane is above glideslope, the meatball appears above, and if low, it appears below the datums. If the pilot is low enough, it flashes red. The goal is to start with and maintain a "centered ball" all the way to touchdown.

The Fresnel lenses actually display horizontal planes of light. Since the lens is located on the left side of the landing area, tilting the lens left or right moves the glidepath displayed for a particular cell vertically up or down over the landing area's center line and all the way up the glideslope. This powerful feature, called roll angle, allows adjustments to two critically important factors.

First, not all aircraft types are the same size. The vertical distance between an F-14 pilot's eye and the aircraft's tailhook is much larger than that for an FA-18. If the lens were not adjusted for each different aircraft type, a Tomcat pilot's and Hornet pilot's eyeballs flying the same glide slope would result in their aircraft landing at different points along the flight deck, with the latter landing much further down the flight deck and probably missing the arresting cables entirely. The ability to tilt the lens according to aircraft type ensures that a "centered ball" puts every aircraft in just the right spot: tilted lower for a smaller aircraft and higher for a larger one.

Second, being able to dynamically tilt the lens enables it to account for a certain amount of deck motion as well. If the lens were fixed, the glideslope portrayed to the pilot by the meatball would move up and down with the deck. On the up cycle, a pilot would see a lower ball and add too much power to compensate. The reverse is true when the deck moves down. After a cycle or two, the pilot would get hopelessly out of phase with the deck's movement, creating a dangerous condition. To prevent this, the lens continually tilts to account for deck movement in order to present a stable picture to the pilot. It's magic, except when the deck is really moving a lot.

If the motion of the deck falls outside the limits of what the lens can handle, or if the lens itself is broken, then the LSOs switch to a completely different system known as MOVLAS. Here a vertical set of fixed yellow lights is placed in directly front of the vertical Fresnel cells. The LSO can move a handle manually up or down to control which of these lights are on. The LSO observes where the aircraft is relative to glideslope and literally transmits that position to the pilot by moving the handle up or down, giving the pilot a presentation that depicts which Fresnel cell would be lit if the lens were working normally. It takes a lot of skill to learn to operate MOVLAS, but its lights are indistinguishable from a normal Fresnel lens to all but the most seasoned pilots.

LSOs are equipped with radios and a "pickle switch" to control the red wave-off lights and green cut lights positioned around the lens. The latter was used in the past for telling pilots of piston-driven airplanes when to chop power as they crossed over the carrier's deck. They are now flashed once in the daytime to initially acknowledge an aircraft on final approach and subsequently to call for the pilot to add power. The LSOs also have a TV camera on the deck center line that looks up the glideslope, mostly to determine whether aircraft are on center line. Oh, and there is a padded net below the platform into which they can jump in case they're endangered by an errant aircraft. Fortunately, I never was forced to bail into the net.

Serving as an LSO in pitching deck conditions, at night, in bad weather is the ultimate test of performance. The ship is counting on the team to only allow aircraft on board that are set up to land safely on a clear deck with the arresting gear set correctly. Pilots count on the LSO to help them down when necessary. Because every landing is graded and debriefed to the pilot who performed it, with no consideration for rank, an LSO's bedside manner is important. It's like being both the catcher and the umpire in a baseball game, and it provides a pilot who serves as one the advantage of having greater knowledge gleaned from serving "behind the plate." Learning the LSO trade further confirmed in my mind how valuable doing the work to master every technical detail of one's chosen profession really matters.

Of course, the most complex piece of equipment required to land an aircraft on a ship is a pilot's brain. A pilot must learn a special type of concentration in order to routinely and safely land on board an aircraft carrier, especially at night. He or she has to juggle the three variables of glideslope (the meatball), air speed (displayed as angle of attack), and lineup in varying conditions and conflicting cues. It is definitely a right-brain activity in which the three variables must be processed in parallel, not in series. It's impossible to describe the discipline required to transition from instruments inside the cockpit to visual cues outside the cockpit on a moonless night under a cloud layer. The lens, the lineup lights, and the yellow glow from the flight deck are barely visible. Everything else above and below the pilot is pitch black and very disorienting. Unlike airfield operations ashore, there are no other lights to provide depth perception and context to the scene unfolding before of the pilot.

A night carrier landing definitely raises the heart rate, particularly when dealing with an aircraft emergency, and it's easy to become disoriented and overwhelmed, which leads to exaggerated throttle and stick movements, which in turn lead to large overcorrections and an unmanageable approach. I always reminded myself that the airplane flies the same way and responds to the same pilot inputs at night as it does in the daytime.

Of course, newer airplanes, such as the FA-18 Hornet series and the F-35C Lightning, have unbelievably good systems compared to the Tomcat, which also suffered from being a bigger airplane with less margin for error. But there's no getting around the fact that pilots who remain calm, believe in the information presented to them, maintain a strong scan pattern, and fight the temptation to make excessive corrections are those who master the art and science of landing on an aircraft carrier at night.

TOP LEFT The F-5 was like flying a sports car. *Winnefeld collection*

TOP RIGHT Every TopGun instructor has a caricature of their call sign on a slide at the beginning of a lecture. *Winnefeld collection*

BOTTOM The TopGun staff in 1986 *Official U.S. Navy photo*

Take My Breath Away

On May 16, 1986, Maverick and Goose launched off USS *Enterprise*, headed into silver screen history in the movie *Top Gun*, which debuted that day. The instructors working at the real TopGun—who helped bring some reality to the script, flew in all of the scenes, and observed the production on the ground—wondered if the film would ever work. They then watched with amazement as it became one of the iconic movies of the 1980s. It was also a major recruiting boon to the U.S. Navy. But what was the real TopGun all about?

Despite the cinematic glamour of the film, the U.S. Navy Fighter Weapons School is a vital component of the naval aviation community. After helping reverse a negative trend in air-to-air combat in Vietnam, the school was institutionalized as a permanent part of the Navy and Marine Corps fighter community under a "train the trainer" concept. It may also have been the most professional organization I've ever known, which is a tall order.

Being selected to serve as an instructor was a dream come true, but not because of the prestige that accompanied the job. I wanted to reach for the

41

most difficult challenge in the business and was impressed with the superb flying, fighting, and teaching skills possessed by the small cadre of instructors at the school. During their debriefs, their poise and tact included an almost uncanny ability to recall every detail of the immensely complex spaghetti that makes up an air-to-air dogfight, often with many aircraft in the same piece of sky. And the lectures they gave to the class were like nothing I'd ever seen—talk about polish!

My experience as a TopGun instructor exceeded all my expectations for working with and learning from the best in the business, and it was an enormous growth opportunity. All pilot instructors qualified in both the F-5 Tiger and A-4 Skyhawk aircraft, which we used to simulate the Soviet fighters of the day. Because I was still allowed to fly the F-14, it was sensational to be qualified in three different airplanes. It was the best flying in the world, often two or three times per day, with the best flight leads and wingmen on the planet.

Before being permitted to fly against anyone besides an instructor, I first had to pass through the school's rigorous instructor training curriculum. This syllabus emphasizes safety, the highest levels of tactical proficiency, and the ability to recognize mistakes and maintain total recall of several complex air-to-air engagements in one flight. The real test is to impart knowledge during a debrief in a manner that "takes the who out of it" so as not to bruise students' potentially fragile egos and teach them the same skill. It was rewarding to feel my own skills sharpened under the tutelage of Navy and Marine TopGun stalwarts like Brian "Beef" Flannery, Lynn "Secks" Seckinger, Bob "Carrot" Foltyn, Charles "Chick" Winship, and several other gifted teachers.

While there are many important elements to being a good fighter pilot, its purest form involves gaining a solid reputation for consistently prevailing in one-versus-one dogfights. Like the back of the boat, you can't BS your way through something like this. Success demands the simultaneous application of several honed skills. Basic requirements include ensuring one's airplane remains healthy, including not running out of fuel while using gas-guzzling afterburners and avoiding collisions with opponents, the synthetic "hard deck," or the actual ground. Near-perfect control of airspeed, altitude, and g-force on the airplane is required to manage the trade-off between one's overall energy (in the form of altitude and speed) and angle advantage gained against an adversary. Maintaining sight of one's opponent, including "managing the sun," is key to revealing the tactics he's using and preventing an almost guaranteed fatal loss of awareness. Accurate assessment of an opponent's airspeed and turning rate relative to the capabilities of his airplane can expose an exploitable mistake. Without precise management of one's own weapons system, the hard work to maneuver to a kill is fruitless. All this is difficult enough. But the pilot must also do everything while countering the effects of high and low g-forces on both body and brain.

As in any competitive profession, knowing you're up against someone with experience and skill can be intimidating. What does he know that I don't know? What maneuver is he going to use that I've never confronted? Is he going to maneuver into the sun and cause me to lose sight? Every pilot's goal is to be on the dominant side of that relationship. In learning this skill, I benefited from my sailboat racing days. But it was ten times harder, like high-stakes boxing and chess matches superimposed on each other. Moreover, if I were going to going to teach it to someone else, I would have to remember everything that happened—and why it happened—accurately during the two or three different engagements conducted during a single training flight and then articulate it all in three-dimensional artistry on a two-dimensional whiteboard.

It gets even more complex when there are many airplanes in the fight. These engagements start, usually at around forty miles, by trying to gain awareness and advantage during a radar intercept. Then, if it gets that far, the fight can devolve into a mass of swirling airplanes, where it can be difficult to differentiate between friend and foe.

My growth and learning weren't restricted to tactical flying. One of the most important beliefs inculcated by my TopGun experience was the importance of accountability and candor in training. The reason American fighter pilots rank as the best in the world is that the truth always emerges in the debrief. It doesn't matter whether we're talking about Navy, Air Force, or Marine Corps pilots. Even though we at TopGun did so with the utmost tact, no stone was left unturned after a flight. Expensive flight hours were too precious to waste on people who could not check their egos at the door.

Indeed, we often found when flying against other nations' pilots that the ego was the most powerful impediment to improvement. It was the epitome of skill to not only thoroughly understand what had gone right and wrong for a student but to present it in a way that advanced his knowledge. A thin-skinned student quickly fell to the bottom of our perceptions.

I also became a better speaker because the school's standards were so high for giving quality lectures. Before an instructor was qualified to present a particular lecture to the class, he had to survive a "murder board" delivered to the assembled instructors. TopGun is where the term originated. The six-hour-long murder board critique after even a short one-hour lecture was a grueling experience, with no guarantee of a thumbs-up from the other instructors. I attribute any skills I have as a public speaker in large measure to the rigor with which I learned to speak to the TopGun class.

Another great benefit of my time at TopGun was that I met my future spouse. We met at the Miramar Naval Air Station Officers' Club in a scary parallel to the then-as-yet unmade *Top Gun* film, except it wasn't nearly as romantic as singing to someone in a bar. One afternoon I was doing my laundry across the street from the club, slipping over to the near-empty club for a beer in between loads. I spotted a table full of young women taking advantage of the one-dollar "all-the-Mexican-food-you-can-eat" special used to lure them to the club on Wednesday nights. Why not wander over and say hello?

Of course, they wisely saw through all this, which is why they arrived early in the afternoon, intending to leave well before things heated up. They referred to me as the "laundry man." But I got a date with a beautiful blonde named Mary Alice Werner, from the little town of Menomonie, Wisconsin. She was in San Diego for the summer taking a course at San Diego State University and checking out Southern California.

Our first date was the TopGun reunion, which I was expected to organize as the newest instructor. I'm sure Mary was not impressed when she discovered that, to get in the door, she had to down a "Kamikaze," a noxious concoction of vodka, lime juice, and who knows what else. I'm amazed she ever agreed to another date, but she did. Even though she loved having a good time, I could tell there was a special heart of gold beating inside this

Midwestern girl. Little did I know how big that heart could be. It sounds corny, but she took my breath away.

Other than meeting my future spouse, perhaps the most enduring benefit I drew from my TopGun experience was the power of positive peer pressure. This group of late-twenties to early-thirties instructors was one of the most fun collection of people I've ever been around, and I've never experienced a more dedicated group of professionals. To a person, they were committed to the success of the organization and worked long hours to make it work. When it came down to high standards, there was simply no compromising.

Like any great work experience, it didn't feel like work. I leaped out of bed every morning, eager to get to the hangar for another day of flying and teaching and learning. For anyone with a true love of flying, it simply didn't get any better than what we were privileged to do.

I especially enjoyed the ability to sneak out in an F-5 in between class flights at China Lake, California, and fly at low altitude across the Mojave Desert or through the high Sierra Nevada mountains. Thousands of other military pilots have experienced this. But I have to say that being able to go anywhere I wanted in the mountains in a fast, agile airplane with a nice bubble canopy was pure exhilaration. It was like living one's own iMax film. A nice barrel roll over a snow-covered ridge, or flashing down a secluded valley, or circling over a milky blue glacier-fed mountain lake, or speeding across a dry lake bed . . . always within the rules we were expected to follow, and all the while keeping the jet as quiet as possible to minimize the disturbance below . . . these were some of the most exhilarating moments of my time as a Navy pilot.

My service at TopGun occurred at the peak of the Cold War. In this regard I had several interesting personal interactions. The first was the opportunity to meet Viktor Belenko, who defected from the Soviet Union in his MiG-25 Foxbat aircraft in September 1976. The United States possessed little intelligence at the time regarding the capabilities of Russian fighters, particularly the MiG-25. The airplane he brought to Japan indicated the Soviets had a long way to go to match our capability, particularly when it came to weapons systems.

For his part, Viktor initially retained high skepticism about the United States, even after he defected. However, once he was taken to an aircraft carrier and observed young Americans operating at a high operational tempo on a flight deck, and after he was given the opportunity to visit not one but several supermarkets, he quickly understood.

My second experience involved participating in a then–highly classified intelligence program that opened the door to what was happening in Soviet fighter aircraft weapons systems and tactics development. I was the only instructor allowed into this new program due to its sensitive nature. I previously attended European Tactics Analysis Team meetings conducted in West Berlin, where it was possible to study, through actual radar observations, Warsaw Pact fighter tactics. But this new program was a completely different level of intelligence.

As I mentioned in the last chapter, we believed the MiG-23 Flogger could only shoot its radar-guided AA-7 Apex missiles in the forward quarter if the plane's radar could look up away from the ground. However, the new program indicated the Russians made progress in "look down, shoot down" capability in the forward quarter, among other advancements. That was a game-changer for us. Based on what I learned and in cooperation with a gifted Air Force exchange pilot named Mike "Boa" Straight, we began reworking Navy fighter tactics to account for this new capability.

It was only later, though open-source material, that I discovered the only reason any of us were allowed into such a highly sensitive program at that time. The Russian who provided the information, Adolf Tolkachev, had already been compromised by at least one American traitor, apprehended, and subsequently executed. At that point it must have been deemed safe to expose it to an audience that could no longer compromise such a valuable intelligence resource.

The specific technical information Tolkachev provided was less important than the newfound realization that we needed to have our act together in a new era of fighter combat. Of course, it was all confirmed later when the Iron Curtain fell and we got our hands on the actual aircraft. I would add that this is a direct example of how our intelligence community does important work that makes a difference down to the military tactical level.

I gained another important relationship via the Center for Naval Analyses, or CNA, which maintained a small cadre of PhDs at Naval Air Station

Miramar to support the fighter community's tactics development efforts. Their lead analyst on the base was a young woman named Christine Fox. Christine was bright and curious—and eager to improve the state of the art of the fighter community's tactical capabilities.

As the new editor of the classified *Navy Fighter Weapons School Journal*, and wanting to elevate the publication to a higher plane, I collaborated with Christine to write an article on the challenging technical topic of electronic warfare. We wanted to explain its concepts in terms an average fighter aircrew (like me) could more easily understand. Our article was a success, and I gained immense respect for her combination of analytical ability and patience. I would work again closely with Christine in the future, first when she became the head of CNA, then when she held two senior positions in the Pentagon, and later as a fellow U.S. Naval Institute board member.

No story about TopGun would be complete without at least mentioning the movie by the same name. A small group of instructors was provided the script in its early draft form, which inaccurately portrayed nearly everything we did. Led by then-lieutenant commander Bob "Rat" Willard, they grappled with whether to help fix the script or walk away from it, hoping for the best. Fortunately, they chose the former, and the movie was a terrific success. Christine Fox was actually the model for actress Kelly McGillis' role.

The flying scenes, which were fairly benign in order to enable their capture on camera, were not terribly interesting for pilots who were used to the violent maneuvering inherent in real air combat training. But it was interesting to watch the film-making process on the ground. I recall thinking several times, "these people are idiots, this will never work," while watching several sessions, only to see the same scene in the movie and think, "these people really know what they're doing." Another lesson for me: be slow to judge people who are doing something about which you know very little. There is more to it than you might think, and they may actually be good at it.

During my tour at TopGun, I was confronted with a career decision that centered on a brief window in which I could accept a $36,000 bonus in exchange for a commitment to remain in the Navy longer. I briefly wrestled with this decision because so many of my peers were leaving the Navy to work for the airlines. I wondered what they knew that I didn't, or whether the prospect of future deployment separations from my soon-to-be spouse Mary would make me regret staying on active duty. However, I quickly decided the Navy constituted something meaningful and rewarding to which I was willing to commit. I enjoyed the flying, the potential for future leadership opportunities, and the notion of service, which I drew from my father. So I took the bonus and promptly paid off my car loan, bought an Apple IIc computer, and invested the rest.

It was fascinating to finally have my hands on my own computer. One of the first things I did was build a spreadsheet to track my finances, including the portion of the bonus I invested. I'm convinced that one of the reasons I emerged at the end of my Navy career in reasonably good financial shape is the discipline that spreadsheet instilled in managing my hard-earned naval officer pay.

Another experience at the weapons school shaped my views of one aspect of military culture for the rest of my career. When I checked in to the command as a West Coast pilot, I noticed my fellow instructors from East Coast squadrons were wearing more ribbons than I was. I hadn't done anything less rigorous, so I assumed it must simply reflect a different culture. At that moment I decided I could either get upset about it or get over it. Napoleon once said, "A soldier will fight long and hard for a bit of colored ribbon." My preference was to follow advice from Joshua Lawrence Chamberlain, the Civil War hero of Little Round Top: "No sacrifice or service of mine merits any other reward than that which conscience gives every man who does his duty." After that, I never worried about awards again (although I wasted plenty of time in future jobs when others did!).

My tour as an instructor wrapped up in 1987, just as TopGun was taking delivery of shiny new F-16s that would simulate a new generation of Russian fighter jets. Sadly, I wouldn't get to fly the Viper, but the whole TopGun experience was life changing. It was hard to leave such a quality organization, but it was time to head back to the fleet as a department head. After a quick stop at the fleet replacement squadron to get refreshed in the Tomcat, I reported for duty with the Fighting Wolfpack of VF-1. Back to sea.

TOP Back to the fleet *Winnefeld collection*
BOTTOM A VF-1 Wolfpack Tomcat on the ramp at Naval Air Station Fallon
Official U.S. Navy photo by Michael Grove

Wolfpack

The USS *Ranger* was steaming seven hundred miles west of San Diego, headed toward Hawaii, a few days out of San Diego on the first leg of a six-month deployment. My radar intercept officer, Lt. John "Woody" Wood, and I were flying a night training sortie under "blue water" conditions, where the only place to land was on board the carrier. Or so we thought.

It was just after a beautiful sunset with a pink undercast low on the water, in the deep twilight high above, when depth perception is the hardest. We were performing a flight that ostensibly was about radar intercept training but was really about keeping pilots proficient at night carrier landings. These flights were generally boring: flying at "max conserve" airspeeds, saving fuel to show up back at the ship with the highest allowable landing fuel in case something went wrong out in the middle of nowhere.

In the middle of one of our practice radar intercepts, I perceived the lights of one aircraft against which we were training to be on a direct collision course with our plane. With a total closure rate of over 500 miles per hour,

I had little time to avoid impact and instinctively pulled the aircraft hard up and left. Unfortunately, this was too much for our Tomcat's Pratt and Whitney TF-30 turbofan engines, both of which entered a deep stall. It was also in a portion of the flight envelope where F-14 was susceptible to entering a flat spin, which is exactly where Woody and I found ourselves.

It's hard enough to get a Tomcat out of a flat spin with both engines running and in the daylight; it is nearly impossible at night with no engines or hydraulic power on the airplane. Passing 10,000 feet and in accordance with rules set in stone for situations like this, Woody pulled on his ejection seat handle in the back seat. We were catapulted sequentially out of the spinning aircraft up into the darkness. I'll never forget the sight of the airplane below as I rocketed up the ejection seat rails. I was rudely jerked to a stop in my parachute, facing a dim orange-red glow illuminating the horizon to the west and a soft pink tinge on the clouds well below.

The many hours of water survival training every naval aviator periodically endures made my next actions instinctive. Flip off the oxygen mask, look up and check the parachute, inflate the survival vest. Then pull on the handle releasing the raft stowed in the seat pan, which dangles on a fifteen or twenty-foot lanyard to help stabilize the parachute. Then prepare for water impact.

Drifting down in the parachute was strangely peaceful and even warm—that is, until I entered the undercast at two thousand feet, which was like descending into a freezer. It was pitch black underneath the clouds, and I only saw the choppy water for a few seconds before I landed. The "Koch" fittings attaching the parachute to the harness that strapped me into the ejection seat were fitted with a clever device that, when exposed to saltwater, would release the parachute's risers. This mechanism was designed to prevent parachute entanglement in the water, which is hard to escape and can result in the pilot being drawn underwater. Of course, every pilot's goal is to beat that system by manually releasing the fittings, which I later learned I did upon splashing into the cold Pacific Ocean.

The water was rough that night, with around twenty-foot wind-blown seas. It took a few minutes to retrieve my tiny life raft on its lanyard. Weighed down by the upper part of my seat pan, G-suit, and harness, I struggled into the raft by pulling myself forward and then spinning halfway around to land heavily on my back.

My first thought was for Woody, who was nowhere in sight in the heavy seas and darkness. I pulled out my radio and signal flares and inventoried my other survival gear. Even though I was only fifty or so miles from the ship, there was no telling how long it would take them to find us in the darkness under the overcast. I couldn't reach Woody on the radio and hoped the heavy seas were interfering with the line of sight of our radios.

Forty-five minutes or so later, I spotted the lights of a helicopter. Helicopter pilots assigned to carriers spend long hours of boredom that are occasionally punctuated by challenging lifesaving events on short notice. These pilots either homed in on my radio, saw my flares, or saw the bright reflective tape on my helmet. The helicopter hovered a few yards away from my raft and slowly lowered its rescue swimmer into the water. While I was fine, this is routinely done in order to assess the condition of the person to be rescued and to ensure conditions are safe for hoisting someone aboard.

It takes a lot of courage and ability to leave a hovering helicopter at night and drop into rotor downwash and cold, choppy water to effect a rescue. The swimmer made his way over and punctured my life raft so it wouldn't be entangled in the helicopter's rotors. He then attached us both to the wire, and up we went. Much to my relief, ten minutes later we picked up Woody, who had landed several miles away from me.

It goes without saying that this was a low point in my career and my life. I hated jumping out of an expensive airplane and cringed over the rumors that must be circulating within the F-14 community back home and naval aviation writ large. Despite my own belief that I was justified in executing the evasive maneuver, there was no technology that could validate how close the other airplane had actually gotten to mine in the dusky haze, and how much of a collision threat it really represented. I went from being a well-respected former TopGun instructor to being . . . well, I wasn't sure. Several other TopGun instructors had jumped out of airplanes, and it had not impacted their careers.

I waited thirty days for an investigation to run its course before I was cleared to fly again. I remain grateful for the support my commanding officer,

Cdr. Don "Puppy" Boucheaux, and others provided to get me back into the cockpit as soon as possible.

In the meantime, I decided that moping about my situation would do no good and that I would try to make the best of things by doing something creative. So I began writing a Visual Basic language computer program on my Apple IIc to simulate the tactic the Navy developed to replace the Vector Logic tactic I despised so much in my first fleet tour. I wasn't sure either tactic would effectively defend the aircraft carrier from fast Soviet bombers armed with long-range cruise missiles, but I needed proof, and the best way was to develop a tool with which to test the existing and new concepts.

I resisted the temptation to start by writing computer code and began the project by drawing a massive flow chart. The effort consumed a good bit of time, which was just what I needed to take my mind off my accident. After suffering the normal glitches associated with writing the program, I produced a workable version. The glitches themselves reinforced a useful lesson: the rigor of putting the tactic into mathematical language and computer code exposed aspects that I might have otherwise never uncovered. There is nothing like running a program and getting an unwelcome result, only to find out there's really no mistake in the code, and it's the tactic that has an embedded flaw. Importantly, the code allowed us to experiment with other versions of the tactic that ended up ramping up our odds of success.

This whole episode was useful background much later for me when I began to see the value of machine learning in revealing important insights that humans are simply not equipped to process. It also offered another powerful lesson I would experience over and over again: a little imagination, determination, and elbow grease can turn a negative into a positive when nobody is expecting it.

Apparently this was a creative period for me, as I also researched and wrote an essay that compared landing on an aircraft carrier to hitting a baseball. I dubbed it "Ball Flying and Baseball." Like most ideas, it stemmed from a synergy of disparate topical interests. First, over the course of my young career I absorbed a lot of knowledge about the technical and human side of landing on board ships, particularly while serving as an LSO. Second, I was increasing my proficiency as a carrier pilot. Third, I had read about the physiology of the brain in Carl Sagan's *The Dragons of Eden*, which my uncle recommended to me. Finally, I was intensely interested in the art and science of hitting a baseball. I devoured books on baseball by George Will and Rod Carew, thereby gaining a finer understanding of the physiological and psychological processes associated with landing on a carrier. The whole project firmly reinforced my twin beliefs that creativity is the result of melding disparate concepts and that broad, lifelong learning is essential to that process.

Both hitting a baseball and performing a carrier landing require good motor skills, spatial awareness, and a special type of concentration. Most interesting is the right brain parallel processing that must occur in both activities. It was a fascinating idea to explore, and the parallels were even more profound than I initially imagined.

In most brains, the left side uses a series, sequential-type of processing. It's responsible for rational, analytical thought—it adds and subtracts one number at a time and performs language and speech functions. On the other hand (so to speak), the right side processes information in a parallel, simultaneous fashion. This side is intuitive—it is here that most spatial processing, pattern recognition, and other similar intellectual activities occur. The right brain is also important for three-dimensional vision. EEG patterns of people performing various tasks confirm all of this: people listening to music and doing little else have active right brains. In contrast, those performing arithmetic problems have active left brains.

The parallels between baseball and ball flying are everywhere. For example, short-term memory resides on the left side of most brains. Good hitters and good pilots have a hard time remembering a particularly successful hit or landing because their right brains work so hard. There are also a host of analogous things good hitters and pilots do. These included the importance of undertaking the right kind of practice, visualizing a few landings before a pilot goes flying, and avoiding verbal distractions during a landing (since the language centers are also on the left side of the brain). The whole point is to put one's mind in a state where "the game" seems to slow down and becomes easier to master. I also walked through other parallels, such as getting out of slumps and the importance of umpires (a threat to fragile egos possessed by both activities).

While the article was too lengthy and technical for publication in any of the normal forums I might use, it was passed around the carrier aviation community as a helpful reflection on our business. I received a lot of positive feedback from fellow pilots who felt it helped them perform better at the back of the boat. I later exposed the essay to professional baseball players I've known. Here is what Adam LaRoche, former Washington Nationals' first baseman, said about it: "Being in the zone is something we as hitters talk about constantly. It's also something that can't be described. I can't tell you how many times over the years reporters, teammates, friends, kids have asked me what I'm feeling/thinking at the plate when things are going well. There is simply no answer that will sound intelligent." Ditto for carrier landings.

Adam made a lot of other great comments that reinforced my feelings about the right brain parallels. But the funniest was, "There was one thing that you are totally wrong about. You said that umpires' calls tend to equal themselves out over time and that you get as many good calls as bad ones. I promise you that is false!!"

This journey of writing about landing on the ship opened my eyes to the importance of thinking more deeply about one's profession than the conventional wisdom and bringing synergies to bear from other disciplines that shed new light and enable new ideas. Good leaders and practitioners are restless about finding new perspectives about their professions.

I deployed twice with the Wolfpack, spending the lion's share of the time right where I spent my first two deployments: outside the Arabian Gulf in the Gulf of Oman. Same ocean, same boredom punctuated by night carrier landings. However, we did enjoy a unique experience in the South China Sea off the coast of Vietnam. The Russian Navy had a squadron of MiG-23s stationed at Camh Ranh Bay airbase and would sometimes launch a few airplanes toward a carrier as it passed by. Of course, this meant we had to get a few of our fighters airborne as well, just in case one of the Russians got too close.

This almost always ended up in what can only be described as an unspoken agreement between pilots to perform aerial combat exercises against each other, with nobody pulling the trigger. A few aircrews would get to tangle with one or more Russian MiG-23s, which were hopelessly outmatched by the Tomcat, and would return to the ship with video and an animated description of the fight. I was fortunate to have a go at it; it was great training and a hell of a way to break up the monotony.

We also obtained a little additional relief further to the west while conducting an exercise known as "Beacon Flash" for a few days with the Royal Omani Air Force. Training against "Jaguar" aircraft and flying down what we called "Star Wars Canyon" on the rough Omani coast was a lot of fun amid a fairly dull deployment.

A few of us were permitted to fly on board our logistics aircraft, known as a COD, into Oman for a debrief with the Omani air force, which was manned partly by British ex-patriots. It took a few ugly looks to tame some of our Navy compadres trying to impress the Omanis and Brits with their debriefing skills, which was robbing precious minutes from our opportunity to wrap up with a visit to the bar. We drank as fast as we could before piling into the COD for the ride back to the ship. The severe discomfort of the bumpy ride back in a cramped aircraft after having downed our first beers in a few months was more than offset by knowing we had visited a bar that afternoon and our shipmates had not.

For the most part, our flights involved boring holes in the sky, orbiting on station off the eastern Iranian cities of Jask and Chahbahar. We were short of flying money and spent many days sitting on deck in the hot and dusty waters east of the Arabian Peninsula. Tensions were still high between Iran, which was at war with Iraq, and the United States. In Operation Earnest Will, the United States reflagged several Kuwaiti oil tankers to help keep the oil flowing out of the Middle East.

The combination of my ejection experience and all this time arcing around off the coast of Iran supplied an idea for a novel, which I started but never finished. In it, our hero experiences an aircraft emergency off the coast of Iran and ejects from his Tomcat. His parachute is driven north by the wind, and he lands on a remote portion of Iranian coast. Not knowing whether the Iranians are aware of his presence, he uses his evasion skills to avoid capture and finds himself at the edge of the Chahbahar airfield, where he spots an Iranian Air Force F-14 parked on the ramp.

He somehow manages to get the airplane started (not an easy task to do by yourself for an F-14!) at dawn and takes off, heading south toward the aircraft carrier from which he started. There were several potential endings to this story, but it was fun to start writing it. I told a few people about the plot, and as of this writing, I'm wondering if I unknowingly planted the seeds for an important scene in the second *Top Gun* movie. Or perhaps it's just a coincidence.

Much later, in 2020, I published a short story in the U.S. Naval Institute *Proceedings* magazine, titled "Reunion," based on the same plot. In Stephen King's book *On Writing*, he urges the writer to let the story lead the author rather than trying to outline the whole thing in advance, and I used that approach in writing "Reunion," in which the Iranian pilot who emerges at the end of the story bore the name of the pilot whose hat I stole in Pensacola some years prior. The story was much better than the unpublished book, which mercifully disappeared with the ashes of the old floppy computer disks used by my Apple IIc.

In mid-October, one of the Kuwaiti reflagged tankers was attacked at anchor off Kuwait by an Iranian Silkworm surface-to-surface missile, blinding its American master. Several days later, in what was known as Operation Nimble Archer, the United States retaliated by attacking two inoperative Iranian oil platforms in the Arabian Gulf used by the Iranian Revolutionary Guard Corps. Our job on *Ranger* was to provide air cover from outside the Gulf but as close to the Strait of Hormuz as we could fly without actually entering it, in case we were needed to protect the U.S. forces inside the Gulf conducting the action.

Everyone wanted to fly these missions, and I found myself as part of a section of F-14s on station at the height of the action. Flying the other airplane was Dave "Barnyard" Bernard, with squadron commander Puppy Boucheaux, who participated in a "MiG kill" during the Vietnam War, in his back seat. I was again flying with Woody.

The Gulf is enveloped in a soup of dusty haze during the autumn months. Naturally, it was critical that we not stray over either Iran or Oman during our flight, but we could only see water or coastline by looking straight down, so most of our station-keeping was performed electronically using, of all things, an Iranian navigation aid.

At one point, an Iranian F-4 Phantom fighter launched from Bandar Abbas airfield in the heart of the Strait and vectored toward our position. We could hardly believe our luck. Any fighter pilot's dream is the opportunity to shoot down an enemy airplane (one of our favorite sayings is "a MiG at six o'clock is better than no MiG at all!"), and here it was. We quickly turned toward the Iranian, gained radar contact, and turned on our "master arm" switches.

Our unclassified rules of engagement essentially dictated that if the Iranians showed "hostile intent," we could shoot first. And nose-on meant hostile intent. We were executing a textbook intercept and were just about ready to pull the trigger on our AIM-7 Sparrow missiles when the Iranian fighter turned around and fled. We were deeply disappointed, but it made for a great story during an otherwise fairly boring deployment.

One of the jobs in the Wolfpack I held while waiting for my turn in the pecking order as a department head was that of assistant maintenance officer. This billet involved none of the glamour and grit of getting cranky F-14 Tomcats ready to fly. Rather, I was in charge of most of the administrative aspects of the maintenance effort, such as inspections and training. But it was the real beginning of opening my eyes to the important needs of our young Sailors. They entered the Navy, trained hard, and worked harder. But it was easy to take them for granted. In many ways, they were still kids, and I found myself encouraging our team to help them grow up.

I will never forget discovering how much one of our young Sailors paid for a brand-new pickup truck, with a horrendous interest rate. I asked our crusty old, physically intimidating weapons officer to take the kid back to the car dealer and threaten him with all kinds of potential (nonphysical) retaliation if he didn't fix it. It's about taking care of your young'uns.

Toward the end of my tour my second squadron commander, Cdr. George "Groceries" Moe, broke the news that I would be receiving the number two–ranked competitive fitness report among all the department heads in my squadron. He said he was taking a chance that, based on my background at TopGun and with so many of my former fellow instructors opting to leave the Navy for the airlines, I held a far better chance of screening for squadron command with a number two competitive fitness report than the colleague with whom I was competing. He thought he might be able to get us both screened by ranking us in that order.

I was devastated. Although I was not fully aware of how the "system" worked, it seemed that my future was now placed in the hands of a gamble that never, to my knowledge, had produced a squadron commander. It caused me to question my decision at TopGun to accept the aviation bonus and commit to more time in the Navy. But I was stuck, understood the logic, and handled it as well as possible. My counterpart deserved the opportunity to command a squadron. It was another case of getting knocked down and having to pick myself up.

Thus, as my tour at the Wolfpack drew to a close, I had to make a difficult choice over where to serve next. Many people advised staying in the cockpit by accepting a billet at the F-14 training squadron, which I was tempted to do as a springboard to the airlines if I failed to screen for command. But the writing on the wall of the Goldwater–Nichols Act of 1987 was also clear.

This legislation was an effort to break down the walls that were dividing the services, which not only resulted in bitter budget battles but also were perceived to have been at least one cause of the Desert One debacle during the Iran hostage crisis and less-than-optimal performance in Grenada. The military was trying to advance multiservice, or "joint," operations beyond mere "deconfliction" into actual "interdependence." The effort included a requirement that to achieve flag rank, an officer must have joint education and serve in a joint duty billet. The Navy also seemed to indicate that one's long-term promotion prospects demanded that an officer serve in Washington, DC, as well. I never oriented my career toward checking blocks, nor do I ever remember waking up in the morning wondering what I needed to do to rise to the level of flag rank. I knew that could lead to really foolish behavior. But I also realized that positioning myself for the long term made it more likely that I'd be selected for the personally rewarding jobs in the near term. If I was to have any hope of screening for command of a fighter squadron, it made sense in my situation to go to Washington and serve in a joint billet.

It helped that nobody in the F-14 community had the slightest interest in such a move, and most of my peers didn't even understand the importance of the legislation. Who in their right mind would want to trade the joy of flying nearly every day, wearing a flight suit to work, and living in San Diego for a desk in Washington, DC?

So, keeping in mind my dad's previous exhortation about running to the difficult jobs and performing well, I accepted orders to the Joint Staff in the Pentagon—one of three times over my career I would serve in that corner of our military.

TOP Lt. Gen. Tom Kelly (*left*) and Rear Adm. Mike McConnell (*right*) briefing during
Operation Desert Storm. *Official Department of Defense photo by JO2 Oscar Sosa*

BOTTOM Gen. Colin Powell (*left*) tapped me to be his senior aide in 1992. *Winnefeld collection*

Beltway Rookie

B y late July 1990 Saddam Hussein had been rattling his sword for six months. But the Soviet Union was also falling, consuming the attention of a town that is really only able to focus on one crisis at a time. The intelligence community was particularly obsessed by the unraveling communist empire due to the opacity of the Soviet system and the enormous potential consequences of a miscalculation during the transition.

But it suddenly looked like Saddam was serious about taking Kuwait. When Iraq began to move forces toward the border, Chairman of the Joint Chiefs of Staff Gen. Colin Powell held a meeting of his fellow chiefs and other senior officers at the round table in his office. Considering the few options available, they were in a tough spot if the worst occurred. And I was in a tough spot, being asked questions about those options.

I was initially told to report upon my arrival at the Pentagon in early 1990 to the Western Hemisphere Branch of the Joint Staff's Joint Operations Directorate, otherwise known in the acronym-filled military world as JOD. I was pleased to be headed to the operations side of the Washington arena instead of crunching numbers or building a budget. But I was not so keen to head to the Western Hemisphere Branch. I knew nothing about operations in Central America and was far more familiar with the Middle East. Moreover, Operation Just Cause—which overthrew Panamanian leader Manuel Noriega for drug trafficking ties and the murder of two American soldiers, among other hostile acts—had wrapped up only a couple of months before. The last thing I wanted to do was show up as the new guy on the cleanup crew.

Fortunately, just as I reported to the Joint Staff, I was suddenly diverted to the Central Command Branch, which covered the Middle East region. I never asked what happened, fearing someone would recognize a mistake. Instead, I simply hunkered down at my desk and learned as much as I could as fast as I could about how the Joint Staff did its business.

Three of us—then-colonel (and future four-star assistant commandant of the Marine Corps) William "Spider" Nyland, then-lieutenant colonel (and future Air Force major general) Bobby Wilkes, and myself—manned the Central Command Branch. Along with the rest of the collegial JOD staff, which included directorates covering other regions, we formed a good team. Our cubicles in the bowels of the Pentagon (but within sprinting distance of the elephants, as we used to say) were as close to the operational world as one can get inside the Beltway.

Whenever a crisis emerged in a region, all the branches threw their lot in together to get through the many tasks that fell to the directorate, including producing briefs and writing deployment orders for military forces. When necessary, we would stand up a crisis action team, or CAT, in the National Military Command Center. There were a host of other talented officers in JOD, including my first exposure to then-Navy captain Vern Clark, who led the Pacific Command branch and would later serve as the chief of naval operations.

Throughout the spring of 1990, and in the wake of the Iran-Iraq War, Saddam Hussein was flexing his muscles. He intimidated Kuwait with invasion and threatened to "burn" Israel. Nobody took him seriously except those of us working in JOD. We urged that we be allowed to draw up plans should his bluster turn into action. But we were told Iraq had been helpful during our various confrontations with Iran, and no planning was required or desired.

In late July, as Iraqi troops began moving toward the Kuwaiti border, the U.S. ambassador to Iraq, April Glaspie, sent a confusing signal, telling Saddam that "the United States has no interest in your intra-Arab quarrels." He interpreted that as a green light for an Iraqi invasion. In debriefs after Saddam was captured, he made it clear he would never have invaded Kuwait had he been told the United States was firmly opposed or that our response would be so robust. It was a classic example of the need to be crystal clear and firm in communications. The severe repercussions of this debacle have led to an enormous amount of bloodshed and wasted effort in the three decades hence, including the Khobar Towers bombing, the attacks on 9/11, the invasion of Afghanistan, the second war in Iraq, and eventually our chaotic withdrawal from Afghanistan.

With Iraq on the verge of an invasion, I was now one of a small group of officers answering a series of tough questions about what options would be available to the president should the worst occur. The paucity of options was daunting. None of the tools we take for granted today—such as Tomahawk missiles, drones, or mass availability of precision-guided munitions—were available, either because they simply didn't exist or they were not configured to strike targets in Iraq.

The questions came from all angles. General Powell once asked me, standing before him in his office with an Air Force general seated at his table, how long it would take to convert Air Force B-1 bombers from their nuclear role to dropping conventional weapons. Having luckily attended an Air Force brief a few days prior on that service's initial development of a B-1 conventional weapons capability, I was able to answer General Powell's question. At least I thought so. I responded, "Sir, the B-1 bomber is not currently capable of doing that; the Air Force is just now developing the capability." His irritation with my response lay just below the surface, and he politely said, "Son, I'm just a simple infantryman. I didn't ask you whether they can do it. I asked how long it would take." I answered, based on the brief I previously received: "About two weeks, sir." First lesson learned: answer a senior leader's question completely and succinctly. Second lesson learned: spare no effort to broaden your knowledge, as you never know when you'll find the opportunity to use it.

Meanwhile, Saddam continued threatening Kuwait with invasion unless they capitulated to his demands, claiming that country as Iraq's nineteenth province. Sure enough, on the evening of August 1, which was the morning of August 2 in Kuwait, I received a phone call at home from the JOD director, Col. Ken Hess, directing me: "Sandy, put on your uniform and come to work." I grabbed a pillow and a blanket and told Mary the Iraqis had probably invaded Kuwait, and I wasn't sure when I'd be home.

It was a busy night. Under the supervision of crusty, irascible, gum-chewing, very Irish lieutenant general Tom Kelly, who served as the Joint Staff Director of Operations, we stood up the CAT and wrote the stack of electronic deployment orders that would start the movement of additional U.S. forces to the region.

I grew to like General Kelly, despite his gruff manner, although we did have one run-in. In the middle of the Iraq–Kuwait crisis, another crisis erupted in Liberia, where U.S. citizens needed to be evacuated in what became known as Operation Sharp Edge. It was my first opportunity to brief the Joint Chiefs in the fabled "Tank," where they hold their formal meetings, and where I spent so much time later in my career. The Joint Staff intelligence chief, Rear Adm. Mike McConnell (who later served as director of the CIA), and I were tasked to brief the situation and our evacuation options.

Just before the meeting started, General Powell came up and firmly told the two of us: "We have a lot to talk about in here today; you have no more than five minutes." Admiral McConnell then proceeded to take four and a half minutes to present the intelligence on the situation in Liberia. As he spoke, and in order to adhere to General Powell's guidance, I began whispering to the audio/visual operators behind the screen, eliminating one by one what I deemed to be the less important slides of the presentation General Kelly personally approved. After all, naval officers are paid to take the initiative and adapt to changing circumstances, right? This was in the day of actual plastic transparencies, and one by one, the slides started to disappear.

When my turn finally came, I presented the remaining slides, and we dutifully departed the Tank. Later I discovered that a furious General Kelly chewed out my boss over some lieutenant commander's initiative in shortening his brief. Fortunately, I was young enough not to worry about my career being torpedoed as a result of my misdeed in the Tank. I felt secure in having obeyed a more senior officer's explicit order. And my immediate boss did the right thing in not coming down too hard on me. I think I also gained a little credibility among some of the other officers in the Joint Operations Directorate, who couldn't believe my chutzpah modifying a brief Kelly had personally approved.

Kelly was a real character. Often several other officers and I—mostly colonels and Navy captains—would huddle as a small group with him to receive his guidance. Just as often, when we walked out, the colonels and captains couldn't agree on exactly what the general had directed us to do. But none of them wanted to go back into the room to face the fearsome General Kelly to clarify the tasking, for fear of the dressing down that might be a part of it.

The initial effort to establish defensive positions for Saudi Arabia, known as Desert Shield, and then the first Gulf War itself, Desert Storm, was a nine-month endurance race for me. I worked a twelve-hour shift in the CAT, then did my normal job and tried to get some sleep in the middle. Worse, we frequently rotated shifts, so I constantly felt jet-lagged. Perhaps worst, I became an early expert in the use of PowerPoint as a briefing tool, which became both a blessing and a curse.

During the runup to the war, then–secretary of defense Dick Cheney made it clear that he was merely a former congressman from Wyoming and wanted to know more about how the military would fight this war. So he requested a brief on one topic from each service that would be relevant to the upcoming conflict. The Army would talk about M1A1 Abrams tank operations, the Air Force would describe the F-16, the Navy would walk through countermine warfare, and the Marine Corps would discuss amphibious operations.

Many years earlier, my uncle Carl Builder wrote a fascinating book titled *The Masks of War: American Military Styles in Strategies and Analysis*, which, among other things, described the differences among the services' cultures. I was about to witness these differences in living color since I was handed the task of guiding them through the process.

The Army's brief was probably the most professional of all—they produced a simple PowerPoint presentation that was quickly approved up the chain of command. A knowledgeable colonel was empowered to give the brief, which went well.

The Air Force put together a beautiful marketing presentation under the personal guidance of their chief of staff, Gen. Merrill McPeak. Their brief was to be given by what appeared to be a professional briefer, closely supervised by McPeak. But it turned out that Cheney didn't want a senior officer in the brief, and much to his frustration, McPeak was not allowed in the room. This was nearly a disaster. Just as quickly as the major slid his gorgeous PowerPoint folder across the table, Cheney slid it off to the side. The professional briefer was on his own, without his slick graphics, but somehow made it through the process.

The Navy handed its task to a "salty" and grumpy senior captain ("why do I have to go brief the damn Secretary?"), who reluctantly put together what I can only describe as a crayon-and-stick-figure presentation. Much to my relief, Cheney also swept this presentation off to the side, preferring to hear directly from the briefer. Fortunately, the latter really knew his stuff and gave Cheney a good feel for the ins and outs of mine warfare in the Arabian Gulf. The Marine Corps' presentation went the exact same way. All four presentations matched almost perfectly what my uncle said about service culture.

The war was over more quickly and with less bloodshed than anyone expected, largely because much of the pent-up capability the nation built for a war in Europe, which now seemed largely irrelevant due to the fall of the Iron Curtain, was moved to the desert and unleashed on the hapless Iraqi Army. It was a showcase for new technology and the Army's lightning-fast ability to overwhelm a lesser adversary in conventional maneuver warfare in the desert. As such, it was hard to watch Lieutenant General Kelly, who was an Army tank officer, grow pale when we showed him a video of Iraqi tanks being taken out like sitting ducks by precision-guided munitions.

Our success in that war shocked both the Russians and the Chinese. The decision by President George H. W. Bush to end the war when our objective—ejecting Iraqi forces from Kuwait and restoring that nation's sovereignty—was achieved rather than continuing on to overthrow Saddam Hussein was one of the wisest in our nation's history. This decision, influenced and supported by thoughtful leaders like Secretary of State James Baker and General Powell, strongly informed my later views on the use of national power.

This war was also a watershed for Joint warfare in many different ways. One of the most important was integration of airpower within the Joint world. In preparation for war in Europe, the Air Force developed an industrial-like process for managing airpower in large and sustained wars. This included a robust air operations center concept that managed a cyclical (although somewhat bureaucratic) process for assigning daily sorties through a vehicle known as the air tasking order, or ATO. It was complex poetry in motion. Meanwhile, the U.S. Navy had oriented itself to one-off, single-day contingency operations, such as strikes against Iranian forces in the Gulf.

Not only was the Navy ignorant of the Air Force's ATO process, but the tactics the two services used were also completely different. For example, in a one-off strike that doesn't take long, it is feasible to lob a near-continuous and preemptive hail of antiradiation weapons into the vicinity of a target in order to suppress enemy air defenses. It is impossible to do this in a large, sustained conflict where you would quickly run out of weapons.

So the Navy and Air Force unintentionally veered away from each other in this and many other ways. The first Gulf War was a handy catalyst to bring the branches back together doctrinally. Similar challenges arose with the Marine Corps, which viewed its aviation assets as part and parcel of its operations and thus had to remain under its complete control. An uneasy truce resulted in which the Marines were essentially allowed to manage their airpower as a major augment to their supporting fires, albeit within the ATO, while offering any excess sorties to the rest of the Joint force. A great debate also occurred over the efficacy of deep strikes to whittle down an enemy's capability (the Air Force position) versus close air support to enable troops on the ground (the Army's position). Most of these doctrinal issues have been resolved over the intervening years.

Not long after the war was over, the Bush administration decided to provide humanitarian relief to the Kurds in northern Iraq, who were being brutally suppressed by Saddam Hussein. Whether they were being starved or gassed by Saddam, the Kurds were in rough shape and pleading for help. When the decision was taken on short notice to support the Kurds late one

Friday afternoon, I was the only one left in the JOD office. Lt. Gen. Martin Brandtner, a Marine with two Navy Crosses from Vietnam who had relieved General Kelly a month or so earlier, called me to his office and directed me to write an order to make it happen.

I dashed back to my computer, pulled up another previous order, "saved as," and began filling in the new details. Needing a name for the operation, and under the somewhat unwieldy rules used by the Joint Staff, I came up with the title "Provide Comfort." I ran back into General Brandtner's office and placed the completed order on the desk in front of him. He smiled, looked up, and said, "you know this name is pretty good, and it's going to make history." Out went the deployment order, and the title stuck. I was sure I had just used my fifteen proverbial minutes of fame. But many other subsequent relief operations used the name "Provide" followed by another word.

Another project on which I worked during this post–Cold War, post–Desert Storm period was aligning U.S. naval force presence with overall U.S. policy. This was not a problem for Army and Air Force units, which were normally either permanently stationed overseas or remained in the United States waiting for a crisis. Conversely, Navy ships, often with Marine Corps units embarked, conducted routine, rotational deployments of the type I had experienced in my first tours of duty. Part of this force would always be deployed, with the rest remaining at home conducting training and maintenance, in a continuous cycle along roughly a 3:1 ratio. The Navy deployed its ships and submarines where and how they believed they could best be used and supported. It was always done this way, and nobody ever questioned the fact that deployment decisions were managed by an office in the Navy that existed for this purpose, rather than something in the Joint world.

But in an evolving global security structure, it made much more sense for forces to deploy to wherever the larger policy community felt the powerful signal of naval presence was most needed. Moreover, I felt the combatant commanders, newly empowered by the Goldwater–Nichols Act, should present their "requirements" for all forces, and the service chiefs should supply that demand as feasible and as adjudicated by an impartial Joint entity. The resulting tension between provider and consumer seemed like a good way to manage the force.

Previously, the Navy jealously protected its sophisticated deployment management model, which gave it a certain power over the question. I was concerned at the time that my leadership of this effort from the Joint Staff could be perceived by the Navy as being disloyal. But, to their credit (and in a very un-Navy-like way), Navy leadership reached the conclusion that it was time to bring forward-presence decisions into the Joint world.

So we cooperatively developed a process known as Global Naval Force Presence Policy, which eventually evolved into overall policy for the entire Joint force, known as Global Force Management Policy. Today it is the process that manages the planned or emergent deployment of any U.S. military unit across the globe.

After all this activity—including having a prominent place in the lower-level Washington, DC, management of the war to liberate Kuwait, Operation Provide Comfort, and force presence policy, I somehow was nominated for the Joint Staff Action Officer of the Year award in the late spring of 1991. Much to my surprise, I was selected. It was a real honor—indeed, an embarrassment—to have been chosen, given the incredibly talented officers with whom I worked over the previous year and a half. It was a real team effort, not an individual performance. The award was generously endowed by Adm. William Crowe, a former chairman, with the annual winner receiving a stack of excellent books on subjects concerning military leadership and policy.

Then, sometime in the late spring of 1991, and much to my astonishment and despite my number two fitness report from VF-1, I was notified that I would be promoted one year early for the rank of commander; shortly thereafter, I was notified that I screened for command of a fighter squadron. You could have knocked me over with a feather. Mary and I were on vacation, staying at the Ballast Point Officer's Club on Point Loma in San Diego, when I received the news on the promotion. My hometown was a great place to hear it.

I was excited about getting back to the fleet and trying my hand at fighter squadron command. It was a real wake-up call for the people who thought I'd made a huge mistake in going to Washington rather than staying in the cockpit. My phone soon began ringing off the hook, with people asking how one might be assigned to the Joint Staff as my replacement. I was looking forward to departing for my command tour within the year.

However, something I did must have resonated with General Powell. Perhaps my acceptance speech at the Action Officer of the Year ceremony, since I kept it very brief. In the late summer of 1991, I was summoned to his office for an interview with his executive assistant, then-colonel Richard Chilcoate.

The chairman was entitled to two aides-de-camp, who were responsible for planning and executing his local, national, and international travel as well as for taking care of some of the mundane details of his life in order to preserve his time for what amounted to an exceptionally busy job. His senior aide had recently been sacked for an unspecified set of conduct issues, and Powell needed someone on short notice.

I was told during the interview that this would be a two-year job, to fill out the end of the chairman's term. I politely thanked Chilcoate for the consideration and said I could not serve for two years because I was selected for command and needed to get back to the fleet. Chilcoate chuckled, said "we'll see," and sent me away wondering if I had just made a huge mistake. After all, a four-star officer, especially the chairman of the Joint Chiefs, can hand-select anyone he wants on his staff. However, either Powell was impressed with my chutzpah—of which he was a real master—or he just needed an aide badly enough. I quickly found out he selected me, and I'd only have to serve one year.

The timing couldn't have been better, for I had been scheduled to fly on the Secretary of the Navy's airplane to the 1991 Tailhook convention in Las Vegas one week later. I could still have gone, but I felt I needed the time to turn over the aide job and get my feet on the ground. Had I been on that flight, I would almost certainly have been swept up in the aftermath of that event, even though I'm certain I would not have been part of the small minority of attendees who brought such discredit on naval aviation through their behavior. But hardly anyone escaped the poorly managed investigation that followed. Sometimes you just get lucky.

I was fortunate to have the opportunity to observe General Powell directly. I was exposed to a wealth of leadership lessons, ranging from how he treated his staff to how he was able to speak in public so eloquently from a stack of handwritten cards he scribbled on the way to an event. And a great deal in between.

Almost immediately after reporting to the front office, I was brought in for an hour-long discussion with Powell on his expectations for his aides. It was a great, condensed learning experience about how senior leaders think and operate. And it was cool at the time to be sitting down at a table with the most senior officer in the military, our first African American chairman, who had emerged as a legendary leader during the Gulf War.

In one amusing moment during our discussion, he directed me to never walk out of the room unsure of any guidance, musing "Kelly—he never walks out of here unless he's certain what I've just told him." I couldn't help recalling many sessions when the colonels and captains didn't want to revisit Kelly's guidance.

I may have been a good officer, but I was not necessarily a good aide. I recall one embarrassing moment not long after we took off in Powell's airplane for a speaking engagement at the LBJ Library in Texas. I went back to the closet on the airplane to verify that his dress military jacket made it on board. To my shock and dismay, I couldn't find it. Walking up to interrupt the general, where he was busily refining the note cards for his speech, I owned up to my mistake. I will never forget how he looked up from his seat, with the same expression my father once used when I told him my brand-new bicycle had been stolen. If it's possible for the reader to conjure an image of "how could this officer have done this to me?" transitioning to "how can I turn this to my advantage?" . . . all in one moment . . . that is what his look conveyed.

Even more to my embarrassment—although also to my relief—Powell's communicators frantically called back to his enlisted aides in Washington, who were certain they loaded the jacket on board. Sure enough, I hadn't looked deeply enough in the aircraft's closet. There was the jacket, deeply buried behind some other gear. Once more, I approached and interrupted Powell, this time with better news. While I was deeply chagrined and was sure he must have been thinking of me as a complete idiot, I gained an important lesson regarding the grace of a senior leader contending with a subordinate's honest mistake. I resolved to emulate that behavior for the rest of my life, and it later paid immense dividends in developing loyalty among treasured subordinates.

Working as Colin Powell's aide offered a host of precious experiences—drawn from both observing the demands of the job of chairman and from the man himself—from which a young officer could benefit. His composure while speaking outdoors at the dedication of the Buffalo Soldiers monument in Fort Leavenworth as a monster thunderstorm loomed behind him was a lesson in calculated risk. Observing him tactfully decline unreasonable requests from his overseas counterparts was a priceless tutorial in international diplomacy (otherwise known as "letting people have it your way"). His somber dignity while visiting Gorée Island in Senegal and Bunce Island in Sierra Leone, where his ancestors may have been sold into slavery, was moving.

These visits were sobering for me as well. I later took Powell's charming wife, Alma, to Annapolis to visit the U.S. Naval Institute to scour their museum basement for art for the chairman's quarters on Fort Myer in Arlington, Virginia. Because the chairman of the Joint Chiefs of Staff position was relatively new and as a Joint billet was not assigned to any given service, there was no sense of history in the quarters, to include a lack of symbolic art. Alma and I found a classic portrait of Commo. Matthew Calbraith Perry, who in addition to opening Japan to trade, also spent 1843 and 1844 commanding the Africa Squadron suppressing the slave trade under the auspices of the Webster–Ashburton Treaty, which called for an end to the trade on the high seas.

One of my most vivid memories was traveling with Powell and his public affairs officer, Col. Bill Smullen, as we became the first three Americans in uniform to visit East Germany after the fall of the Iron Curtain. Months before, I sat outside in an anteroom with a couple of senior Russian colonels while Powell met with his Russian counterpart privately in an obscure house in Vienna. When our host brought out a platter piled high with sandwiches and a vast amount of beer, I couldn't believe how quickly those two Russian colonels made their way through both plate and pitcher. It was as though they hadn't eaten in days, although their physiques didn't indicate it.

Now, after the fall of the Berlin Wall, we flew deep into East Germany in a Russian-built helicopter as guests of the chief of the German general staff, Gen. Klaus Naumann. It was unforgettable to see the bewildered faces of young East German conscripts as a Black American four-star general walked down their troop line, shaking their hands and making small talk.

As the horizon drew closer on working as Powell's aide, along came the process of where I would be assigned for my tour as a fighter squadron commander. The variables were: location (east, west, or all the way west to Japan) and which of three variants of the F-14 (A, B, or D) would be in the squadron to which I would be assigned.

It seemed that every officer who screened that year in the F-14 community desperately wanted to be the first commander of the newest variant of the Tomcat entering the Navy inventory: the long-awaited F-14D, with more powerful engines and a new radar. In my calculation, the opportunity for deploying as a squadron commander was far more important than the airplane flown by my squadron, and it wasn't clear when the F-14D would be making its first deployment anyway. So, taking a contrarian view, I told the detailer to send me wherever he wanted, realizing it meant I would likely be going to a squadron with the oldest F-14s in the Navy.

Sure enough, I was assigned to the "Fighting Checkmates" of VF-211. Due to the needs of aircraft inventory management, this squadron had recently traded in their newer F-14Bs—which had more powerful, more reliable engines than the ones that stalled during my spin accident—for the oldest F-14As in the fleet. No matter: this squadron maintained a solid reputation and would be deploying overseas rather than potentially struggling to bring a new model of Tomcat into the fleet.

So Mary and I packed up our stuff and moved back to San Diego.

My journey back to the fleet passed once again through the F-14 training squadron. One day toward the end of my requalification process to join VF-211, a friend and I decided to play golf at the Naval Air Station Miramar club. He said he would have to join after nine holes, so I wasn't surprised when I approached the clubhouse that there was an announcement on the loudspeaker saying I had a phone call in the pro shop. But the phone call was not from my friend. Rather, the chief of staff at the fighter wing informed me a Navy F-16 used as an adversary aircraft had crashed in Twin Falls, Idaho. I was assigned to conduct the accident investigation and was directed to get on an airliner in a couple of hours to fly up to the scene.

This was the most bizarre accident I'd ever encountered. The pilot, who was visiting a relative who lived in the area, did a high-performance takeoff in a snowstorm, pulling straight into the vertical into the heavy snow. He and his aircraft plummeted to the ground a couple of miles downrange, and he was killed instantly.

It is remarkable what can be discerned from the various components of an aircraft in the aftermath of such an accident. Based on witness marks indicating the position of the flight control surfaces at impact, we knew he tried to pull up when he broke out of the low undercast at a high rate of speed. There was strong evidence there was nothing wrong with the aircraft based on the microscopic condition of filaments in light bulbs, which fracture differently if they are warm, and which indicated which warning lights were lit or unlit at impact. It appeared as though he simply became disoriented due to his maneuver up into the clouds. The question was: why?

It became evident to my fellow board members that this accident was a poster example of what is known as "human factors" interfering in a pilot's ability to both make sound judgments and fly competently. This pilot had been immensely distracted by a host of personal issues in his life, along with a consistent theme of maneuvering out of performance challenges on the ground. Every rivulet we followed turned into a raging torrent of human factors. I took great care in writing the report, and it became the classic case study of the importance of human factors in aviation.

Recovering the crash scene was exceptionally challenging since the aircraft landed in deep snow in the middle of nowhere. I likened it to Napoleon's march on Moscow. Digging the many pieces of wreckage out of the snow was hard work, but we managed to recover most of the major parts that survived the impact.

One night when the area was afflicted with heavy snow, high winds, and subzero temperatures, I ordered the Air Force personnel from a local base who were guarding the wreckage to go back to their hotel. I was concerned their vehicle would run out of fuel or experience a mechanical problem, and they would be stuck out in the cold in survival conditions. Surely nobody would want to go out in that kind of weather.

I shouldn't have underestimated the ability of the hardy local Idaho population to survive in such conditions. When we arrived on the scene the next morning, many of the parts we neatly set aside that were most important to our investigation—most notably the hydraulic actuators whose witness marks would tell us the position of the flight control surfaces at impact—were missing. Apparently, they were picked up in the middle of the night by snowmobilers looking for souvenirs. Fortunately, we were able to recover them by broadcasting on local radio stations how essential these parts were to the investigation and offering amnesty for their return.

Two investigations are conducted for every military aircraft accident—one to examine human and technical performance and another to determine whether any legal or other culpability is involved. Sadly, the legal investigating officer, who almost completely missed the human factor issues associated with the pilot, spent most of his report taking me to task for temporarily losing custody of the parts. No good deed goes unpunished. Mercifully, I later received a call from the fighter wing commander himself saying I would not be disciplined for my misdemeanor.

I learned a great deal from this accident, most notably that I would need to keep a close eye on the pilots in my future command lest they end up in the same place. After the investigation was complete, VF-211 conducted its change of command, and I found myself as the number two leader in a fighter squadron. I would help shape it into what I always believed a fighter squadron should be for when I would eventually assume command. It was a dream come true.

Anchor #1:
Lead Yourself

"Would you have a great empire? Rule over yourself."

Publilius Syrus

Character First

"All reality hinges on moral foundations."
Dr. Martin Luther King

"Where principle is involved, be deaf to expediency."
Commodore Matthew Maury

"Rest satisfied with doing well, and leave others to talk of you as they please."

Pythagoras

Know Your Stuff

"Leadership and learning are indispensable to each other."
John F. Kennedy

"It's what you learn after you know it all that counts."
Coach John Wooden

"Try to learn something about everything and everything about something."

Thomas H. Huxley

Commit or Quit

"Success flourishes only in perseverance . . . ceaseless, restless perseverance."

Manfred von Richthofen

"The harder I work, the luckier I get."

Samuel Goldwyn

Manage Your Brain

"Never let 'em see you sweat."

Colin Powell

The man who can do the average thing when everyone else around him is losing his mind.

Napoleon's definition of a
military genius

ANCHOR 1
Lead Yourself

CHARACTER FIRST

For leaders, character matters more than anything else—without it, any effort to develop oneself is wasted. Its key components are *humility, integrity,* and *courage,* which do not develop naturally and must be learned, lived, and projected. They are the first thing scrutinized—and emulated—by the led.

Authentic humility stems from the deepest sense of personal security. If it's not genuine, people will quickly see right through it (even though a leader who takes himself or herself too seriously will not detect this). It is what allows a person to, in the words of my Aussie friend Roger Eaton, "cheer on your peers." Integrity is doing the difficult right thing rather than the easy wrong thing, regardless of whether someone is looking or not. It is the only thing that cannot be taken away from a person—it has to be given away. As J. R. Ewing from the television series *Dallas* said, "Once you give up integrity, the rest is a piece of cake." Courage is, as Samuel Johnson once said, not an absence of fear; rather, it is the willingness to go forward in spite of one's fear. Physical courage is what enabled men getting off the landing craft at Normandy to keep going up the beach and to the cliffs in spite of withering German fire. Moral courage, which is more commonly tested, is what allows people to take personal risks in the name of a principle or an ambitious project. It is also what allows a change of mind when one is confronted by new facts, and to admit when one is wrong.

Buying into these critical traits can be challenging for young people eager to make their reputation in the world, as there are many tempting shortcuts to success if that is the only goal. Although people who come up short in humility, integrity, and courage can be named or elected as leaders, they will never be wise or worthy, and they can be spectacularly ineffective if not downright dangerous.

KNOW YOUR STUFF

It is impossible to overstate the importance of lifelong learning, both within and outside one's chosen field. Those who put in the extra effort to learn a little more each day will rapidly outpace their peers. The knowledge "interest" compounds rapidly over time. Moreover, I've seen the benefits of an organization demanding that its members gain more than the minimum level of knowledge required to operate, which builds confidence in handling unknowns when they arise. The U.S. Navy's nuclear propulsion program does this because when a submarine is under the ice or when a ship is in the heat of battle, the operator has to make emergency decisions with the right knowledge firmly in hand.

Lifelong learning also enables people to think for themselves rather than the "groupthink" that causes many people to fall prey to twenty-four-hour news media and social media echo chambers. Because of their unrelenting curiosity, learning leaders see things others don't and are more willing to confront what seems wrong. Learning is also the engine of the creative process that enables one to bring different ideas together in previously unknown combinations that yield new opportunities or solutions to problems. The only way to lead that synergy process is to feed a relentless curiosity by pursuing additional knowledge not only in one's own field but in others as well.

It helps to be well organized to quickly get your hands on the knowledge you need. I also find it useful to structure knowledge and experience (including, for example, my thoughts on leadership expressed in this book) within a set of lists, or hooks, in my mind that I can rapidly access. Finally, knowing the history of one's profession can lend a great deal to routine operations, strategic planning, and crisis response.

COMMIT OR QUIT

It is not unusual for people to enter into a leadership role, especially for the first time, thinking "I've arrived, and now it's time to give the direction and let everyone else do the work." This is a terrible mistake. Leaders of the most successful organizations are usually the hardest-working members. They run to work and actively search for the hardest parts of the job.

Commitment is a synonym for "will," which Jim Collins identifies, after humility, as the second essential trait common to the most successful leaders at the helm of the hundreds of companies he studied. Your team will quickly sense whether you are committed, and they will act accordingly.

Commitment is born of a combination of factors. *Belief in one's mission* is contagious. *Determination* enables leaders to understand that high-level success is found just after most people give up. *Energy* translates into the daily grind required to develop oneself, to innovate, to hire the right people, and to simply get things done. *Enthusiasm*, expressed clearly and consistently, firmly signals the leader's commitment. Finally, *focus* helps one prioritize the "important and urgent" over the "not important and not urgent." A good leader should get something important done every day.

MANAGE YOUR BRAIN

It's almost impossible to predict with certainty how someone will perform under competitive or real-time stress. Being entrusted with pressure is a privilege to be relished, and handling that pressure requires self-control and discipline. When a sudden and difficult problem arises, it helps to have the requisite skill and confidence that allows you to rise to the occasion. Your team will feed off your poise and will panic along with you if you crumble.

When that critical moment arrives, you will be too busy thinking through a problem at light speed to waste time on agitation.

Experienced leaders find ways to either eliminate stress or compartmentalize it out of sight of their subordinates. In naval aviation, we're taught to just "put stress in a box in the corner and to control when and where you let it out." Accept bad news gracefully, avoid the temptation to shoot the messenger, and calmly turn to understanding the problem and finding a way to mitigate it.

Further, the accomplished leader knows that remaining calm and managing stress demand a good dose of personal security. That means keeping your ego in check, taking responsibility for your actions, and avoiding placing blame on others. When thinking about their personal success, leaders don't confuse skill with luck, don't confuse conviction with stubbornness, and develop thick skins. They don't have to constantly remind others of their own accomplishments. Finally, it can be tempting when one is under pressure to rationalize violations of policy, law, or ethics; history is filled with those who failed in this regard. Don't be this person.

TOP The Fighting Checkmates squadron patch *Winnefeld collection*

MIDDLE VF-211 Tomcat *Jim Caiella*

BOTTOM Deployment homecomings are sweet. *Winnefeld collection*

Checkmate

I n 1994 Forrest Gump and the X-Box burst onto the American scene and the last Russian troops left East Germany. There would not be a World Series that year due to the Major League Baseball players' strike. It was also the year I took command of the "Fighting Checkmates" of VF-211 at Naval Air Station Miramar in San Diego, California. It was finally a chance to put in motion all the leadership lessons and ideas I'd developed over the previous sixteen years. I started with building the team.

Naval aviation has a long tradition that the commanding officer of a squadron first serves as its number two ranking officer—otherwise known as the executive officer, or XO. One of the benefits of this system is that a proactive XO can assemble the team that will man the squadron once he or she takes command. I was determined to bring on board the best leaders I could find to fill my department head and senior enlisted maintenance positions. This required actively recruiting people as well as working closely with the "detailers" who make these assignments happen.

The latter were reluctant partners because they were rightfully interested in spreading quality around and not putting too many of the Navy's best people into competition with each other. But enough banging on the table got the job done. It was a bit selfish, but having quality senior leadership made all the difference in the world in our performance as a unit. It was a lasting lesson.

The squadron deployed to the Arabian Gulf on board USS *Nimitz* while I served as XO. Having participated in the first Gulf War effort from inside the Pentagon, it was fascinating to fly as part of Operation Southern Watch. After all, I had drafted the operation's "execute order" in 1991, which imposed the no-fly zone over portions of Iraq. We launched daily combat air patrol missions intended to prevent Iraqi aircraft from entering the restricted airspace. We also conducted reconnaissance missions using a camera pod known as the Tactical Air Reconnaissance Pod System. Our job was to scour the Iraqi countryside for unauthorized activity.

These missions were dangerous due to the presence of an Iraqi surface-to-air missile site in the no-fly area, combined with the slow airspeed—around 220 knots—required to acquire good photographs from the pod, which left us few maneuver options if we were targeted. But we had the threat well covered with jamming and strike assets if the missile site ever became active. Nonetheless, it was a bit disconcerting at night to see the trails of antiaircraft artillery fire headed up toward us, even though we always flew above it.

The only exciting moment occurred when an Iraqi MiG-23 headed south one night at high speed from Baghdad toward the edge of the no-fly zone. My wingman and I were vectored north and came close to launching a weapon with a near-perfect shot just before the Iraqi turned around, just short of the no-fly zone border. Apparently Saddam Hussein's Air Force wanted no more a part of us than the Iranians did a few years earlier over the Strait of Hormuz.

I took command several months after returning to San Diego from our deployment. The night before the ceremony, the junior officers from the squadron raided our home on short notice and drank every drop of alcohol we owned. In a gracious gesture, Mary took most of the shots intended for me so I would not be a mess during the ceremony, and she still somehow managed to look beautiful the next day. I don't know how she did it.

One of my first goals as a new F-14 squadron commander was to do my part to transform the fighter community from having a pure air-to-air mission to assuming the additional air-to-ground role. Tomcat aircrews had long-resisted taking on this additional mission, even though the airplane was designed with some capability in that area. To many fighter pilots, "making mud bounce" seemed to be beneath the pure dignity of air-to-air combat. But this approach was about to render the community irrelevant. The Russian threat seemingly evaporated overnight with the fall of the Iron Curtain, and now the premium was on air-to-ground capability, not so much on air-to-air. Our efforts in Iraq were "exhibit A" of this shift. It only made sense to make precious room on carrier flight decks for aircraft that could perform more than one mission.

This was an example of what is known in biology as genetic drift. Richard Pascale and his coauthors of *Surfing the Edge of Chaos* tell us an organism continually refines its winning concept to the point that it becomes overly specialized. It can then become extinct within a generation when an environment it can't handle suddenly emerges. It happens in business—to wit, the demise of Polaroid with the advent of the digital camera, even though company executives saw it coming—and it can happen in the military as well.

Like Polaroid, the F-14 community, which refined its air-to-air culture over a couple of decades, was about to be wiped off the map. It was time for Tomcat aircrews to get with the program, and I wanted VF-211 to be the first to push forward with the "Bombcat." It helped that we managed to bring on board a talented pilot from the A-6 Intruder community, which was eliminated due to the age and expense of its airplanes. The prodigious air-to-ground knowledge he brought with him was priceless.

Unfortunately, and not long after becoming the new Checkmate skipper, I received a phone call from the fighter wing that would define the first portion of my tour. Because we recently returned from a deployment, I was told that we would have to manage a 70 percent cut to our funding for the final three months of the fiscal year due to budget shortages. Moreover, we would only have access to three of our fourteen Tomcats to prevent us from robbing parts from some of our airplanes to enable us to fly others.

This was a potential morale-crushing blow for the squadron. I was told by my chain of command to "show the pain." But I viewed that as something

I would later codify as "vicious compliance"—not what I desired as the defining philosophy of my command tour. My mission was to forge the most combat-ready squadron I could with the resources provided by the American people. I saw the funding reduction as an intriguing challenge, which got my creative juices flowing. I also knew that human beings are adept at making themselves feel miserable, and I wanted nothing to do with that, either for myself or for the young people I was leading. The bottom line for me was: "do the right thing; don't waste this crisis."

I told my officers our attitude would be: "you're going to have to try a lot harder than that to jack us around, and we're going to somehow come out of this better than when we went in." We rose to the bad news in two ways.

The first involved challenging our people, before we lost our funding, to do something no other F-14 squadron had ever done before: a fifty-sortie day involving live air-to-ground weapons deliveries. This effort was not without risk: our pilots would be dropping live weapons, sometimes at lower altitudes, while flying three or more times the number of sorties in one day normally flown by a squadron operating "on the beach." But we felt the risk could be managed, and we prepared well. The team pulled the day off without a hitch. Led by talented maintenance MC Danilo Abrajano and weapons CWO David Thigpen, our team performed flawlessly on a day that started early in the morning and ended late at night.

But even after this accomplishment, we still had to deal with being severely underfunded for the final three months of the fiscal year. Thus, our second goal was to emerge stronger than we entered. We worked to gain special permission to access all of our airplanes to conduct corrosion control under the solemn promise we would not "cannibalize" any parts. We flew the daylights out of the simulators to keep our muscle memories intact and maintain our knowledge of emergency procedures. We took a field trip to Nellis Air Force Base to view former Eastern Bloc airplanes in their museum. We gave people leave. We held more ground training than ever before—and tried to make it as interesting as possible.

The effort paid off. We kept our spirits high and flew eleven of our fourteen Tomcats less than a week after our funding was restored, which was a monumental accomplishment given how cranky these airplanes could be when not flown for a while. So much for having the oldest jets in the fleet! While we didn't reinforce much bad news on funding cuts, our Sailors were proud of having safely achieved a stretch goal.

Two other events contributed to further molding me as a leader, each tragic in its own way. The first involved the unfortunate and fatal crash of Lt. Kara Hultgreen, who was the first woman to fly as a pilot in the F-14, on October 25, 1994.

Kara—who was in a different squadron and whom I did not know personally—crashed while in the final turn toward an aircraft carrier during a qualification period. In the landing configuration, the aircraft is closer to stall speed. Given the relatively wide separation between the Tomcat's engines, it was more vulnerable than most other aircraft to the loss of an engine, especially if the one on the inside of the turn failed. Kara lost her inboard engine at the worst possible time and was unable to recover the aircraft. Sadly, she did not survive the ejection attempt.

Bringing women into the male-dominated halls of Navy carrier aviation was not without considerable controversy, and their first cadre was under enormous pressure to perform. Thus, this accident became immediate fodder for the media and opponents of women flying carrier jet aircraft. But it occurred to me that VF-211's pilots—especially younger ones—might not have handled this situation any better than she did. We constantly rehearsed procedures, reinforced by simulator flights, for the loss of an engine on a catapult shot, when the aircraft is heavy as well as slow. But we hardly ever rehearsed the loss of an engine while landing—probably because most single-engine situations occurred during some other phase of flight.

So we trooped our pilots over to the simulator and put them in the same situation, and most of them crashed on their first try, even though they knew what was about to happen. After some coaching and practice, they did it again and all survived. Our experience as a group of pilots was used by my chain of command to help debunk the myth of women not being able to serve successfully as fighter pilots.

The other event—less tragic but hard nonetheless—was the need to end the flying career of one of my pilots. This is easy to do when it involves "sins of commission," such as repeated instances of a lack of flight discipline. It's more difficult when the person is trying hard and wants to succeed. This pilot—a collegial and well-liked person—demonstrated all the characteristics of a failing aviator, including trying to make up for poor performance in the air with hard work on the ground.

But when several dangerous carrier landings came on top of other incidents that had caused us to put him on a form of probation, I decided to pull the plug. It was at once one of the easiest and most challenging decisions I've ever made. Fortunately, my chain of command—namely, my air wing commander, then-captain Timothy Keating—supported my decision.

Keating and I were soulmates. When he was the air wing's deputy commander and I was squadron XO, we saw eye-to-eye on the difference between the important issues we faced and the trivial things other people wasted time complaining about.

I got a bit lucky one day when, during an air wing detachment to Roswell, New Mexico, one of my talented department heads, Lt. Cdr. Bobby "Tree" Rountree, led four of our big Tomcats into a perfectly executed "fan break" at low altitude over the field. This was a difficult maneuver that required all four aircraft, flying in an echelon formation, to bank 90 degrees nearly simultaneously into a tight turn, then open the distance between themselves at exactly the same rate. They then had to achieve the same landing interval, all while remaining at the same altitude on the downwind leg of the landing pattern. Performed improperly, it was at best embarrassingly ugly and at worst dangerous.

Keating and I happened to be in the tower at the time, observing the air wing's return from a practice strike. He chuckled a little bit, but I could tell he was impressed. He was also smart enough to know the difference between me leading a maneuver like that and developing a squadron full of aviators capable of executing such a maneuver. I was under no illusions: it was the four talented pilots who executed the maneuver, not me, but it was a great statement about the culture of the command.

One amusing event during this tour involved the mounting frustration experienced by the Navy rank and file over an ever-increasing peacetime paperwork load imposed on our people. This sense had gotten back to someone important in Washington, and down came a directive called the Paperwork

Reduction Act. The next guidance we received was to submit a new report at the end of each month outlining the actions we took during that period to reduce the amount of required paperwork. You can't make this stuff up.

Kara Hultgreen was not my only experience with the advent of women on sea duty in the Navy. The Checkmates were among the first squadrons at Miramar designated to bring an initial cadre of enlisted women on board. Life is tough for the troops on the flight line and living in cramped quarters on board aircraft carriers, and it was going to be tough for women to break into this male-dominated culture safely and securely.

I always felt that if someone was qualified to serve, it didn't matter whether they were male or female, although I was somewhat concerned about the social aspects of mixing men and women in close quarters. But my father had served as commandant of midshipmen at the Naval Academy when women were first allowed to attend, and I knew it could work as long as we applied good leadership.

I also knew I'd need some senior female senior leadership, so I took the controversial step of naming a female command master chief—the senior enlisted person in the command—when I got the opportunity. We welcomed on board YNCM Valerie Johnston. Candidly, Johnston received mixed reviews from the crusty senior enlisted personnel manning the squadron. As has understandably sometimes been the case, perhaps she sometimes felt as though she had to try too hard to fit into her new role. But it had to be hard for her to break this glass ceiling, so I give her a lot of credit for courageously stepping into an unknown environment and taking on the associated risk. She provided much-needed senior leadership to both the young women we brought on board and their male peers.

This episode was the beginning of my long-standing belief in the wisdom of empowering women in the service. To be sure, there are personal factors—such as the opportunity to bear children—that can cause women to leave a career earlier than their male counterparts. There are physical differences that can make it challenging for women to succeed in some of the more demanding jobs. Let's face it, carrying a hundred-pound pack over many years can place more stress on an average woman's physique compared to men. But these factors are usually overshadowed by the immense talent our nation's women bring into the workforce, to say nothing of doubling our recruiting pool. So I went out of my way to support women professionally for the rest of my career, and I'm glad I did.

Part of taking care of Sailors involves looking after their health. It never ceased to amaze me how poorly most Sailors performed on their physical readiness test, or PRT. Now that I was in command of a unit, I could have some small influence over their fitness. Our Sailors had a hard time understanding why they needed to be physically fit if all they would be doing was maintaining aircraft or doing paperwork, rather than performing the hard, physical activity of ground forces. And it just wasn't cool to perform well on a fitness test—it looked like you were trying too hard.

The Navy was beginning to clamp down on body fat and on underperformance on the PRT, including mandatory sessions if a Sailor didn't measure up. Because the retention statistics our commands produced were closely scrutinized, and because I felt healthy Sailors would work better and live better lives, I decided to incentivize PRT performance. Sailors who scored in the top category would get a day off and not attend any of the mandatory sessions. And Sailors who advanced from a lower category to a higher category would also get a day off.

I was amazed at the immediate turnaround in our squadron's PRT scores (and we watched closely to ensure there was no cheating). It seemed to be important enough that I decided to write a personal message to the chief of naval operations. I wanted to make two points: the good news that our Sailors were in better shape than we thought, alongside the bad news that they didn't feel motivated to demonstrate it. When I think back, the CNO must have thought it bold for a random squadron commander to send in a personal message on any subject, much less physical readiness.

Unfortunately, my time in command of VF-211 drew to a close too quickly. I was ordered to leave command six months early and report to Orlando, Florida, to the Navy's Nuclear Propulsion Training Command, which would open an entirely new chapter in my life and career.

The F-14 community was shrinking at the time, and command slots were precious—at least one other officer was scheming to be a direct input to be my relief. But I wanted to be loyal to my capable XO, Cdr. Gerry "Steamer"

Beaman, who worked incredibly hard and supported everything I wanted to accomplish in VF-211. So I pulled the administrative tactic of preemptively sending out invitations to my change of command with Steamer listed as my relief. That was that.

When I left the Checkmates, the Navy was slowly drawing down the F-14 community by decommissioning one of the two squadrons in each air wing. Because the rivalries were so intense between the two squadrons within a typical air wing, most squadrons that remained in commission wanted nothing to do with their decommissioning sister squadron's people or culture. Our sister squadron (VF-24, my first squadron) would be retired not long after I departed.

However, VF-211 and VF-24 were originally spawned from a Vietnam-era squadron that flew F-8 Crusaders, which had both a checkmark *and* a checkerboard in the design on their tails. In the transition to F-14s, VF-24 retained the checkmark on their tail, and VF-211 retained the checkerboard. It seemed like such an easy and sensible thing to do to engineer a "friendly takeover" and draw in the best of VF-24 and restore the old tail insignia. I was secretly pleased when Steamer did precisely that. I was even more delighted when he later rose to three-star rank and commanded the Navy's Third Fleet, based in San Diego.

After my first experience in command, and after enjoying sixteen years of flying at sea on board aircraft carriers, I was about to enter the fascinating world of learning to drive them.

TOP It's never fun to drive an aircraft carrier through "the Ditch." *Official U.S. Navy photo by PHAN Javier Capella*

BOTTOM USS *John C. Stennis*, like most carriers, had eighteen amazing department heads and their deputies. *Official U.S. Navy photo*

Splitting Atoms

Captains of aircraft carriers are required by law to be nuclear-trained naval aviators. Before that can happen, they need to obtain three indispensable elements of knowledge and experience: how an aircraft carrier works as a complex system, how to safely navigate and otherwise operate a ship at sea, and how to safely operate a nuclear propulsion plant.

Achieving this knowledge and experience is a long process, and there is no guarantee an officer will make it all the way through—there are many potholes. But, if successful, the officer is then exposed to a final screening process to be chosen to command a carrier, which is also not guaranteed. It takes a lot of experience, hard work, academics, sea duty, and a bit of a roll of the dice to be selected. But the effort is well worth it in the long run. And, for an officer completing squadron command, it beats the living daylights out of many years sitting in an office in the Pentagon.

The most intimidating portion of the journey is the Navy's nuclear propulsion program, which came into existence in the 1950s under the firm guidance of an almost fanatically dedicated engineer named Hyman G. Rickover. The program he designed has operated nuclear propulsion plants on board hundreds of submarines and ships for over seventy years, steaming hundreds of millions of miles without a single accident or harmful release of radioactivity from a reactor. It is an amazing accomplishment but not surprising to anyone who has been through the program and understands its internals.

The Navy does not like to send post-command squadron commanders—who have been out of college for twelve to fourteen years—through the difficult nuclear training pipeline by themselves. Placing at least two in the same class enhances the odds of them both graduating. I was selected for the program because one of the officers in a two-man group had dropped from the program before he even started. The system needed someone quickly, and I possessed two characteristics that made me ripe for the plucking. My airwing commander, Tim Keating, had already written a fitness report good enough to eventually screen for command of an aircraft carrier, and I possessed an engineering degree from Georgia Tech.

After passing interviews with Adm. Bruce DeMars, who was in charge of the Navy's nuclear propulsion program, and with several of his key staff members, I entered the program in Orlando, Florida.

The first step was Class 95-05 at nuclear power school, which involved six months of challenging academics I liken to obtaining a master's degree in nuclear engineering (except no degree was granted due to the sensitive nature of the subject matter). This crash course was followed by six more months of academics and hands-on experience operating an actual nuclear reactor on board a former ballistic missile submarine welded to the pier in Charleston, South Carolina. This was followed by three months of intense academics at the Navy's nuclear propulsion program offices in Washington, then a course in operating surface ships at Newport, Rhode Island. If I made it through all of that, I would report as the second in command of the aircraft carrier USS *John C. Stennis* in Norfolk, Virginia.

Mary and I thought carefully over whether she would accompany me through this process. She was both working and pregnant, and the conventional wisdom was that getting through the program was easier without the distraction of having a spouse and kids nearby. Mary and I didn't buy that approach at all—we have always wanted to be together. And we didn't have kids yet who would be disrupted by all the moves. So she found a way to make her job portable and suffered through the summer heat of Orlando.

For the first six months of the intense academic portion of the program, we senior aviator students would relax on Friday nights via what we labeled the "Stalag-235 tunneling committee," named after the Uranium-235 that powers nuclear reactors. Every few weekends, Mary would pick me up from my study session at noon on a Saturday. We would travel someplace like Disney World, Cape Canaveral, or St. Petersburg for Saturday night. Then she would drop me off again at noon on Sunday. I confess I spent many of those twenty-four hours of bliss sitting by a pool trying to memorize all the formulas I needed to know.

Miraculously, I managed to graduate first in my class in Orlando. "Miraculously" is not false humility because I walked into every test thinking I was going to fail. I give full credit to my Georgia Tech education, maturity as an older person going through the program, and hard work. I did every homework problem the program offered, which proved invaluable going into the tests. When it became apparent that I might have a chance to excel, I thought it would make a great statement for naval aviation to have one of their own come out ahead of all the young submariners and surface officers in the class, so I redoubled my efforts.

And that was only the beginning. Once that part of the program was complete, we headed to Charleston, South Carolina, where I discovered a new aspect of heroism when Mary delivered our first child, James, via cesarean section at around ten o'clock at night. Once the birth was complete, nearly the entire staff left the hospital, leaving Mary high and dry in intense pain while a bumbling, incompetent nurse searched for the combination to the safe that held the pain medication. I saw a new dimension to my spouse that night as she forced her way through the pain while I felt angry and helpless. I would see that same strength many more times in different ways.

The program in Charleston was about continuing to expand each student's academic knowledge while bringing them into the hands-on environment of operating a nuclear power plant. Even though any sane person would be much happier flying an airplane, I have to admit that the nuclear program was transformative for me. To begin with, it was a real culture shock. But even though the academics were difficult and tedious, the way the Navy's propulsion plants are designed and operated was fascinating on many levels. In learning about the combination of physics and thermodynamics that makes these plants work, I was stunned by the brilliance of the people who designed them.

To give the reader a sense of the technical elegance of this system, it suffices to merely describe how these plants regulate their power with only minimal input from the operator.

There is a myth that nuclear fission involves "smashing" atoms apart using neutrons released by previous fissions. This is only partly true. Uranium-235 atoms split when their nuclei simply absorb another neutron and become unstable. The forces that normally hold the nucleus together are suddenly unable to do so, and the nucleus splits. When the daughter nuclei are released, they shrink, with their nuclei becoming bound more tightly than the original uranium atom. This causes a loss of mass that converts into an enormous amount of energy in accordance with Einstein's $E = mc^2$ formula. The process also releases, on average, around 2.4 neutrons traveling at high speed. To keep a reactor exactly critical—not too many reactions and not too few—exactly one of these neutrons needs to be absorbed by another nucleus, and the rest must either leak or be absorbed by something else in the reactor plant.

Moreover, because atoms absorb neutrons rather than being blown apart, these "fast" neutrons actually have to slow down, much slower than when they're born by a fission event. The way our propulsion plants make this happen is to have them ricochet off the water molecules in which the plant's fuel plates are bathed and which absorb the energy of the fission process and carry it off to steam generators. When that water is cooler and denser, more neutrons will slow down, and more fissions will occur. The reverse is also true. And that is where the magic begins.

In the case of a nuclear-powered ship, when the throttles are opened, it pulls more heat out of the steam generators, which in turn cools the water down flowing into the reactor across the fuel plates, which in turn causes more neutrons to slow down, which causes more fissions, which causes the plant to produce more power, heating the water flowing out of the reactor to the steam generator. The same thing happens in reverse when less power is required—the water flowing in has less energy removed and is thus hotter, which results in fewer fissions. The way our plants are designed, that process balances itself out perfectly. Nobody has to move control rods in and out constantly. They just open or close the throttle. I was blown away by this beautiful combination of physics and engineering.

Even more transformative than all the wonders of how a nuclear propulsion plant works is the culture of operational excellence I found within the nuclear program. It quickly became clear there was something special about this program that fit well with my personal beliefs about how to operate complex systems safely and effectively. Here was a culture where excellence was a way of life.

Admiral Rickover knew that the mystique associated with all things nuclear meant a serious accident could cause the quick demise of a program that had transformed naval warfare. So he set about creating what is known in other circles as a "high-reliability organization." He brought the highest possible technical capability to bear on the problem. His reactors use only the highest quality materials and most conservative designs. They employ redundant systems and multiple safeguards that will automatically shut the reactor down if there is a problem. He introduced rigorous testing, and the highest quality maintenance procedures. But he also realized that technical safeguards were not enough—humans still had to operate these plants, and there were any number of ways human error could endanger them.

So how did Admiral Rickover fight his battle against human error? He started by taking ownership. He realized that ultimate responsibility for the safety of his program was on his shoulders. There is an old saying that "culture is the collective behavior of the senior leadership," and in this case, it started right at the top. Rickover personally interviewed every officer who entered his program—a practice that lives on. He also trained his people relentlessly, forcing them to learn more than most operators probably thought they needed to know about the propulsion plants.

Further, Rickover believed in the power of checking up on how things are really working. He instituted a system of both scheduled and spot inspections, always done by a third party. The scheduled inspections are tough and thorough. They look under every rock. You do not want to fail. The spot inspections mean an outside observer can step on board the ship any time of day or night while the ship is in port and do a complete walk-through of the plant. The next morning, the ship's captain has to explain to a regional technical authority anything found to be out of order.

Rickover also instituted a culture of accountability through required self-reporting, including a quarterly personal letter from the captain of every nuclear-powered warship directly to him, along with special incident reports to document any deviations. He believed that unless you can point to who is accountable, no one is accountable, and he laid accountability squarely on the ship's captain's shoulders. These requirements endure to this day.

But above all, Admiral Rickover instituted a set of interrelated and enduring operational excellence principles that govern every aspect of how our Sailors operate our nuclear propulsion plants. Even though, to my knowledge, he never explicitly stated them in a single list, they permeate the program. They are not just words. Every operator in the nuclear Navy lives and breathes these principles—and they are a valuable framework for any leader seeking to establish a similar high-reliability organization. They include integrity, level of knowledge, procedural compliance, formality, forceful backup, and a questioning attitude.

I'll describe them in a little more detail later in this book, but these principles work extraordinarily well. Their sum is mightier than their parts. Each one reinforces the others, amplifying a culture of professionalism. Any Sailor deeply ingrained with these principles will feel a tingle of guilt when violating even a single principle. I expected my people to know them—not just in my propulsion plants but also on the bridge, on the flight deck, and during underway replenishments. I even used them in organizations I led much later as a flag officer.

Mistakes still happen in a business that uses machinery as complex as the Navy does. When they happened in my organizations, I required my people to debrief them in the context of the principles that were violated, which only reinforced them. I've found that, for any given mishap or close call, generally more than one principle was violated.

I believe in these excellence principles so much that I wrote about them in *Harvard Business Review* in the context of cybersecurity and in the U.S. Naval Institute's *Proceedings* magazine during a recent period of challenges to the Navy's safety record at sea.

Once I completed nuclear power school, the next step on my journey—and my first opportunity to test my newfound nuclear knowledge—was to serve as executive officer on board the brand-new aircraft carrier USS *John C. Stennis*.

An aircraft carrier is a massive operation and the biggest leadership challenge I had faced to date in my career. Over three thousand Sailors made up *Stennis*'s crew, with two thousand more embarking when the ship got under way with its air wing and flag staff. A carrier normally has eighteen departments, including engineering, reactor, air, operations, combat systems, navigation, supply, aviation intermediate maintenance, weapons, intelligence, security, medical, dental, deck, administrative, legal, public affairs, and our chaplains. It is critically important that the ship and air wing operate as a seamless machine, even though they're commanded by two different officers competing for fitness reports.

I reported on board *Stennis* and immediately discovered that my biggest leadership challenge was not the crew but the captain. Bob Klosterman was always gracious and polite to me but was rough and abrasive with nearly everyone else around him. By nature, he was paranoid, deeply suspicious of people, and could be quite incendiary when provoked or otherwise let down. We've all seen leaders like this. He was deeply resentful that he was assigned to the ship as its commissioning commanding officer, which meant he would not lead a deployment, which in turn meant he would likely not make flag rank.

It was my job to make the ship run smoothly and to insulate the department heads where possible from our volatile captain to maintain their morale. We were blessed—as I would discover again in future ships—with great department heads. One of them was our weapons officer, Cdr. Perry Driver, who reached mandatory retirement age during my tenure. He could have easily disappeared to an easy life and his favorite pastime of bird hunting, yet he was so dedicated to the mission that he asked for a waiver so he could make one more deployment. We had to move heaven and earth, but we got the waiver.

I was also lucky with my principal enlisted partners, our two superb command master chiefs. The first was Rick Tick, a crusty aviation boatswain's mate who was a good foil for me when we would host bingo and answer the crew's questions on the ship's closed-circuit TV system. The second was a genial nuclear machinist's mate named Phil Russell, from Antlers, Oklahoma.

How can I ever forget, when we were conducting some important ceremony on the ship's massive hangar deck, and nobody could find the singer who was supposed to render our National Anthem? Master Chief Russell just stepped forward to a nearby microphone and belted it out like a gifted tenor, even though he had no formal training. It was a superb metaphor for the American Sailor. Adapt and overcome.

Stennis was the third aircraft carrier in the Navy to include women as part of the crew, and the first to do so from the very first day its crew came together while the ship was being built. *Stennis* had an advantage in this regard because doing it from scratch was a more natural fit than changing an existing, male-only ship. The presence of women was never a major issue while I was on board. If anything, any behavioral issues associated with having young people from both sexes on board were offset by the excellent work many of our female Sailors did and a better general decorum. It also opened the door to improving nutrition on board the ship, as the female officers demanded healthier food, which propagated to the main chow lines.

The entire crew felt a sense of relief when Capt. Doug Roulstone checked on board as the new captain. He was a thoughtful and innovative leader who struck a fine balance between holding the crew accountable and looking out for their best interests. Doug took great interest in the ship's namesake's heritage, and we forged a close bond with the John C. Stennis Center for Public Service Leadership. This organization, based on the Mississippi State University campus and led by Senator Stennis' former chief of staff, the remarkable Rex Buffington, was most generous to the ship. The leadership awards program sponsored by the center was a model of public–private cooperation that I "borrowed" in a subsequent command.

Although he was capable in his own right, I was fortunate in that Doug trusted me implicitly, which enabled a much steeper learning curve. Together we took *Stennis* on her first deployment. Because of some long-forgotten yet pressing need to have an aircraft carrier deploy quickly to the Arabian Gulf in 1997, we made a record transit from Norfolk, Virginia, through the Mediterranean and Suez Canal, and finally to our destination. The ship steamed at an average speed of 29.4 knots—and when you consider the waiting time and slow average speed through the Suez Canal, you get a sense of how fast these ships can really move at sustained speeds—a huge strategic advantage attributable to nuclear propulsion.

Stennis was the beneficiary of a Navy program inspired by several visionaries, among them Vice Adm. Arthur Cebrowski and Adm. Archie Clemins, that strived for better communications connectivity for these powerful ships. As such, we deployed with a relatively new system that leveraged a specific commercial satellite communications capability to connect the carrier into a larger network. This kind of connectivity is something we take for granted today, but it was a great innovation in its time. For the first time, we could use the full range of classified and unclassified Internet capability.

The system was supported by a large antenna with a fiberglass dome just below the aft port side of the ship's flight deck. One day, to our horror, an EA-6B Prowler conducting a high-power test of one of its engines blew the dome apart, with all of the large curved triangular pieces that formed it splashing down in the middle of the Arabian Gulf, exposing the delicate antenna to the elements. We were in the middle of conducting flight operations in light winds, and the ship needed to keep moving, so the dome's components were left floating lazily in our wake. It seemed as though there was nothing we could do. It would be unwise to try to operate the system with its antenna exposed to the elements. Our newfound connectivity was doomed. Or so we thought.

The pieces were somehow still floating. I asked the bridge team to mark the spot and, on a subsequent "reset" from launching and recovering aircraft, asked Roulstone if we could quickly send a boat to go out and pick them all up. Sure enough, we recovered every piece, and they all appeared to be intact if lightly damaged.

But what to do now? I asked the engineering team to suspend their disbelief and find a way to stitch the dome back together. The hundreds of plastic bolts that held the pieces together were sheared off and blown away. No problem. We rounded up all the zip ties we could find on the ship, and our engineers, led by Cdr. Ray Duff, and our combat systems professionals, led by Cdr. Bruce Lewia, painstakingly put Humpty Dumpty back together again within about twenty-four hours. Our engineers didn't trim the loose ends off the ties, and we affectionately referred to our repaired radome as the "chia pet." But it was good enough to get us through the rest of the deployment. I was secretly proud to have pushed our team not to give up on the system, but it was an even greater testament to their ability to improvise to get the system back up.

As a naval aviator, I'd always had the need for attention to detail drilled into me, but I learned a broader application involving, of all things, dessert. While deployed, our supply officers ordered ice cream for our crew by using one line item with the agents who provided food: "assorted flavors of ice cream." Then, of course, the agents would scour their warehouses for any unpopular flavor that might be about to expire and send that out to the ship. Once I insisted that the supply team stipulate the flavors Sailors most coveted line-by-line, our ice cream socials became better events.

I departed my tour on board *Stennis* as a much more seasoned leader, although my journey home was delayed a month because my relief took extra time finishing the nuclear power syllabus, which nearly caused me to miss the birth of my second son, Jonathan. *Stennis* was a faster work tempo than I'd ever experienced. I went for months with no more than five hours of sleep per night—and usually much less—learning firsthand the expression coined by our operations officer: "There's plenty of time for sleep when you're dead." I learned how to efficiently move three thousand Sailors' worth of paperwork, bring many disparate organizations together, get them rowing in the same direction, and maintain their morale under difficult circumstances. I was eager to try my hand at commanding a ship and would soon get my chance on board one of the oldest ships in the Navy.

USS CLEVELAND

Our Mission

To safely conduct Operational Maneuver From The Sea in support of
our Amphibious Task Force Commander and the finest team in the world.

Our Vision

To consistently be the safest, most combat ready LPD in the Navy
through leadership of the finest Sailors and Marines in the world
and the enthusiastic pursuit of operational and engineering excellence.

Our Guiding Principles

Honor--Integrity and honesty.
   Dignity, and equal opportunity for every Sailor and Marine.
Courage--Both physical and moral.
   Choosing the difficult right over the easy wrong.
Commitment--To combat readiness; to our people; to quality; and to safety.
   Holding ourselves to the highest possible standards.
Ownership of our ship--Cleanliness, material condition, economy, security.
   Not walking past anything that is wrong.
Tactical excellence--Intelligent aggressiveness, flexibility, principles of war.
   Always ready. The leading edge of tactical innovation in the LPD community.
Professional watchstanding--Integrity, level of knowledge, procedural
   compliance, forceful backup, questioning attitude, formality, and foresight.
Safety--Seamanship, experience, judgment, and concentration.
   Thinking ahead, recognizing hazards, fighting complacency.
Continuous improvement--Data based decision making & process improvement.
   Listening to the smartest people on our ship: our Sailors and Marines.
Leadership by example--Being a Sailor or Marine 24 hours per day.
   Top notch military bearing, behavior, physical fitness.
People--Genuinely caring for those who serve. Permitting honest mistakes.
   Communications, personal involvement, and timely recognition.
Teamwork--We will win if we operate as a team everyday.

On time, ready on arrival to fight!
If you're not having fun, you're not doing it right!

J.A. WINNEFELD, JR
COMMANDING OFFICER

TOP Trying to codify leadership along the way. *Winnefeld collection*
BOTTOM The Steamin' Cleve *Official U.S. Navy photo by PHCS Terry Cosgrove*

Gators

I joined the amphibious Navy in early August 1998, assuming command of USS *Cleveland* (LPD-7) in Pearl Harbor, Hawaii. My job was to not only operate a vessel with the mission of transporting U.S. Marines and Navy SEALs but also to navigate another leg on the learning journey toward potentially commanding an aircraft carrier.

Tom Clancy once said, "LPDs are a national asset . . . little-loved but heavily used." These ships were among the oldest and most tired ships in the entire Navy, much less the "Gator Navy." Indeed, they had been run hard: my father had commanded another LPD, USS *Trenton* (LPD-14), over twenty years earlier. That ship was still in commission and younger than *Cleveland* when I took command! How many people can say they commanded a ship older than the one their dad commanded?

But these amphibious transport docks were (and their successors are) wonderfully versatile ships. Measuring around seven hundred feet, with a flight deck and ample storage room, they possessed a large "well deck" that, when the ship was ballasted down, allowed smaller amphibious craft to offload the ship's Marines and cargo.

Cleveland was a seamanship-intensive command because of the frequent operations these ships conducted in shallow water while moving heavy equipment and launching and recovering helicopters, amphibious craft, and small boats. They were also among the last ships in the Navy to use boilers to generate steam for propulsion, which demanded constant care from an understaffed, hot, and tired engineering crew.

It was also what one might label the backwater of the Navy. These were not the "slick and perfumed" high-speed destroyers that were most surface warriors' command ambition. Instead, they were slow, unglamorous, vulnerable, and anything other than sleek-looking. But I loved them, and the lack of attention given to these ships gave me considerable license to be innovative with how we both configured and operated her.

But I had another amphibious operation to conduct first. My next-door neighbor in Del Mar—a former University of California football player, self-taught piano player, medical doctor, and the funniest person I have ever known—asked whether I knew how to surf. When Brad Buchman heard me reply that I previously tried it once or twice with no success, he urged me to try it for two weeks, and if I wasn't hooked by then, we could drop it.

Surfing at 5:30 in the morning fed my habit of waking up early and fostered a built-in delay that allowed me to arrive at the most dignified time for a captain to return to his ship. I was also eager to learn a new sport that required skill and balance and that would also help keep me in shape. And who better to learn from than a six-foot-six, 250-pound former offensive lineman who could pluck me right out of the water if I got in trouble?

I was hooked after a few days of initial frustration. I spent the rest of my tour whenever *Cleveland* was in port sharing a spot in the Del Mar "lineup" with an eclectic group of other early risers—from university professors to drywall installers. Every surfer is the same in the egalitarian lineup. The only thing that matters is courtesy to the person on the inside of a wave and respect for the more able surfer. The sense of calmness waiting for the next set, an early morning train roaring along the coast breaking the soft rhythmic sounds of the surf, the beautiful sunrises and moonsets, the camaraderie, and the exhilaration of catching and riding a wave are lasting good memories. It was an incredibly refreshing way of preparing for a day on board ship. I only had to watch out for the occasional drip of saltwater out of one of my ears betraying my early morning recreation.

One of my pre-command moves was to pay an office call on my amphibious squadron commodore, who was in charge of our three-ship group consisting of flagship USS *Boxer*, USS *Cleveland*, and a slightly smaller amphibious ship named USS *Pearl Harbor*. Capt. Terry Labreque was a quiet yet highly professional officer who was an absolute joy to have as a boss. I might have gotten off to a rough start with him when I complained before taking command that I'd been required to go through the helicopter survival trainer one more time despite, as an aviator, having done it so many times already. I was mortified when he informed me that his brother had died in the same dunker. I thought this was the end, as in: "how do you like me so far?" Fortunately, Terry was as gracious a human and leader as anyone can be, and we got along well during my tour under his command.

I joined the ship for a week of turnover at what felt like the perfect time, just before it entered Hawaii for a port visit and right in the middle of its workup cycle for a deployment. I would get a lot of time at sea, put my imprint on the ship's culture, and take the Cleveland on an overseas deployment.

The first thing that struck me was the crew's sense of being micromanaged from a distance. What this meant was that senior leadership tended not to visit the deck plates, especially the engineering spaces (which was anathema to anyone who ingested the Navy's nuclear culture). It also meant that the ship's navigation team was utterly dependent on the captain. I was not sure whether this was due to paranoia over a potential mistake by a subordinate that could end a career or whether my predecessor had actually almost been burned by some major mistake made by his team. But it was clear the team looked to the captain for approval for each move it made.

I was determined to correct this, and it took nearly a month. I started at the first navigation brief departing Pearl Harbor, after our change of command. My navigation team was told that they had better not look at me, that the ship was theirs to drive, and that I would serve as a safety observer. If the conning officer was ten feet right of where I might have the ship in the channel but it was in a safe place, I would not say a thing. Sure enough, as Cleveland wound down the narrow, twisting channel past Ford Island and Hospital Point, the young officer directing the ship's movements kept nervously looking over at me, seeking approval for every helm order.

Old habits are hard to break, and I eventually resorted during an inbound transit to San Diego to taking the conning officer alone up to *Cleveland*'s open-air flying bridge, requiring that he give his orders through an old-style speaking tube down to the bridge. The navigation team was initially acutely uncomfortable, but they got the message. This was about trust and seamanship. In the long run, I believe they ended up having much more rewarding tours on the ship, and we were safer for it.

The second thing I discovered was the backward configuration of the ship's bridge. It was right out of World War II, including an ancient radar display with a rubber boot into which one would peer to attempt to determine what was on the surface within about twenty miles of the ship. It was horrible. I knew my young officers, who joined the Navy with visions of the most technically advanced fleet in the world, were bitterly disappointed. So I used my first month or so of goodwill with the regional maintenance authorities to ask that an electronic chart information display system, or ECDIS console, be installed on *Cleveland*'s bridge. It cost about a hundred thousand dollars. The maintenance people grumbled, but I was both surprised and delighted when the request was approved.

This system not only provided an electronic chart, it integrated the ship's radar onto the chart to provide a superb graphical display, fully manipulable by my young officers. It turned out that the ship's radar was perfectly fine; it was just the old black boot display that was so awful. The fact that my officers could now see an electronic chart, with radar contacts superimposed on it, with the names of nearby ships displayed next to the contacts, was a huge morale boost. In fact, I now had to push them to look out the bridge windows since it was so tempting for them to go "head down" to use the ECDIS to serve their situational awareness.

My Sailors were delighted as well since this modern system reduced our requirements for manual tracking in my combat information center, or CIC. Contact information was previously passed via sound-powered phone from a watchstander in CIC to a Sailor on the bridge, who would then write the information backward in grease pencil on a glass panel on the bridge. It was ridiculous. Eliminating this chain meant more sleep and time for professional development for my Sailors.

Amphibious ships carry ground forces and move them to and support them on the beach. In my case, I would deploy with four key components. My main customers were our embarked Marines, which included an artillery company and an infantry company that operated a small fleet of rubber raiding craft. A platoon of Navy SEALs and their two sophisticated fast boats, which we lowered from our flight deck using a large crane, were also embarked. A large landing craft, known as an LCU, lived in the ship's well deck and would be used to move the artillery company and other equipment ashore in the traditional amphibious way. Finally, we also embarked a small detachment of Pioneer unmanned aerial vehicles. What a rich field for innovation!

One of my first tasks was to shape *Cleveland*'s culture. Two of my key leaders were vital to getting this done. Like most Navy units, *Cleveland* was blessed with a fantastic chief petty officer's mess, led by MCPO Dwayne Patrick. Patrick was a gifted bowler who was constantly trying to quit smoking. We worked hard together to solidify our team and have fun at the same time. He somehow managed to convince the other members of the chief petty officers' mess, or "goat locker," that they ought to support what this crazy fighter pilot captain was trying to do. He was also indispensable in building teamwork with our embarked Marines.

My longest-serving executive officer, Lt. Cdr. Mark Cedrun, was the vital other half. I nicknamed him "The Sultan of Schmooze" for his ability to get things done for the ship. He came up with a nickname for the ship: "The Millennium Falcon," after the rebel spaceship flown by the character Han Solo played by Harrison Ford in the movie *Star Wars*. We named USS *Boxer*, which was our flagship and where the atmosphere was not so collegial, "The Death Star."

Just as I felt it was my job on board *Stennis* to ensure the air wing had whatever it needed to succeed, I took the same approach on board *Cleveland*. This has not always been the case between the amphibious Navy and the

Marine Corps. I claimed to be a fighter pilot who was too stupid to know that the Navy and Marine Corps were supposed to hate each other. The key was to keep our egos out of it, assume the attitude of "the answer is 'yes,' now what's the question," and then count on our goodwill being reciprocated.

We worked hard on this, including ensuring that the cramped berthing spaces for our embarked customers were as comfortable and functional as possible. We took great pride in the atmosphere of relaxed precision we fostered. I permitted my Sailors to wear special T-shirts and shorts in the Arabian Gulf heat (except for my poor engineers, who needed protection from a host of hazards found in a steam plant). Our Marines quickly picked up on the culture and eagerly helped us with our underway replenishments and other projects.

Equally important to supporting our embarked units was finding new ways to make them more effective in executing their missions. This led to several innovations that would pay off during our deployment.

Our SEAL platoon brought two large rigid-hulled inflatable boats, or RHIBs, on board as their primary means of mobility. These highly maneuverable and sophisticated boats could travel long distances at high speeds and do so fairly quietly. By necessity, they were stored on our flight deck, which brought up two opportunities.

First, this meant we needed to use our old boat and aircraft crane to put them in the water. This involved connecting them to a sling, hoisting them up and over the side, and lowering them into the water. But the LPD's relatively flat bottom and lack of stabilizers caused the ship to roll quite a bit, especially in the ever-present swells in the Pacific Ocean. Sailors would hand-tend heavy lines attached to the boats in an attempt to stabilize them as they were launched using these cranes. It was hopeless to try to cleat and uncleat the lines to keep them taut while the boats swayed when lifted off their trailers. Without constant tension, the boats ended up slamming against these lines in concert with the ship's rolls. After time it would crack the delicate fiberglass sterns of the SEALs' boats. We needed a better way.

With my sailing background in hand, I hauled my engineer and first lieutenant, Lt. Cdr. Ron Cook and Lt. Cdr. Gary Brennan, off to the West Marine store on Point Loma that served all the big marinas and yacht clubs in San Diego. We bought medium-sized sailboat winches and twenty-thousand-pound test nylon line, along with a few of the blocks (or pulleys, as most people might know them) used on sailboats. Our engineers welded special fittings for the winches, and we set off to experiment with the new rig. Brennan was certain we would be taken to the woodshed by operational inspectors for such an unconventional boat handling setup. But it passed the test. Not only were fewer Sailors now required to tend the RHIBs while they were hoisted, we were also able to effortlessly keep the lines tight, which meant safer and more expeditious movement of the boats into and out of the water.

The other problem was that placing two of these RHIBs on the flight deck meant one had to protrude just enough into the landing area to inhibit the number of Marine helicopters that could land at one time. This was due to the presence of what was formally known as "the alongside refueling winch," but was informally known by much more derogatory terms. This winch was a holdover from when LPDs were envisioned as refueling smaller ships using a highly complex rig that used the boat and aircraft crane, with the offensive winch serving as a key component. No one could remember when this winch had ever been used, and it was in terrible material condition. Worse, it was in the way. So, my engineers cut it off and stowed it on a pallet in the ship's cargo area. We stretched the tolerance of the local authorities by promising we could put it back quickly if we needed to. Our Marines and SEALs were delighted.

USS *Cleveland* also had the unique opportunity of embarking a detachment of Pioneer unmanned aerial vehicles, or UAVs. This was in the early days of using UAVs to support combat operations, and the Pioneer had not operated off ships for very long. Launching these snowmobile engine–powered little airplanes using a rocket bottle to get them up to flying speed was always an anxious moment. Waiting to see if the engine would continue running also kept us in suspense—if the plane made it through the first thirty minutes of flight, it was usually good to go. When the engine failed, it was heartbreaking as an aviator to watch through the UAV's camera as it glided into the water.

The ECDIS system we installed when I first got on board became instrumental in helping us employ the Pioneers. Instead of using GPS to navigate, these very basic UAVs only reported their range and bearing from the ship. If we wanted to precisely move the Pioneer around, we first had to translate that range and bearing onto a chart, then figure out where we wanted the bird to fly, then draw a line on the chart and figure out the course to the new point, then transmit that to the UAV. It was horribly ungainly, time-consuming, and—worse—inaccurate in the tight airspace of the Arabian Gulf, where we needed accuracy above all. However, the ECDIS was particularly adept at quickly formulating and displaying this type of range and bearing solution. All that was required was good communication between the bridge and the little trailer that controlled the UAV. Our ability to maneuver these birds became dramatically easier and more precise, which paid dividends later. Score another for the innovation team.

I was also confounded by the fact that the Marines launched their rubber rafts—twenty or so at a time—from *Cleveland*'s stern gate, but I had no way of observing the operation from my position on the bridge. This was an inherently dangerous operation, with the gate down into a horizontal position to provide a little beach for the boats, with waves sometimes violently crashing on board. I asked my electricians to install a video camera that looked down at the aft area inside of our cavernous well deck. It sounds simple, but once again it was modifying a ship. It made huge addition to our situational awareness on the bridge whenever we were operating boats of any type, and greatly enhanced our ability to do so safely.

Finally, I discovered to my dismay when I took command that there was no classified computer network on board the ship. This meant we would not be able participate in the increasing dependence of the fleet on the Navy's version of the Secret Internet Protocol Router Network, or SIPRNet. Without this system, we could not electronically transfer classified e-mails or files to and from the ship. We were essentially in the dark other than routine, slow traditional message traffic. Moreover, the computers we did have were ancient. So I charged our combat systems officer, Lt. Mark Mukanos, with scrounging up some computers and building our own network.

This was a massive undertaking. Fortunately, Mukanos was a good "scrounger." He discovered that the sprawling Space and Naval Warfare Systems Center, or "SPAWAR," complex in San Diego, which is the Navy's center for all things electronic, had recently purchased new computers for all their engineers. It goes without saying that I was irritated that their engineers received new computers long before my ship. But their old machines (which were still newer than ours!) were just sitting on a loading dock, waiting to be carted off to the dump. Mukanos and his team grabbed enough of them to not only replace many of our older unclassified computers but also to build a separate SIPRNet on the ship. Mark then persuaded the Navy's Pacific Fleet communications team to allow us to transmit encrypted traffic through an unconventional satellite network. Even though our ability to move classified information on and off the ship was a bit old and clunky, at least we had it. It would later make a huge difference during our deployment.

On a sleepy Saturday morning in December 1998—the same day as the Army–Navy game—we got under way from San Diego for our six-month deployment, with elements of the 13th Marine Expeditionary Unit embarked. Our transit west from San Diego soon turned into a no-sleep event. We were battered by howling winter winds and towering seas from a large storm in the northern Pacific Ocean for seven days straight. Both sea and wind were directly on our starboard beam, so *Cleveland* was both heeled over and rolling hard the whole voyage, at the expense of much of our galley's dishes and an absolutely miserable crew and embarked Marines. Toward the end of our transit to a port stop in Hawaii, the ship was stressed enough that a seawater pipe broke in our engine room. Thanks to the brave and quick actions of several of our engineers, the leak was stopped. But it caused a lot of lost liberty for our engineering team as they frantically worked to repair the pipe so we wouldn't miss any of our scheduled movements.

Heading further west, Commo. Terry Labreque produced a meaningful surprise for the embarked Marines in our amphibious group. He somehow managed to divert the group a hundred or so miles toward the Japanese Ogasawara Archipelago. In one of the most thoughtful gestures I've ever seen, each of our ships called their Marines on deck as we silently cruised past the island of Iwo Jima at sunset. We were all moved, and it jacked up our Marines' morale during a portion of the deployment that was as boring as it can be for an embarked Marine.

After a rainy port visit in Singapore, we got under way toward the Indian Ocean. Turning west into the Strait of Malacca, which is the narrow passage between Singapore and Indonesia, I was exposed to yet another example of how hazardous it can be to operate at sea. The strait is the busiest area for maritime traffic in the world and is where the USS *John McCain* collided with an oil tanker in 2017. Transiting this confined area is particularly dangerous at night, as mariners can easily become disoriented, and many do not speak English or carry the automatic identification system, or AIS, that helps ships avoid collisions.

Sure enough, transiting westward with ships both in front and in trail of *Cleveland*, we were confronted by a merchant vessel crossing from left to right in the crowded channel. With "constant bearing and decreasing range" between our two ships, we were destined to collide if neither ship maneuvered. In accordance with the international rules of the road, as the ship on the right it was *Cleveland*'s duty as "stand-on" vessel to maintain course and speed and allow the "burdened" vessel time and space to maneuver clear.

However, this vessel neither responded to our radio calls nor changed course or speed to avoid a collision. With every decrease in range, we drew closer to a situation where it would be too late for the two large ships to avoid an accident. Yet, for *Cleveland* to maneuver when she was supposed to be predictable could result in a collision becoming more likely if the master of the other ship woke up and suddenly maneuvered. It could also result in a collision with the ship directly in trail of us. However, at some point, even the stand-on vessel must turn. Thanks to a spot-on bridge team and an alert ship in trail, we slowed *Cleveland* and turned to starboard as the burdened vessel blithely sailed across our track.

Our first stop in the Middle East was not the Arabian Gulf operations we were expecting. Rather, we parted company with the two other ships in our group and detoured to the Red Sea solo to support a potential noncombatant evacuation of American citizens during one of the periodic squabbles between Ethiopia and Eritrea. In what was to become a tradition for me, I conducted a swim call by flooding our well deck and then closing its ramp, which shut out the numerous sharks swimming around the ship.

After a month or so we were finally relieved of the duty off Eritrea and headed off to our original destination in the Arabian Gulf. There we were plunged into the heart of attempts to interdict Iraqi oil smugglers. The Iraqis would modify small tankers, then try to sneak out of the port of Basra and into the Gulf on their way to offload cargo in some other port. There were only a couple of locations where we could catch them in international waters.

Our interdiction effort led to a few unforgettable nights. *Cleveland* would be positioned far to the northwest in the Arabian Gulf, with only a few feet under her keel, navigating through thickets of fishing boats with their nets trailing hundreds of yards behind them. Our SEALs would get under way on their RHIBs, our large landing craft would sortie from our well deck supporting them, our helicopters would operate from our flight deck, and our UAVs would be airborne as well.

This was a complicated ballet that I equated to an hours-long night landing on an aircraft carrier. These operations, while exhilarating to lead, involved managing an enormous variety of risks. It was all executed with a small crew that could easily feel the effects of fatigue in the hot and humid Arabian Gulf weather conditions.

I suppose there were people higher up in my chain who, had they been aware of the complexity of these operations, would have been highly nervous about them. We could have pushed back and said it was too much. But we trained hard for this type of operation and were at the height of our proficiency. We carefully thought these operations through and trained a good, alert team on the bridge. We put the right mitigating factors in place to control the risks, including making sure we had extra people involved who were well rested.

One of the tasks we were given for our UAVs during these operations was to try to help find a surface search radar the Iraqis installed on the al-Faw peninsula, which is a war-torn piece of land lying between Iran and Iraq that extends all the way to the Arabian Gulf. This radar could potentially threaten our operations by providing targeting information to Iraqi surface-to-surface missiles. Central Command's intelligence assets had been unable to find this radar using overhead still photography. Yet we almost immediately found it using our UAV because the little bird transmitted full-motion video back to our ship, which exposed the movement of the radar's antenna.

It was during one of these Pioneer sorties that we discovered to our alarm the Iraqis had indeed positioned a surface-to-surface missile on the peninsula, and we were right smack in its envelope. We quickly maneuvered the ship out of the way. Because we had installed SIPRNet on the ship, we were able to transmit still pictures plucked from our UAV video back to the Fifth Fleet commander's headquarters. The following day USS Enterprise, which was in the Arabian Gulf on a deployment, was instructed to have a pair of its FA-18 Hornets returning from a sortie over Iraq destroy the missile on their way back to the ship.

Since we discovered the missile, we were anxious to watch its destruction. So we launched a Pioneer, keeping it well clear of the Hornets' bombing path but with its camera focused on the target at the appointed time. A young representative from the State Department was on board at the time for an orientation visit, and we invited her into our CIC to watch. Just before the scheduled time on target, a truck stopped at the missile site and a man got out to take a look around. We all held our breath.

Moments after the Iraqi got back in his truck and drove away—and at precisely the advertised time—the missile disappeared in a huge explosion and cloud of smoke. We cheered, and our State Department representative's eyes bulged wide open. The truck was no more than a hundred yards down the road. The man stopped the truck, got back out to see what happened to his missile, then quickly jumped back in and drove away at a high rate of speed. We could only imagine what he was thinking.

Playing the tape repeatedly for my crew was a huge morale boost for a team that would ordinarily have no role in something as sexy as blowing up an enemy missile. This was long before use of UAVs became ubiquitous. Although I had no idea of how far the capability would later evolve, it was a huge introduction to the immense potential for UAVs to influence the battlefield. In one event, it also vindicated many of the disparate, out-of-the-box things we did to enhance the ship's capability.

It was not all work, though. The Super Bowl was played while we were deployed in the Gulf, and, unfortunately, there was no way for Cleveland to download TV shows in real time. There was no way for us to watch or even tape the game, but flagship USS Boxer—the Death Star—had an antenna that could download the game in real time.

So the morning after the game was over, I grabbed one of our Marine rubber boats and drove over to Boxer with a couple of gallons of Baskin Robbins chocolate chip ice cream pulled from a case I brought along on the deployment. The Super Bowl tape was dropped to us in the boat, and we hurled up the ice cream to eager hands waiting above. I forbade my communicators from reporting the score of the game overnight, and we enjoyed a terrific barbeque on the flight deck while watching the Denver Broncos defeat the Atlanta Falcons on a large screen in our helicopter hangar.

I was certainly not the first ship's captain to ever employ a special touch for a deployed crew, but it was not lost on my team how important such things are to break up the monotony of a long deployment and bring a crew together.

Cleveland was also the victim of an innovative prank. At one point during our deployment, a group of midshipmen on a training cruise on board USS *Harpers Ferry* asked to visit us while we were under way. We were flattered that they would go out of their way to visit an LPD, so we graciously gave them the tour of the ship. Little did we know that they found our large battle flag and cleverly mailed it to themselves on the other ship in a large box.

This flag, which was used during underway replenishments, homecomings, and other important events, already had a checkered history. It was one of the large banners used by the Cleveland Indians baseball club to portray their then-mascot, Chief Wahoo. My predecessor had not permitted the ship to fly the flag out of deference to the Native American community.

When I had arrived, I asked Master Chief Patrick to survey the crew to see if there were any of Native American heritage. Sure enough, there were a couple. They expressed that they had no problem whatsoever with the flag and were, in fact, disappointed that we never flew it. In subsequent years the Cleveland Indians have found it necessary to stop using Chief Wahoo, which is completely understandable. But at the time, and after such due diligence, we found we could use it without offending anyone on our crew.

During a group underway replenishment event a week or so later, *Harpers Ferry* drove up alongside the oiler proudly flying our flag. Of course, we had to rectify this humiliating situation. Later that evening, a RHIB full of *Cleveland*'s SEALs scaled the side of the offending ship and kidnapped her operations officer, who we held for ransom until our flag was returned (of course, *Harpers Ferry* said we could keep their officer). The whole matter confirmed for me the inherent creativity and spirit beating inside the hearts of our young people. We are in good hands.

After the ship was decommissioned in 2011, I was privileged to return the Chief Wahoo battle flag to the city of Cleveland, Ohio, during a home Cleveland baseball game. This was the second time the ship's flag was returned to the ball club. The first flag was presented to the crew in 1993 and, having been well-used, was returned in 2006. Cleveland Indians great—and former Navy chief petty officer—Bob Feller presented a new flag in return, which is the one my crew used. The press release in 2012 stated: "The flag was an essential part of the 'Steamin' Cleve's' esprit de corps . . . and now serves as a constant reminder of the bonds the Cleveland Indians and the City of Cleveland have with the U.S. Navy family."

While I served on board *Cleveland* I was blessed with a terrific chaplain with the most appropriate name I've ever known for such a position: Lt. Randel Livingood. He placed a sign on his office door that read, "Jesus turned water into wine; I can't turn your whining into anything." That said, he was full of compassion and care for an exceptionally hard-working crew. When our amphibious squadron received an order to send a chaplain ashore temporarily to some highly undesirable place, the three chaplains on board USS *Boxer*—the Death Star—tried to foist the order onto Chaplain Livingood. It was not hard to firmly parry this unpopular order since dropping from one chaplain to zero seemed much worse than going from three to two.

Finally, we departed the Arabian Gulf via the Strait of Hormuz and headed home to San Diego. During the transit that evening, I witnessed the most bizarre phenomenon I have ever seen in my many years at sea. As we approached the strait, my bridge team started to see what appeared to be long waves of green phosphorescence in the water approaching the ship. As we got closer, we saw these waves of light actually spinning in a large pinwheel shape, perhaps half a mile across. After we passed by one, we would enter yet another one. This went on for about twenty miles. I called USS *Boxer* ahead of us to see if they were observing the same phenomenon, and indeed they were. I've never produced a satisfactory explanation. Perhaps it was a form of large marine life trying to herd fish, which might have energized the plankton in the water. Or maybe it was some sonic event from an underwater source.

In any event, we left the pinwheels in our wake and commenced the long voyage across the Indian and Pacific Oceans to San Diego, with port visits to

Australia and Hawaii along the way. Threading our way through the historic Solomon Islands included an equatorial "crossing the line" ceremony at the 180th meridian, thus bestowing upon the entire crew the vaunted title of "Golden Shellback."

During this transit my crew and I were treated to sunsets in the South Pacific, which are the most amazing on the planet. Their blazing arrays of colors, brilliant cloud formations, and radiating rays captured in the Japanese flag are simply spectacular. Sailors develop a fascination with sunsets at sea, including for many remaining ever-alert for the elusive green flash that sometimes appears for a second or two in the last liquid-like drop of sun before it drops below the horizon. For centuries sunsets have been a source of camaraderie for a ship's crew, which on a peaceful day will gather topside to observe it, then quietly return below decks to continue the ship's routine. We enjoyed many such moments on the long transit to Hawaii on our way home. You never know when you're seeing your last one, which is a great reminder to make the most out of every day one is privileged to live on earth.

Not long after we arrived in San Diego, we underwent a dreaded INSURV inspection, conducted periodically by the Navy's Board of Inspection and Survey. These inspections are cursed by Sailors, as they dive deeply into a ship's every nook and cranny, requiring each space and system to be beautiful, clean, and in perfect working order. These inspections are hard enough on a new ship. Preparing for one on a forty-year-old LPD is an absolute nightmare. Much like preparing for a college exam, the only real way to prepare is to try to keep everything working all the time anyway. Our final preparations brought to mind the "hay is in the barn" comment I used to give to my fraternity brothers preparing for final exams. Thankfully we passed the exam and shortly thereafter headed into drydock for an overhaul.

It was depressing to see the ship up on blocks, with all its systems torn apart, after she had performed so well on our deployment. The next big event was the aviation major command screen board, in which I would either be selected to command an aircraft carrier or would fall by the wayside and likely retire not long after. With a delight that rivaled finding out that I would be a TopGun instructor or being selected early for the rank of commander,

I gladly received the news that I had indeed screened and would command USS *Enterprise*.

I do not know, but I may have been chosen for the oldest carrier in the Navy because *Cleveland* just passed its INSURV examination, and *Enterprise* had one coming due soon. Or perhaps it was because I had performed well in nuclear power school, and *Enterprise* carried the most complex propulsion plant in the Navy. Who knows? All I knew is that I was walking on air.

One of my final acts as *Cleveland*'s captain was to host a meeting of the amphibious group based in San Diego, which included all the captains of all the ships. The admiral's new chief of staff was none other than Terry Labreque, who was my commodore while deployed.

Terry and I were both big fans of Patrick O'Brian, who authored the series of books that were the inspiration for the movie *Master and Commander*. These meetings were normally boring affairs held in the drab venue of a basement room in the Naval Station San Diego Officers Club. Terry asked me to host the meeting and a dinner afterward on board Cleveland "in the Patrick O'Brian style." He gave no other guidance, but I knew exactly what Terry wanted. I also knew that because my fitness report fate was already sealed, I couldn't be accused of sucking up to the admiral if I did it right.

We pulled out all the stops. First, we requested all the captains to arrive in their ships' boats and judged their appearance and handling as they came alongside. We greeted each captain with sideboys in uniforms from the early nineteenth century, after which they were ushered to a large tent erected on our flight deck, where the meeting was held. While the meeting was under way, we reconfigured the side of the ship to accommodate mooring a large Hornblower yacht we rented at a good price based on the good graces of Herb Zoehrer, a longtime family friend and Naval Academy classmate of my father's.

As the meeting drew to a close, our spouses were escorted on board, and we descended a ladder on the water side of the ship to take a harbor cruise with, of course, USS *Cleveland*–labeled wine and beer. While we were on the cruise, the tent was reconfigured into a dinner venue. We arrived just in time for the evening colors ceremony on the flight deck and then entered the tent, where a string quartet was playing music from the Patrick O'Brian novels. The meal was drawn from a wonderful book named *Lobscouse and Spotted Dog*, which is based on the superb description of nineteenth-century meals portrayed in O'Brian's novels. It was a very nautical conclusion to one of the most enjoyable tours of my Navy career.

My next stop was to pass through the Naval Reactors office in Washington, DC, for a month-long session designed to teach me as much as possible about the unique propulsion plant on board *Enterprise*, which was just coming out of the shipyard and beginning her workups for deployment. I was headed to command the most storied ship in U.S. Navy history.

Anchor #2:
Lead People

"You manage things; you lead people."

Rear Adm. Grace Hopper

Build an Awesome Team

"You can be bad at hiring people, or bad at firing people, but you can't be bad at both."

Former Walmart CEO Lee Scott

"I always try to hire people who are smarter than me."

Enterprise Holdings Chairman
Andy Taylor

Connect with Your People

"You can only understand people if you feel them in yourself."

John Steinbeck

"Failure is the opportunity to begin again, more intelligently."

Henry Ford

High Standards & High Care

"All I demand is that every man do his best."

Dwight Eisenhower

"The simple act of caring is heroic."

Edward Albert

Trust & Teamwork

"Talent wins games, but teamwork and intelligence win championships."

Michael Jordan

"The best way to find out if you can trust somebody . . . is to trust them."

Ernest Hemingway

ANCHOR 2
Lead People

BUILD AN AWESOME TEAM

In most organizations, 80 percent of the results come from just 20 percent of the people. In his book *Good to Great*, Jim Collins tells us to first "get the right people on the bus and the wrong people off, and then figure out where to drive it." Getting those people on your team takes relentless research, energy, and working the system, but it's well worth the time.

I quickly learned in my first command how important it is for leaders to scour their profession to find those who live and breathe excellence and to be eager to hire people who are smarter than themselves. They quickly spot subordinates who have a hunger to learn and weed out the knuckleheads to get to the talent. They aren't looking for "cookie-cutter" fits, either—they want curious, hard-working, creative people with high integrity. They recognize the true value, not just the symbolic virtue, of diversity of all types. Once on board, people have to be developed, which sometimes requires letting them go away for additional development, which is especially hard to allow for that top 20 percent.

Leaders also have to tolerate—even encourage—certain kinds of failure. Although "sins of commission" should be fatal for membership in a high-performance organization, "sins of omission" should be expected and used as a learning opportunity. However, leaders must be willing to compassionately remove underperformers for the betterment of the entire team. This is incredibly difficult if the person's failure is not attributable to a lack of effort or integrity, but it must sometimes be done.

CONNECT WITH YOUR PEOPLE

There is a yawning gulf in effectiveness between connected and disconnected leaders. People are not merely a market commodity that obeys the laws of supply and demand. You either care about your people or you don't, and they will quickly sense it.

The best leaders I've known had an uncanny knack for this. Our ground forces—in which everyone in a unit is exposed to the same dangers, hardships, and training—usually pick this up more quickly than other military specialties. They understand that *knowing* people as individuals means really *caring* about them. Because as a young officer I was so focused on being the best possible fighter pilot, I didn't initially appreciate the hard work put in by the young people who maintained our airplanes. However, over time I discovered how important it is to get to know those who put in the long, unglamorous hours. Unfortunately, the larger the organization, the greater the challenge of getting to know individual people. It's difficult for all but the most capable leaders to know more than a critical mass of about a hundred individuals well.

Knowing people also requires understanding the generation you're trying to lead. Even though most of leadership is grounded in time-tested principles, each generation has a unique combination of characteristics shared by most of its members that demands a little different touch. It has a lot to do with the economic and technical environment in which people grew up—boomers, millennials, or subsequent generations—and what they drew from their parents. The information on leading different age groups is out there, and you should find it.

HIGH STANDARDS & HIGH CARE

One of the most important things I learned about leadership traces to a simple statement I overheard from Gen. Colin Powell: "The essence of leading people is holding them to the highest possible standards while taking the best possible care of them." If you take nothing else about leadership away from this book, other than the importance of character, remember that imperative. It is an obvious yet profoundly important combination. It works for children, troops, athletes, and any other group I've ever observed.

Properly executed, high standards and high care work together in an almost magical way, and one does not work without the other. If you only hold people to high standards, they will perform but will soon drift away. If you only take care of them, they'll take you for granted and fail to perform.

Holding people to high standards has two threshold requirements. It first means firmly and frequently ensuring they know exactly what those standards are. Second, it means having leaders who strive to exceed those standards. This can be hard for young people moving up in responsibility, or for those who lead people older than they are. As we say in the military, morale never rises when standards fall.

At the same time, one of the most profound factors governing whether a person is happy is whether they look forward to going to work every day. There are a host of things that contribute to this, including treating people with dignity, celebrating a team's success, having solid internal communications, recognizing individuals with special touches, and ensuring a safe mental and physical work environment. One of the most important things a leader does is to pay attention to whether his or her subordinate leaders are good leaders. If there is a trend of poor retention within a business unit, it may mean there is an underperforming leader in that part of the organization.

TRUST & TEAMWORK

Good leaders are fanatical about building trust, both inside and outside their organizations, which in turn leads to good teamwork. The first question I ask myself about anyone with whom I work is "can I trust this person?" And my biggest fear is that those above, below, or alongside me would somehow lose their trust in me.

In the military, where one's life can literally depend on the reliability and performance of the person next to you, one develops a dependence on trust at an early age. We hand an unbelievable amount of responsibility to young people for expensive equipment and precious lives. If you can't trust the nineteen-year-old Sailor hooking your airplane up to the catapult or setting the arresting gear for your landing, you're in the wrong business. If you can't trust the Marine next to you in your foxhole, you have a real problem when the bullets start flying. Our heavy reliance on trust is what makes it so devastating when it's violated through an ethical transgression.

Building trust in your people includes assessing their integrity, ensuring their technical competence in the job at hand, and training them in your beliefs, vision, and ways of doing business. This takes a certain amount of time for a new leader, but it enables that leader to start building trust *outside* the organization. This latter kind of trust derives from solid performance and careful cultivation of relationships. As the saying goes, when your house is on fire is not the time to start a relationship with your neighbor.

So much has been written about teamwork, and examples abound in all professions for how it leads to success, so I will not belabor it. But teamwork is in large measure an outcome of building trust. A special form of teamwork is required to make the ballet of carrier flight operations work safely. Our special operations forces forge their teams at both the internal, high-skill "actions on the objective" level, and with the military and the intelligence partners they bring into the fold to work a problem. Shared hardships and bonding experiences build teamwork . . . and when people on the team are able to check their egos at the door, it really blossoms.

TOP Forty years under way on nuclear power. The similar February 1965 *National Geographic* cover inspired me as a kid. *Official U.S. Navy photo by PH3 Douglass M. Pearlman*

BOTTOM Dad and I are under way together on Big E's bridge. *Winnefeld collection*

The Big E

I assumed command of USS *Enterprise* (CVN 65) on a bright and beautiful day in March 2000, relieving Capt. Marty "Streak" Chanik, my first flight lead in my first F-14 squadron. As with *Cleveland*, my timing was good, as this historic ship was exiting the shipyard and beginning workups for her eighteenth deployment.

This command was a dream come true. As an eight-year-old boy, I saw a photograph of a relatively new USS *Enterprise* on the cover of the February 1965 *National Geographic* magazine, steaming in company with the nuclear-powered USS *Long Beach* and USS *Bainbridge*. She had "E = mc²" traced on her flight deck by Sailors in their white uniforms. The eighth U.S. Navy ship bearing the name, she was now almost forty years old and going strong—our oldest aircraft carrier and the oldest ship in the entire Navy. Unlike the newer *Nimitz* class ships, which have two large nuclear reactors, *Enterprise* had eight smaller reactors installed, with thirty-two steam generators of different designs and chemistries and a lot of older equipment throughout the ship. She was known as a particularly tough ship to command from an engineering standpoint.

I didn't care. It was *Enterprise*, the most famous ship in the Navy, whose name would take the breath away of any naval officer possessing any sense of history.

The first ship in the series was a sloop-of-war captured from the British in 1775 during a raid on St. John and renamed *Enterprise*. The third ship of the name served honorably under Capt. Stephen Decatur in the Barbary pirate wars. Her crew burned the captured frigate *Philadelphia* in Tripoli Harbor in what Lord Horatio Nelson called "the most daring act of the age." The seventh ship in the series, CV 6, was the most decorated ship of World War II. Known as "The Big E" and "The Galloping Ghost of the Oahu Coast," she served from the beginning to nearly the end of the war, including in the Battle of Midway. She was in the process of being broken up while CVN 65 was a-building and gave up both the portholes in her captain's cabin and her "Big E" nickname to a new ship of the name. If all goes well, those same portholes will find their way into the next USS *Enterprise*, CVN 80, which is under construction as of this writing.

CV 6 also gave her name to Enterprise Rent-a-Car, whose founder, Jack Taylor, flew F-6F Hellcats off her in World War II on the wing of the leading U.S. Navy ace of all time, David McCampbell. Jack actually flew more sorties during the war from USS *Essex*, but when it came to naming his car leasing company, there was no question in his mind which name was better. Jack and his son, Andy, were generous in helping pay for construction of a legacy room on board *Enterprise* used for reenlistments, VIP tours, family videos, and other events. Thus, I met and got to know Jack and discovered what a real character he was. He brought my romantic vision of the World War II Navy fighter pilot to life.

Quietly dashing, with penetrating blue eyes, a flair for style, and a disarming sense of humor, Jack was a real ladies' man with business savvy to give away. He brought his military values into his family-owned business, which evolved to lead the rental car industry. I became lifelong friends with Andy and his wife, Barbara, who took his father's company to even greater heights. Andy also personally commissioned models of all eight *Enterprises*, which grace the atrium of their headquarters in St. Louis.

Nearly twice as many Americans have been into space as have commanded a nuclear-powered aircraft carrier. It is at once an exhilarating and exhausting experience to have hands-on responsibility for such an enormous and complex piece of machinery and its large crew. The captain is the only person on the ship who has the requisite experience in the disciplines central to operating such a ship. In addition to leading a large organization, it requires mastery of how an air wing operates off the carrier and how the carrier supports the air wing, intimate knowledge of the ship's nuclear propulsion plant, and exceptional competence in safely navigating a large ship in a wide variety of hazardous situations. Several officers assigned to the carrier have vital pieces of this knowledge. The "air boss" and operations officer know how to work the air wing. The reactor officer and engineer know how to operate the machinery. The navigator knows how to operate on the surface of the ocean. But only the captain has the requisite knowledge to master all three.

Soon after I took command of Big E, our workup cycle for deployment went into high gear. In a painful "déjà vu all over again" from my experience on board USS *Cleveland*, our cycle would include the necessary evil of an INSURV inspection. Poor performance could ruin a captain if traced to a ship being underprepared. I was well aware of how challenging these visits are for older vessels. So we knew we had to work extra hard to get *Enterprise* ready.

One of the toughest tests during an INSURV inspection is a full power run, in which the ship is expected to operate at its fastest speed for a certain length of time. As we prepared on the evening before this test, our chief engineer, Capt. Faris Farwell, reported a pinhole leak in one of our main steam pipes that would preclude the test until it was repaired. So we shut down that plant and began the arduous cooling process, conducting a weld repair, and heating it back up. The inspectors asked that evening when we might be ready to conduct the test, and we provided an estimate of ten o'clock in the morning. The repairs were slightly delayed such that, when ten o'clock rolled around, we were within thirty minutes of being able to start the test. Unfortunately, we did not know the inspectors intended to hold us to the estimated time, and they failed us on the test.

My engineers were stunned and demoralized after working all night to fix the pipe. I angrily told the inspection team we would do the test on this forty-year-old ship anyway, and they were welcome to watch if they wanted. *Enterprise* accelerated to full speed and performed beautifully, and our engineers felt deeply vindicated. This was about backing up my people. I reported my extreme displeasure with the inspection team up my chain of command and never heard about it again.

There are many reasons for the success we enjoyed on board *Enterprise*. Perhaps foremost among them was the high quality of the many department heads and senior enlisted personnel assigned to the ship. Because of the many highly different disciplines organic to an aircraft carrier, we were blessed with people at the absolute pinnacles of their professions. This included our command master chief, Norm Wood, who was as calm, effective, and candid a leader as I've ever met.

One of the defining characteristics of my tour was the close relationship formed among the leaders internal to our strike group, most of whom embarked *Enterprise* as the flagship. Our strike group commander, Rear Adm. Harry Ulrich, assembled an extraordinary group of leaders, including destroyer squadron commander Mark Ferguson, cruiser captain Rick Hunt, and air wing commanders Phil Godlewski and, later, Dave Mercer. I found it hard to keep up with these incredibly talented officers. Without really openly discussing it, we just arrived at the common conclusion that we all would look better if we cooperated rather than competed openly. It was a singularly rewarding experience to work closely with these officers.

There is risk in assembling such a concentration of talent: the subsequent fitness report competition can result in good people being left on the cutting room floor at selection board time. I had reflected on the same concern when I assembled a highly talented group on VF-211. But in the end, Ulrich managed to get all of these officers promoted to flag rank.

Ulrich once asked me during our workup cycle, when I joined the air wing for its overland training at NAS Fallon, Nevada, to whose "coattails" I was attached. My response: "Nobody. I want to be recognized independently for my own good work and don't want to be tied to someone who may fail and take me down with him." It was just how I felt, derived from similar advice

Colin Powell had given years before not to allow one's ego to become attached to a particular position, lest the ego fall with the position.

Operating military units is a hazardous profession, and none more so than working on the flight deck of an aircraft carrier. Perhaps the only thing I regret about my tour on board *Enterprise* is that we lost a young airman named Trevor Maki one night while conducting carrier qualifications. Maki had finished chocking and chaining the landing gear on his side of an E-2C aircraft that was to be refueled. Unfortunately, he turned the wrong way exiting the wheel well, ran into a spinning propeller, and was mortally injured. All of his shipmates dearly loved him, and his tragic loss was a real blow to our morale. He was a real gym rat, too, so we named our newly renovated ship's gym after him.

If looking after the Sailors in my previous two commands was a learning experience, doing so on board USS *Enterprise* was a varsity learning experience. Three thousand crew members and two thousand members of the air wing when embarked yielded every imaginable problem a young adult could experience. I had to handle many of these issues at "captain's mast," which is the nonjudicial proceedings that empower commanding officers to maintain discipline in their units. Some specific problems escalated as we got close to deployment, especially those that could preclude a Sailor from going overseas—but the volume was small, as most of our Sailors were excited about what lay ahead.

Building on my experience back to being a department head in VF-1, a fairly significant portion of the hour I spent with every group of new *Enterprise* Sailors in the "school of the ship" was talking about financial issues, mostly because I felt no one could do it better. Listening to my various friends and associates growing up in the business, I was convinced that few possessed the financial literacy and discipline to develop and accumulate any wealth, much less manage money on a day-to-day basis. So I spoke to these Sailors about the importance of managing their money wisely, including keeping a budget, avoiding all manner of debt and frivolous expenses wherever possible, and having a well-crafted investment plan. I also told them to avoid paying confiscatory rates to the car dealers, furniture retailers, and investment firms that, unfortunately, prey on young military folk.

Again, I was blessed with a group of department heads who also looked after their Sailors. One standout was our first lieutenant, Lt. Cdr. Don Smith, who led the Deck Department, which sported the youngest and roughest Sailors on the ship. He was previously the first lieutenant on an LPD, which was near and dear to my heart, and he came to the ship highly recommended. His team handled lines, anchors, boats, and refueling rigs and was responsible for painting the ship. They were the least technically trained of any of our Sailors. In an amazing accomplishment, especially for an aircraft carrier, he turned around a moribund organization, somehow managed to get all the young Sailors on his team their Enlisted Surface Warfare Specialty badge during our deployment, and had remarkably few disciplinary problems. It probably had something to do with the old Navy way—I never asked.

Don also resurrected the ship's rigs previously installed to refuel other ships, which had fallen into disrepair since it was rare for carriers to refuel other ships under modern operations. But I wanted to have the capability in case we ever needed it. So, against the wishes of a grumpy regional maintenance organization, we managed to get the parts, fixed the rigs, and tested them out by refueling several of the ships in our strike group. It would pay dividends later.

During our workup cycle we were obliged, like all aircraft carriers, to host landing qualifications for new pilots. We were fortunate on board *Enterprise* to do this work in the Gulf of Mexico, which is closer to the training command bases and normally enjoys nice weather during the winter. Because the Army Corps of Engineers had just finished dredging the sand bar at the entrance to the channel leading into Pensacola, Florida, and *Enterprise* was not heavily loaded at the time, we were also scheduled to conduct the first-ever port visit by a nuclear-powered carrier to the cradle of naval aviation.

As we were steaming down the east coast of Florida toward the Gulf on a beautiful, calm late afternoon, my officer of the deck spotted a large radar contact 10 degrees right of the bow that the bridge team could not quite make out visually. He asked to divert a bit to the right to check it out. In keeping with my philosophy developed on *Cleveland*, I wish he hadn't even asked. But the contact turned out to be a beautiful yellow thirty-foot center-console fishing boat bobbing on the gentle swells—with nobody on board.

Worried there might have been foul play, and certainly concerned that the boat represented a hazard to navigation, we turned our massive ship around and "hove to" a few hundred yards away. I sent our burly air boss over in a boat with a security team, and they found nothing. No dead bodies, no weapons, no drugs. Under an obligation to remove a hazard to navigation, we reported the boat to the Coast Guard, hoisted it on board *Enterprise* and gently placed it on ammunition carts covered with mattresses in the hangar bay. The boat was so tricked out that we put a security watch on it to make sure no Sailor tried to take any souvenirs.

However, within twenty-four hours, the Coast Guard reported they found the owner, who wanted to talk on the phone. He turned out to be a wealthy older man who flew P-40s with the Flying Tigers in World War II. He said he was moving his large yacht, named *Cookie Monster*, from Florida to Newport, Rhode Island, for a boat show. As many large yachts do, they were towing the smaller boat, which served as a tender. They checked the tow every hour and discovered late one night it had broken free. Despite an extensive search, they could not find it and presumed it sank. He was so grateful to pick up his boat when we pulled into Pensacola that waiting on the pier along with his large boat trailer was a truckload of Pepperidge Farm cookies for my crew. We got a little seamanship training, and the crew got a lot of cookies.

We successfully completed our workup cycle and, on a gray Norfolk, Virginia, day in the spring of 2001, headed east for a six-month deployment, *Enterprise*'s seventeenth. We spent the first half in the European theater, making spectacular port visits to Cannes, Naples, Rhodes, Portsmouth, and Lisbon. Undertaking five port visits in three months was an extraordinary bonus for our crew, and they performed admirably while on liberty ashore.

Mary was able to join me for several of the visits. During our port visit to Cannes, at the invitation of the prefect (or governor) of Nice, we enjoyed the surreal experience of flying via his helicopter to see the Monaco Grand Prix. We dined at the Automobile Club of Monaco (which hosts the race), watched the contest from the tower from which it is controlled, and then flew back to Cannes. This only reinforced my belief that every naval officer is given a glimpse of the "lifestyles of the rich and famous" at least once during his or her career.

Our stop in Naples was especially poignant since I lived there as a child in the early 1960s. On our first day in port, after Mary and I enjoyed a beautiful lunch overlooking Naples Bay with Harry Ulrich and his spouse, Mary, we took the opportunity to swing by the home in which my family previously lived.

Mary Ulrich, who grew up in a Neapolitan family, served as interpreter at the gate to the home's spacious courtyard. I was delighted to discover the couple living there were the same people who had rented the place to my family four decades earlier. We were invited inside for a look around. The olfactory memories stimulated by the massive wisteria vine winding around its trellis flooded back from my childhood many years before. It goes without saying that the longtime owner of the home, who was a lawyer in Naples, and his family received an awesome tour of USS *Enterprise* later during our visit.

Heading east for the Suez Canal in late July at the end of the European portion of our deployment, the crew was sky high from spring and early summer in Europe, even though we knew we would be spending the second half of our cruise in the worst heat of the summer in the Arabian Gulf. As we prepared for our transit through the Suez Canal, the "noise on the net" in the intelligence world indicated some sort of big event was imminent. We thought there was a strong possibility that *Enterprise*'s Suez transit might be that big event, and under Ulrich's watchful eyes we prepared especially hard for force protection during our Suez transit.

Suez transits are exhausting for any crew and captain, as the transit south from the Mediterranean Sea normally begins early in the morning and ends late at night, with almost nonstop action and piloting the ship in unbelievably close quarters. Our transit had the not-uncommon added dimension of commencing in heavy fog. Imagine navigating a 95,000-ton ship through a narrow canal where one normally cannot see water on either side of the ship due to the flight deck overhang. Now we were unable to even see the bow due to the fog. Fortunately, we had installed the same state-of-the-art electronic chart display information system I put on board *Cleveland*, which, along with the embarked Egyptian pilots, helped keep us on the straight and narrow.

Largely due to uncertainty over terrorist threats, I asked one of my dentists, who was of Egyptian heritage, to remain on the bridge during the entire transit listening to the pilots, who were not aware she spoke Egyptian Arabic.

I wanted to be able to detect any signs of danger of which the pilots were aware but were reluctant to share with me. Fortunately, the only interesting thing she overheard was the pilots' belief that I would be giving them all Rolex watches when they disembarked at the end of the transit. Fat chance! But it underscored the advantages we have as a nation to have such a richly diverse population in our military.

We frequently refueled and replenished while we were deployed overseas. Obviously, a nuclear-powered vessel needs no fuel for propulsion, but we did need jet fuel for our aircraft. We needed a host of other supplies as well: mainly parts and food, and sometimes ammunition. These replenishment operations involved driving *Enterprise* close aboard another ship. The standard procedure is to maneuver within 160–180 feet of the delivery ship, stabilize alongside, then fire shot lines to the opposite ship that end up being the leads for steel cables from which fuel hoses or pallet transfer mechanisms are suspended. Normally we would simultaneously conduct vertical replenishment, in which helicopters would fly a highly coordinated pattern between the ships in which they transferred pallets slung from nets.

This is one of the most hazardous operations for any ship's captain. All it takes is one wrong helm order or an inattentive conning officer or an engineering casualty, and the ships end up "swapping paint," with rather obvious consequences for a captain's career. It is especially dangerous when there is a lot of other surface traffic in the area where the replenishment is conducted, even though ships that are "tied together" are considered "restricted in their ability to maneuver" and have the right of way over most other ships.

This is not ordinarily a problem. I was used to merchant ships being aware of the rules and staying clear of refueling aircraft carriers. That is, until one day when a merchant ship quickly came over the horizon off our port bow on a collision course while we were fully engaged in a replenishment. Usually, we would call the approaching ship on the radio, express our situation, and expect her master to maneuver to avoid us. Not so this time—the other ship either ignored us or, more likely, was on autopilot with nobody paying attention. They didn't answer or budge, and things began to get uncomfortable.

During a normal emergency breakaway—which we practiced at the end of each replenishment operation—we would rapidly disconnect the two ships, and *Enterprise* would sprint ahead to get clear quickly. That simply wouldn't work in this case—if we broke away at full speed moving ahead of the oiler on our starboard side, we would drive straight into the path of the oncoming ship and would never have gotten both ships clear in time. We improvised by conducting a particularly tricky, nonstandard emergency breakaway in which we disconnected and backed *Enterprise* down hard in order to allow our replenishment ship to ease in front of us, see the danger clearly, and then maneuver on her own. I cleared the oiler's captain to cross to the left across our bow if he needed to (which was not a problem since we were going backward at full speed). We both safely escaped to the left of the oncoming ship, whose master was oblivious to the havoc he just caused, and which sailed blithely down our starboard side.

We had practiced just this maneuver once before—much to my crew's either puzzlement or amusement. Why would we do an emergency breakaway backing down? I wasn't sure whether I would ever need to conduct such a maneuver but wanted to shake my team out of the mindset of always having to do it the normal way. The maneuver ended up coming in handy—the master of the replenishment ship called over after the event and said it was the finest act of seamanship he'd ever witnessed. That made this old fighter pilot feel pretty good. It also reminded me that leaders are really put into place for two principal reasons (although there is plenty to do in between): to establish a culture and vision for the organization and to handle a crisis nobody else on the team is equipped to handle.

Enterprise's mission in the Gulf was threefold: deter Iranian malign behavior, help prevent Iraqis from smuggling oil out through the Arabian Gulf, and support our troops' efforts in Iraq by flying hundreds of sorties in support of Operation Southern Watch.

During our workup cycle, I used my experience from building boarding teams on board USS *Cleveland* to build teams for *Enterprise*. Everyone thought I was crazy—after all, why would an aircraft carrier ever need to conduct a boarding mission? But Navy ships have boarded other ships throughout our nation's history—to wit, the *Enterprise* Sailors who burned the *Philadelphia* in Tripoli nearly two hundred years earlier. I had seen firsthand the shortage of trained teams in the Gulf while on board *Cleveland*. Moreover, it provided an opportunity for a few of my Sailors to qualify in something difficult and special. So I pushed for it, and after the usual pushback, the system finally yielded. We ended up with no shortage of enthusiastic volunteers to go through the training and eventually built two fully qualified teams. I participated in some of the training myself.

The Navy leadership in the Arabian Gulf was both surprised and delighted when we arrived with boarding team reinforcements. With a proliferation of oil smugglers and growing success in apprehending them, the Combined Coalition Task Force 50 commander needed prize crews to man "Comiskey Park," which was the code name for the area where we held detained Iraqi smugglers' vessels. We spent "no-fly" days on board *Enterprise* cruising up and down the Iranian coast looking for smugglers. For a few days we were assigned the services of the Australian ship HMAS *Anzac*, which carried specially qualified boarding teams that could conduct more difficult opposed boarding operations.

The Aussies were tough—if the rules of engagement permitted them to break a window to get into the target ship's bridge, they would break all the windows. We would have them apprehend an Iraqi smuggler, then we would relieve their specialized team with one of our boarding teams as the prize crew, which in turn released the Aussie team to move on to the next ship. We took quiet pride in knowing *Enterprise* Sailors made a difference and that training them was a good investment of time and money, despite the skeptics.

As busy as we were, we still managed to have some fun, including a swim call. We anchored in a secure corner of the Gulf, trailed a couple of lines with buoys attached behind the ship in the light current, put a couple of boats in the water with safety observers, lowered one of our aircraft elevators, and commenced swim call. I would only allow people in the water who were willing to jump the twenty-five feet or so from the elevator to the water. I figured if they weren't confident enough to do that, they didn't belong in the water. The rule was that Sailors left their shoes with their ID card tucked inside on the elevator, jumped in, and then drifted or swam back to the stern of the ship. They could then get out and reclaim their shoes and ID, which had been carried to the stern; this was how we maintained track of who was in the water. I was the first one to jump off the elevator, along with our navigator, Cdr. Tighe "Tiger" Parmenter. Sure, a few sea snakes drifted past the ship, but no one got hurt and it was a great day. Ulrich thought I was nuts, but taking a little personal career risk to give my crew a well-deserved break seemed to be worth it.

Our support for Operation Southern Watch involved flying sorties over Southern Iraq to enforce the no-fly zone imposed after the first Gulf War. Here it was, ten years after that war ended, and we were still sending planes into Iraq every day. And, when necessary, our pilots eliminated surface-to-air missile systems that could threaten our aircraft.

This was a real cat-and-mouse game. We would find a mobile radar driving around and start to position aircraft to strike it. The Iraqis figured out that we would not hit them when they were moving (although they may not have known why: this was purely to ensure we avoided collateral damage). They also knew that if they stopped for longer than a few minutes, we would strike them. Whenever they stopped, the drivers would quickly get away from their trucks. The Joint Forces Air Component Commander team would frantically check the coordinates for collateral damage and obtain a legal review to determine whether we could strike the target. If all was satisfactory, authorization would be given and the aircraft vectored in for the strike. However, it was often too late because the driver got back in the truck and drove off. So we learned a great deal during this time about preclearing areas and other ways to expedite procedures to strike a mobile point target that proved to be essential during the "drone" operations of more recent times.

The strike we conducted on our final night of flight operations in the Gulf was particularly challenging for both the air wing and for me. An Iraqi radar had been detected at rest in a grove of palm trees, and aircraft from *Enterprise*'s Carrier Air Wing Eight, led by then-captain Dave "Merc" Mercer were assigned to take it out.

We launched nearly every aircraft on the flight deck into the night in several waves in order to conduct this strike, and we were short of aerial refueling aircraft. With all of the respotting required to keep the landing area clear when bringing a large number of aircraft back on board, it was going to be challenging to recover them when they returned, likely all low on fuel. We moved *Enterprise* as far northwest as possible to shorten the distance they needed to fly. It was a dark night with a moon that would not rise until after we finished flight operations. We were also challenged by the confined, shallow waters of the Gulf, the numerous oil rigs and fishing dhows scattered around the area, and the fact that there was zero ambient wind. All of this meant *Enterprise* would have to steam at a high rate of speed to recover her aircraft while dodging all of the obstacles and turning around frequently to avoid running aground. Because of the lack of wind, we operated in a mode we labeled "Chinese," which meant recovering aircraft in nearly any direction we drove.

In the end, we managed to get everyone on board in what we thought was the final big event for the ship and the air wing during our deployment. Little did we know that there were more challenges just over the horizon.

We settled in for a long, boring trip home.

TOP We rebuilt *Enterprise's* ability to refuel other ships under way, and it paid off on the journey home. Here we refuel USS *McFaul* during workups. *Official U.S. Navy photo by PH3 Josh Kinter*

MIDDLE The flag flown by the Arlington Police Department at the Pentagon on 9/11 was sent to *Enterprise. Arlington Police Department photo from Winnefeld collection*

BOTTOM The Arlington Police flag flying on board *Enterprise* on the first night of strikes into Afghanistan. *Winnefeld collection*

First Responders

On Tuesday afternoon, September 11, 2001, *Enterprise* was speeding south along the coast of Oman, heading home after a highly successful deployment. The ship and airwing planned a brief pause that evening to requalify a few pilots in night landings, but we were otherwise wasting no time heading home via the first-ever nuclear carrier port visit to South Africa.

At around three o'clock in the afternoon in the North Arabian Sea, or nine o'clock in the morning on the East Coast of the United States, our safety officer called telling me to turn on the TV because something was happening at the World Trade Center in New York. I immediately saw the gut-wrenching sight of the top of the North Tower pouring smoke and flames, followed not long after by the sickening impact of an airliner into the South Tower. The attack altered both the course of *Enterprise*'s deployment and, more importantly, our country's history. It was immediately apparent to those in leadership positions on *Enterprise* that we were not heading home any time soon.

What happened next is the subject of much folklore. No, I did not immediately whip *Enterprise* around to the north toward the coast of Pakistan
without any orders. I've been privately embarrassed numerous times when
some well-meaning person pulled that story off the Internet and introduced
me to an audience using it. While on active duty, I always instructed my aides
to preempt such an introduction. But, to my chagrin, it didn't always work.

What actually happened is much simpler and should strike the reader as
more realistic and in keeping with how these decisions are made.

After the tragic attacks unfolded, I approached Rear Adm. John Morgan
(who had relieved Harry Ulrich just days prior) and air wing commander Dave
Mercer to determine whether we should still fly that night. I felt the crew's
preoccupation with the tragedy and the spike in human factors involved could
affect safety of flight. Within an hour or so, we slowed down and loitered,
pending a decision from our chain of command regarding our track. After a
few fits and starts regarding whether to send us back to the Arabian Gulf, the
Fifth Fleet commander directed us to turn northeast toward a point in the
northern part of the middle of the North Arabian Sea. We were to join the
Vinson Battle Group, which had just rounded the southern tip of India at the
beginning of their deployment on their way to the Arabian Gulf to relieve us.

Enterprise and her crew did well in executing a complex process of sailing
overnight from the coast of Oman to our station just south of Pakistan,
with an air wing ready to fly on command. Once we were clear of the Gulf
of Oman, we had largely "buttoned up" the air wing for the long transit to
South Africa. But we now needed to conduct a host of aircraft elevator moves
to reconfigure the air wing for potential combat operations. It's standard
procedure to run the elevators with the ship steaming at no more than twenty
knots. Any faster and a hard turn could heel the ship enough to cause a
lowered elevator to dig into the water, with the potential loss of people and
aircraft. However, our navigation team said we needed to average twenty-five
knots to make it to our assigned station on time.

It seemed like an intractable problem to my team because the ship would
ordinarily maintain a steady speed to reach its destination. I directed that
we sail at thirty knots, then quickly slow to twenty knots for the periods in

which we would move all four elevators on their down and up cycle, then quickly resume the higher speed. We would make a series of these moves and average twenty-five knots. It seems so simple in retrospect, but members of an organization in a time of urgency can sometimes think inside their own stovepipes. The person at the top may be the only one who can see through the problem with a simple solution.

We made it to our station the next morning, ready for combat against Osama bin Laden, al-Qaeda, and their Taliban hosts. We then settled in for the waiting game as diplomacy ran its course.

Sailing once again in the North Arabian Sea was reminiscent of my formative years as a naval aviator. With the summer monsoon having died out, the water was a familiar flat calm, with the horizon always seeming closer than it should be. Puffy clouds gave promise to possible rain squalls that never seemed to materialize, frustrating our eagerness to wash the Arabian Gulf dust off the ship. At least the water and air were cooler than in the Gulf: our flight deck and propulsion plants were far more habitable than before.

It was a tedious time. For one thing, it was the only time in my career when I felt safer at sea than I did for my family back home due to the uncertainty over the potential for additional terror attacks. Nonetheless, until we gained greater clarity regarding where Pakistan stood on the whole issue of support for al-Qaeda, we had to remain alert for potential attacks from that direction, most notably from a couple of Pakistani submarines that were under way. I was relieved that *Enterprise*'s antisubmarine warfare module, supported by Mark Ferguson's destroyer squadron staff, passed with flying colors when our skeptical strike group commander visited to see whether it was up to snuff.

Meanwhile, both Mary and I were trying to help manage morale on the ship and at home. Our families were anxious to know their Sailors were safe, and they remained incredibly supportive of our need to extend the deployment. I sent an initial e-mail to our family e-mail tree, explaining what we were doing as best I could. The message explained that we turned off the outgoing e-mail every so often to avoid telegraphing our intentions should hostilities begin, but our Sailors could always receive e-mail.

Mary found herself presiding over family support group meetings that had previously averaged around twenty attendees but now swelled to hundreds following the attacks. She had to be very forward-leaning with news media that tried to overplay our deployment extension, as well as push a family support structure that was unprepared for this kind of event. Out on the ship, while our Sailors were anxious to get home, they were bound and determined not to leave before they had the opportunity to participate in our nation's response to the 9/11 attacks.

At one point I had fun showing our crew a *Los Angeles Times* article with a map of where all the military forces were in the theater, with various silhouettes of ships. While we were unhappy the media would put out our forces' rough positions, I noted that *Vinson*'s silhouette was that of a *Nimitz*-class carrier, while ours was that of the World War II carrier *Enterprise*, CV 6. This was somewhat spooky, especially since that *Enterprise* was also on her way home during the last treacherous attack on our country and drew first blood on the Japanese in an attack on the Marshall Islands on February 1, 1942. But it gave me an idea I would use on the day we started combat operations.

Operating for an extended period in the North Arabian Sea presented a host of logistical challenges. We were far from our traditional regional hubs in the Arabian Gulf, and the system had to support two carriers (and, later, more) simultaneously. We used considerable creativity to keep parts and mail flowing. At one point we conducted the most complex underway replenishment I had seen to that date, moving ammunition, groceries, fuel, and parts in an event in which we connected to two different ships in the same morning. I was proud of my team, who designed the scheme of maneuver for four ships to replenish from three others and then executed it flawlessly.

The only blemish occurred when I discovered that the congratulatory message I personally wrote to the other participating commanding officers was retyped by our communications center. They transmitted it despite my previous guidance that any message directly from me that needed to be retyped for some reason must be brought back to me for review. It was loaded with embarrassing errors and was the only time I ever recall being upset with my otherwise-excellent combat systems officer. Responding to the ribbing from the *Carl Vinson* folks was a good test of character.

Another example of logistics complexity arose when we executed a carefully conceived plan to move a couple of heavy E-2C Hawkeye engines from Fujairah in Oman to the ship. I asked my team to carefully design a daisy chain of ships and helicopters that were not normally used for this kind of movement, which would place them at the edge of their operating envelopes. The only alternative was to take *Enterprise* off station for a couple of days to steam over to Fujairah and back.

On the two-week anniversary of the attacks, I went flying for the first time in a couple of months. I had been holding off out of concern that all our F-14 pilots would not get one hundred arrested landings during the deployment. I didn't want a pilot who failed to reach this milestone to feel cheated because the carrier captain went flying a couple of times. That was no longer a problem now that our deployment was extended.

My flight was a one-hour cycle with the commanding officer of VF-41, Brian Gawne. It was interesting to talk with him about their upcoming transition into the F/A-18F at the end of the deployment. We did a couple of intercepts, some good tail chase with another airplane, then practiced a couple of high-altitude laser-guided bomb deliveries and returned to land on the 3-wire. It was a motivating and welcome break.

As I would find out again in a later tour, it's important for leadership to fly with the frontline team because it can open windows on problems that might be frustrating them. In this case, I was able to see from the pilot's perspective just how slippery our flight deck had become due to its painted nonskid profile wearing off at the end of a long deployment. The accumulated spills of aviation fuel, engine oil, hydraulic oil, and a host of other lubricants, often in areas where the nonskid was completely worn away—something with which land-based pilots never have to contend—created a slick surface. We redoubled our efforts to maintain the flight deck as best we could.

This dead time between the attacks and our response was full of symbolism. We named the operating "boxes" we drew in the North Arabian Sea: "Pentagon" (closest to Pakistan), "World Trade Center West" and "East" (a little further south), "NYPD" and "NYFD" (even further south), and "Pennsylvania" (in the Gulf of Oman). I wondered whether anyone told the NYPD and NYFD we named our boxes after them. We also heard a touching story of a British warship that saluted USS *Winston Churchill* by flying an American flag at half-mast as they sailed by, with a "lead the way" banner displayed.

Another symbol involved a small model of the World Trade Center someone on the ship found and brought to me on the bridge. It was a cheap tourist souvenir but, sitting on my console along with a couple of FDNY and NYPD ball caps, was quite a motivator for my bridge watch teams. We also received the actual American flag flown by the Arlington police force at their command post at the Pentagon on 9/11, which we flew from *Enterprise*'s masthead and presented to the department after we returned home.

While we were waiting for combat operations to begin, I received a phone call from Adm. William "Fox" Fallon, saying my next job would be as his executive assistant. I had enjoyed a luxury few Navy captains have: serving on sea duty during my entire time at the rank of captain. Now I was heading to a desk. Fox kindly said I could arrive in January. I replied that if he didn't mind nursing someone who had been on sea duty since 1993, it would be an honor to have the job.

Of course, we continued to keep ourselves proficient, preparing for our forecast role as the "night shift" carrier when combat finally commenced. I recall waiting for one dusk, or "pinkie," launch to occur. It was exhilarating to be sitting in the captain's chair on *Enterprise*'s bridge as we ran south away from Pakistan to build sea space. The setting sun off our starboard side highlighted the flight deck. The rippled steel blue water rushed past at thirty-plus knots, with our broad, foamy wake stretching to the horizon and our escort ships breathing hard to keep up with us. In my very near field of view was the smoothness of our bridge watch team as it prepared to turn back into the wind and avoid a couple of nearby tankers. The near field was filled by the busy flight deck . . . aircrews starting their aircraft, the flight deck swarmed with flight deck personnel and movement of tractors and helicopters. Beyond were our escort ships, with their white wakes flashing a few miles away. The sun was a brilliant orange ball sinking into the brown smudge of the horizon to the southwest as it tracked through the bridge windows while we turned into the wind. It is a feeling and a sight I will always miss.

I found time in the days before our first strikes to descend into a weapons magazine deep in the bowels of the ship, where the bombs were assembled for our first night strikes. I helped put one together, wondering where it was destined to land. I also provided supplemental orders to my bridge and combat direction center watch teams for combat operations, focusing on additional vigilance, clarifying self-defense procedures in this unique environment, and a reminder that we would not take the first hit.

I woke early on the morning of our first strikes to the unpleasant sensation of looking at the radar scope in my at-sea cabin and seeing a contact at five miles with a "closest point of approach" of only two and a half miles. In normal circumstances, the bridge team was supposed to call me when a surface contact was at ten miles with a closest point of approach of five miles or less. My night orders stressed trying to stay five miles away from all contacts during a period of heightened uncertainty. The officer of the deck stated that he wanted to wait to call until my wake-up call, which would have been in ten minutes. I didn't want to start the first morning of a war upset at someone, so I remained calm but reset the standard on the spot.

That afternoon we welcomed a group of reporters aboard the ship. Many of them had little or no experience with the military. When they emerged after sitting for several hours in their cramped C-2 Greyhound aircraft, they were unprepared to see red-shirted weapons personnel loading bombs on aircraft everywhere on the flight deck. Earlier that afternoon I had my picture taken in my red weapons shirt wearing an "FDNY" hat and wrote in chalk on one weapon: "COLE, Pentagon, WTC, FDNY, NYPD." Other bombs bore inscriptions that would be inappropriate to relate in this book.

That evening Operation Enduring Freedom began with Tomahawk missile launches from surface ships in the North Arabian Sea. One of these ships was USS *McFaul*, only a few miles off our port side. Watching a couple of her missiles boost into the night sky and transition to cruise flight felt like the beginning of something that might last a long time.

We began moving north at around 7:30 p.m. to get the air wing within fifty miles of the Pakistani coast since no Air Force tankers were available for our first strikes. That put more pressure on our pilots' fuel planning, so the closer we could get to their targets, the better. With light winds generally from the north, working inside fifty miles from the coast required us to use all of our sea-room-preservation tricks. But our experience flying in the heat, light winds, and cramped confines of the Arabian Gulf prepared us well.

At 9:45 p.m., I made an announcement to the crew on the ship's public address system. Not fancying myself as a great orator, much less a historical figure, my speech didn't rise to the level of a Nelson exhorting his Sailors before Trafalgar that "England expects that every man will do his duty." Nor was it as simple and eloquent as Dwight Eisenhower stating, "All I demand is that every man do his best." Moreover, our Sailors certainly didn't need any extra motivation on this night. But I wanted the crew and air wing to understand the historical significance of the moment and to focus all their energy on the difficult task ahead. So, leveraging an idea I obtained from the flawed newspaper article of a few weeks before, here is how it read:

> Aboard ENTERPRISE, good evening shipmates. The last time America actually went to war to defend against an attack on our homeland was almost exactly sixty years ago, when a treacherous enemy conducted a surprise attack on Pearl Harbor. During that attack, a different ENTER-PRISE was at sea on her way home, and was ultimately an integral response to the difficult and bloody task of soundly defeating that enemy.
>
> Ever since then, whenever America has gone to war, it has been to protect freedom and our vital interests and those of our allies. We have not had to defend our homeland. However, on September 11, our ENTERPRISE was at sea on her way home during a treacherous new attack on our country. And tonight, a ship named ENTERPRISE will again be an integral part of our nation's response. And like 1941, this war is a little more personal than merely defending our vital interests. We are defending our families.
>
> About two hours ago, our battle force launched Tomahawk missiles towards targets in Afghanistan involved in supporting terrorism, and those targets were struck about 15 minutes ago. Additional strike assets from coalition forces are hitting other targets as I speak. In a couple of hours, Air Wing 8 will be launching aircraft from ENTERPRISE to strike even more targets.

Tonight, and for who knows how long, our brave aircrews will be taking the fight to the enemy. They do not think of themselves as heroes. The real heroes are the 17 Sailors who died aboard USS COLE; they are the 42 Sailors and Navy civilians and all the other innocent victims at the Pentagon; they are the firefighters and policemen and thousands of other innocent people who died at the World Trade Center, they are the innocent people who died thwarting hijackers in Pennsylvania, and they are those who worked tirelessly to look for survivors.

We do not call what we are doing tonight revenge, for revenge only belongs to God. What we are about tonight is the first real step to ensuring terrorism cannot happen again in our country, though it is likely to happen again before we are finished. Our cause is just, for unlike those against whom we are fighting, we will take pains to only go after the guilty, not the innocent.

You have done a tremendous job preparing for this. You are ready. I ask that you do several simple things. Say a prayer for our aircrews and our country. Concentrate very hard on what you are doing. Do not let the enormity or excitement of what we are doing distract you from what is a difficult and dangerous business that we have to get right.

God bless you shipmates, and God bless our great nation.

We commenced launching airplanes forty-five minutes later, including four S-3 tankers to support a package of two FA-18s and two F-14s going to Afghanistan on our initial strike. Among our first targets were caves in which bin Laden might have been hiding and buildings at suspected terrorist camps. We hit nine of eleven targets, with a nice video of a damaged surface-to-air missile shooting out of a burning storage facility. The air wing and flight deck performed flawlessly. After the launch, I stopped by the makeshift press room to ensure the reporters knew what we were doing, and several demanded to be allowed to call their editors. I told them they could do so only after our aircrews returned "feet wet" from their initial missions. I also sent an e-mail to our families telling them we commenced strike operations from a safe area.

We conducted strike operations for sixteen days before offloading our few remaining weapons and beginning our transit home. On *Enterprise* we flew all night and replenished during the day, including once actually launching and recovering aircraft while connected alongside a replenishment ship on our starboard side, with a helicopter moving ammunition from a ship on the port side. All of this was tiring for both the crew and the air wing, but we were running on adrenaline. The crew knew they were stepping up, and it only made them feel and operate better. We were doing so well that Fifth Fleet Commander Vice Adm. Willy Moore told us he was having second thoughts about letting us go. We were victims of our own success, but we didn't want to leave a moment before the time was right.

Trust became a helpful factor for me during this time. *Enterprise*'s navigator, Cdr. Tighe "Tiger" Parmenter, had left the ship just after the 9/11 attacks on emergency leave due to the death of a relative. When he returned to the ship from the United States just before our combat operations began, I had a precious asset: someone I knew could competently run flight operations yet whose sleep cycle was preadjusted to the night hours.

There are many carrier captains who would simply not leave the bridge in the middle of night combat flight operations. But I knew this was a marathon and not a sprint. I was picking up a lot of tasks during the day, such as conducting underway replenishments and working with the media, for which our embarked admiral and air wing commander didn't have time. So I took the "chair" for the first half of night flight operations, and Tiger took the second half. Ernest Hemingway once said, "The best way to find out if you can trust somebody is to trust them." I never would have given Tiger this key responsibility had he not been trained well. And I knew he would call if he needed me. It must have given him an incredible boost to know I was comfortable with him on the bridge during these operations.

We sometimes had to improvise. Once a Tomcat returned to the ship with so much trapped fuel that it would have to land four thousand pounds heavier than what the recovery bulletins said was permissible. After a bit of searching, we found that this weight could actually be set in the arresting gear even though no fleet airplane was ever supposed to be "trapped" at this weight. The question was whether the aircraft could handle it. Knowing margins are built into these operations, I made the call, with our air wing commander's concurrence, that we would step up the wind as high as possible and land the jet instead of trying to do a complex divert to Oman that might collapse our entire tanking program.

The airplane landed just fine. I suppose that's one reason they put people in command: to make the call when the rules don't cover a situation and when judgment, knowledge, and experience have to take over. I was glad to have trained as an LSO, with all the attendant knowledge about arresting gear, as well as being nuclear-trained to better understand the energy tradeoffs involved in the landing. I was also grateful for a fantastic air wing commander in Dave Mercer, who was willing to share the risk.

Although it felt right to be using a great deal of military power to bring the perpetrators of an attack on our nation to justice, our future in Afghanistan seemed murky to me. After receiving a brief from the Fifth Fleet staff during the initial days of our efforts, I wrote in a diary I kept at the time: "The ultimate goal is to transform Afghanistan into a productive, responsible country that does not support terrorism. That is a tall order. How does one transform the drug trade? How does one integrate the tribal culture?" Events have, sadly, seen this observation come true, despite the many sacrifices of our remarkable ground forces.

We finally departed the North Arabian Sea on October 23, but not without one last bit of predeployment preparation and innovation coming home to roost. Because we had resurrected *Enterprise*'s ability to refuel other ships during our workup period, we were able to bring the guided-missile cruiser USS *Philippine Sea*, commanded by Capt. Rick Hunt, along with us on the way home. With so many thirsty ships now in the North Arabian Sea executing operations in Afghanistan, there was no way to break an oiler away to meet us in the Red Sea. Don Smith's hard work saved the logisticians a head-scratching problem and got the cruiser home on time.

We were tired but pleased with how we contributed to our nation's response to the terrorist attacks of 9/11. After a Suez Canal transit and a brief stop in Souda Bay, Greece, we would be the first warriors home from the war. A huge crowd on the pier greeted us seven and a half months after we left, with Neil Diamond's "Coming to America" blaring from our loudspeakers. A stiff current running down the Elizabeth River in Norfolk forced us to drive a bit past the pier before turning the ship 90 degrees bow-in. Most of the crowd thought we had miscalculated and overshot, but under the guidance of Norfolk's expert docking pilots, we drifted downstream and back into perfect alignment with the pier. It was heartwarming in the extreme to be reunited with family after such an eventful deployment.

Our first two tasks upon arriving home—other than trying to get as much of the crew as possible off on leave—were to host what we called GB1 and GB2. GB1 was a huge concert put on by Garth Brooks on *Enterprise*'s flight deck. It was amazing to watch these professional entertainers transform the ship into a concert venue, and then see the performance shown on live television.

GB2 was a visit from and speech by President George W. Bush. We transformed the flight deck again, although with far less glitz. The president was warm and gracious, shaking hands with as many Sailors as possible and delivering an uplifting speech. This was not his infamous "Mission Accomplished" speech on the flight deck of USS *Abraham Lincoln* later. Instead, it was an important moment in which the president used the ship as the backdrop for making a reassuring statement to a nation shaken only a few months earlier by the 9/11 attacks.

Not long after the festivities were over, we brought *Enterprise* into Norfolk Naval Shipyard for a long-awaited dry-docking period. After the water was drained from the dock, I walked all around and under the ship's massive hull. Satisfied, I sent a note to my old mentor and predecessor, Streak Chanik, that there were no marks on the bottom of the ship he would have to explain.

While I was waiting for the date to transfer command of *Enterprise*, I visited the Naval Reactors office in Washington, DC. There I presented their leader, Adm. Frank Bowman, with a riff on the photo that had inspired me as a child: *Enterprise* with "$E = mc^2 \times 40$" traced on her flight deck, to indicate how many years this remarkable ship had been in commission. She was to have a photo with "$E = mc^2 \times 50$" before she was decommissioned.

I was able to engineer a modest change-of-command ceremony in what began a tradition for me. I've always been bashful about large change-of-command ceremonies—they seemed to be too ostentatious, more about a single person than the people who made really things work. That's not my style. I also didn't want the ship to lose a precious full day of shipyard work through having to orchestrate a large ceremony. The post 9/11 security and safety requirements were the perfect foil for keeping the ceremony small and brief. On a chilly winter day in Norfolk Naval Shipyard, Vice Adm. John Morgan and I spoke to the assembled crew and a few guests, and shortly afterward Mary and I were "bonged" off the amazing Big E.

It was finally time to go ashore, at least for a while.

TOP I worked for a demanding boss in Navy Vice Chief Adm. Bill Fallon (*right*), and I couldn't have done it without our deputy executive assistant, Cdr. Dave Radi (*left*). *Radi family collection*

BOTTOM Adm. Vern Clark asked me to assemble a team to figure out carrier readiness. *Official U.S. Navy photo by Jo1 Brandan W. Shulze*

Shock and Awe

T he words "shock" and "awe," used later to describe the initial strikes of the second war with Iraq, were apropos as I entered my new job on the Navy staff. My job was to serve Vice CNO Adm. William "Fox" Fallon as his executive assistant. Transitioning from being the captain of an aircraft carrier to life as a staff officer was less a matter of ego than it was about wondering whether I could make a difference.

Fallon was the number two ranking officer in the Navy behind CNO Adm. Vern Clark. Because my only previous Pentagon experience was on the Joint Staff, I initially felt uneasy because I was in a critical enabling position but knew nothing about how the Navy staff operated. But I received an excellent turnover from my capable predecessor, Capt. Charlie Martoglio, and jumped on the oars with the rest of the team.

I quickly discovered how lucky I was to have inherited Cdr. Dave Radi as a deputy, a collegial and effective naval intelligence officer with a great sense of humor. Dave, who is a second-generation American whose father came to the United States from Czechoslovakia, was also one of the quickest thinkers

I've ever known. He had moved to the office from the Navy Command Center just a few weeks before the 9/11 attacks. Several of his former colleagues working in that area were killed or injured on that fateful day. Dave kept me out of trouble long after I thought I had learned the ropes. He also taught me that "Google" is as much a verb as a noun (remember, this was 2002).

It didn't take long to learn how much power was wielded by an executive assistant, and I was determined to use it to my boss's advantage, not mine. My initial discovery centered on the many paperwork packages from the various Navy staff elements that would land on my desk for submission to or through Fallon. Clearly, the three stars on the staff were so busy they didn't have time to read the actual contents of their staff's packages before initialing and forwarding them. But Fallon would not tolerate substandard staff work—and I didn't want to feel the heat from passing it to him.

I was initially a bit unsure about rejecting paperwork—after all, who was I to tell a three-star admiral that one of their packages was unsatisfactory? What I quickly learned, though, was how grateful these officers were for my suggestions on how to successfully get their paper through with minimal wrath from our boss. Nonetheless, I spent a great deal of my time personally bringing awards packages and other items up to our quality standards—a far cry from what I did in command of an aircraft carrier.

A few months after I arrived in the Pentagon, I was informed I was selected for flag rank, along with around thirty other officers. I was not at all overconfident about this selection; I had seen too many strange career twists and turns. But I felt a successful tour on board USS *Enterprise* might carry the day. Selection to be a one-star admiral felt like vindication in one way: I never once woke up in the morning asking what needed to be done to make flag rank. I felt doing so would cause me to make bad decisions and be overly risk-averse. Perhaps more importantly, the combination of gaining my required "joint education" via a correspondence course while the executive officer of VF-211 (thereby saving the Navy a full man-year) and my shortened squadron command tour gave me more time to serve as a flag officer before I would statutorily have to retire, which opened more doors to the future.

About this time, I began to take a different view of the overused word "humble," as in the many people I heard say something like, "I'm humbled to have been selected for flag rank." While their words were undoubtedly sincere, I thought "fortunate," "grateful," or "downright lucky" seemed more appropriate for me, especially in light of the other unbelievably talented officers who were not selected for whatever reason. "Deeply honored"? Of course. But "humbled"? No. There was nothing humbling about it. Humbled was what it felt like to be on top of the world as a TopGun instructor and then jump out of an airplane a few months after rejoining the fleet. "Humble" came across as false modesty from people who couldn't think of anything else to say. My most charitable interpretation of the use of the word in these situations was as a reminder to actually be humble in the new role. I didn't hold it against anyone, but I resolved to strive for genuine humility and never use the word in that way.

The commonly accepted practice was to immediately start moving newly selected flags into flag officer positions, as more such posts existed than there were newly promoted officers available to fill them. As I began speculating how soon I might escape the drudgery of being an executive assistant and to where I might move, Admiral Fallon quickly informed me: "not so fast." He had hired me for a reason, and I would spend at least a year in the job, watching my fellow selectees move into their initial baby admiral billets. While I was anxious to get going and initially a bit worried about falling behind, there was no reason for panic—I sensed it would all equalize over time, and I was learning a lot in my current position.

Throughout that summer and fall of 2002, the momentum began to build for a different kind of "shock and awe"—namely, that associated with a U.S. invasion of Iraq. Dave Radi and I watched with interest on the TV in our office as twenty-four-hour news coverage unfolded of accusations over nuclear and chemical weapons inspections and Iraqi complicity in the 9/11 attacks. However, I felt the information connecting Iraq to 9/11 was pretty thin—rather more like a pretext for an action that had already been decided. To be sure, there was a strong case for not allowing Saddam Hussein to possess nuclear weapons or other weapons of mass destruction. But a combination of the Bush administration's expressed belief that spreading democracy was the answer to the world's problems, lingering resentment over the attempted assassination of Bush's father in Kuwait, and a desire to end the drawn-out no-fly zone operations predetermined that Saddam Hussein had to go. At least that's the way it appeared to me.

I captured two important leadership lessons during the buildup to the second Gulf War. First, be wary of allowing your preexisting worldview to act as a filter between you and potentially contrary facts, otherwise known as anchor and confirmation biases. And, second, be especially sensitive to organizational momentum gathering in an unwise direction to the point that it is nearly impossible to stop.

During the buildup to the war, the Navy was asked how many aircraft carriers were available to participate in strike operations in Iraq. The Navy previously surged several carriers for post-9/11 combat operations, but this consumed much of their hard-earned readiness. So the service reentered a cyclical deployment model in which only two carriers would be overseas at any given time, with the other ten in maintenance or training.

Secretary of Defense Donald Rumsfeld didn't like this. It seemed to him as a businessman that having only two of twelve expensive capital assets in service at any given time was wasteful, and he questioned the wisdom of continued investment in the capability. This challenged a significant element of the Navy's investment strategy, to say nothing of its ingrained beliefs. Fortunately, it was also an unintended misrepresentation of the Navy's true readiness.

As it turned out, through herculean effort, the Navy managed to break out of the cyclical routine and get six carriers on the line ready to fight fairly rapidly, in varying degrees of readiness, before combat operations started in March 2003. As with our ground forces, we were lucky Saddam Hussein once again was foolish enough to give the United States time to build up its forces. We cannot count on this in the future, but I fear the lesson has been missed, and it could cost us in a conflict with a more capable adversary such as China.

The drama of obtaining a UN Security Council resolution, with my old boss Colin Powell in the spotlight as secretary of state, gradually unfolded. As Radi and I watched the first strikes on TV followed by the ground invasion of Iraq, I began to wonder why we hadn't tried a little more coercion first rather than a full-scale invasion. Perhaps a few carefully aimed strikes would convince Saddam to allow the UN weapons inspectors to have full access if that was the ultimate goal. I also wondered what the plan would be for Iraq if their population didn't lay flowers down in front of our troops once Saddam's regime was overthrown. What would come next? Would we bear responsibility for cleaning up the mess? I thought of Powell's "Pottery Barn" rule: "if you break it, you own it."

We were about to find out exactly how far the impact of the war—which came to be known as Operation Iraqi Freedom—would reach across the Middle East in both space and time over subsequent years. What started over a decade earlier with a blown diplomatic signal over the Kuwait invasion would, through another miscalculation, gradually engulf much of the Middle East and sap a tremendous amount of U.S. power and goodwill.

The war ran its initial course with the rapid overthrow of the Iraqi regime thanks to the superiority of U.S. combined arms in a conventional fight against an overmatched adversary. As Iraqis and Americans tried to sort things out in the aftermath, Iraq descended into chaos. We found ourselves in an untenable situation, simultaneously countering a Sunni insurgency and defending against attacks from Shia extremists backed by Iran. Like Afghanistan, we were driven by the hubris that we could transform a nation that was not ready for change.

As the heavy combat of the war ramped down, the Navy was anxious to get its carriers home, recover their readiness, and place them back into the familiar cyclical deployment regime. However, the sting of Rumsfeld's skepticism about the viability of the Navy's carrier fleet lingered, and CNO Admiral Clark searched for a way to more accurately reflect their true readiness state. Before the war the Navy only really counted as ready its deployed carriers, which was what had drawn Rumsfeld's ire. Even though I worked for Admiral Fallon, Clark asked me to assemble a small team to take a look at the problem.

We determined that our first task was to determine how long it would take the Navy to recover from the war effort. We aligned all the actual carriers' forecast schedules in rows on a spreadsheet, with color-coded blocks in each month representing how ready each would be over time. Once we placed them vertically adjacent to each other and sorted the rows by readiness levels and deployment dates, a clear pattern leaped off the page. In addition to counting carriers, with their air wings, that were deployed, there was also reason to take credit for the ones that were "worked up" but not deployed. In addition, we could take partial credit for carriers that were in the middle of their workup cycle, were almost ready, or could be accelerated. We could even take credit for carriers that could be made ready in an emergency.

We formalized our ideas into what we called the Fleet Response Plan, or FRP, in which we made a case for a "6 + 2" scheme: six carriers that were deployed or readily deployable and two that were "emergency deployable." This was more than cosmetic: it established expectations, a rule set, and a cost structure for how ready the Navy's carrier fleet would be. It seems so simple and obvious now, but it ran against the then-existing risk paradigm that a carrier was only ready when it was fully ready (and not a moment before) and that schedules were inviolable. The 6 + 2 number may have been optimistic over the long term, but the idea was correct.

I found Vern Clark to be an extraordinary CNO. He had survived briefly leaving the Navy to pursue a business career. Many told him he was nuts—that his Navy career was in tatters due to the gap—but he persevered in no small measure by leveraging what he learned while outside the Navy. He was a great example of the benefits of gaining diversified knowledge rather than sticking with a cookie-cutter success pipeline. I first met him during my earlier stint on the Joint Staff, when he served as the head of the Pacific Command branch in the Joint Operations Directorate. I think he viewed me then as a diamond in the "very" rough, and I'm grateful for his patience when I was a young lieutenant commander.

Clark was deeply religious and was a good listener and commonsense professional who applied his earned business acumen to his job as CNO. He also demanded a businesslike approach from his flag officers. I couldn't help chuckling in recalling the character Raymond Stantz in the film *Ghostbusters* saying, "I've WORKED in the private sector—they expect results!"

Even though the Navy was not strictly a business, it made sense to apply lessons from industry to our processes. So I quickly read every business book I could find, which turned out to be helpful for the remainder of my career and beyond. These books include, among many others, Larry Bossidy's

Execution, Michael Collins' *Good to Great*, Michael Watkins' *The First 90 Days*, and William Kotter's *Leading Change*. Even though they could be trendy at times, I digested them completely, attempting to meld together their many themes.

To say Clark was frustrated is an understatement. While the Navy was being provided more money by Congress, he was getting less for it in capability, capacity, and readiness. One of his famous statements regarding the latter was, "We understated the requirement, and then we underfunded the understated requirement. That's no way to run a Navy." He was convinced that one of the solutions was to produce readiness more efficiently, and he was actively searching for ideas. But he was frustrated that all the budget increases the Navy received during his tenure resulted in essentially zero recapitalization, stating that "the executive corps just doesn't get it."

Because I was a flag-select, I attended the annual all-flag officer conference. Clark wanted advice on shaping the agenda for the conference and asked, "What is the one thing you would do as CNO?"

So I stepped out of my lane as a baby-flag-select executive assistant and wrote Clark a memo suggesting he follow Jack Welch's practice of paying hard-nosed visits to his business units to personally drive accountability that would make the business more profitable. I opined that when CNOs are not trapped in Washington, DC, they normally do glad-hand, morale-building visits. While those were fine, he needed to step in more actively and hold his leaders' feet to the fire. I told him his budget-building process was much healthier than the processes we used to drive execution and that he needed to shift his emphasis toward the latter. It wouldn't be as much fun as shaping the future Navy, but we wouldn't get to the future Navy unless he did this.

I closed my memo by saying: "It will require bold, well-thought-out, carefully articulated action to transform the Navy into an organization with a more efficient approach to business but whose key focus remains on combat readiness. You will need to shift your emphasis to force this change, as well as making your intentions clear in your 2003 guidance, and the Navy will follow."

He agreed, and the memo became the foundation for a series of visits he paid to the various fleet components, which I believe ultimately saved important top-line money for the Navy that could be reinvested elsewhere. Of course, it was still a Sisyphean task. For instance, some in the target audience believed, with some justification, that if they became more efficient, the system would only pass along their savings to those who were not. So why waste their time? But the CNO's increased emphasis had a real effect. I was particularly proud of how naval aviation responded, with leaders like Vice Adm. Mike Malone and Vice Adm. Wally Massenburg stepping up to drive efficiencies into their end of the business.

Finally, Fallon indicated his willingness to cut me loose to move on to my first flag billet. It turned out that Radi was retiring the same month I would transfer, so I made sure we left on the same day—I couldn't do the job without him. As a farewell gift, I gave him a Salvatore Ferragamo tie with camels and elephants on it, symbolic of how he carried me and kept us both in stitches for a year and a half.

My next stop was to follow Fallon back to the fleet, but only to another shore job in a supporting role at Fleet Forces Command, which was charged with being the Navy force provider to the Joint world. I could smell the saltwater, but that was as close as I was going to get to it for now. It seemed like Fallon was employing what a friend of mine once called the "Tonto school of leadership"—find a good horse and ride it until it drops.

My job was to help shape the requirements the Navy staff in the Pentagon would, at least in theory, turn into programs. Part of the idea was to parallel what the Air Force was doing with its Air Combat Command based in Langley, Virginia. I was also expected to bring transformational ideas to the fleet. But the office was understaffed and underpowered. There was no way a baby one-star admiral stationed outside Washington, DC, with three people working for him was going to change how the Navy viewed its warfighting requirements.

In the meantime, little did I know that my advocacy for Welch-like visits to the fleet from the CNO was about to be visited upon me. Sure enough, Fleet Forces Command was his first stop in scrutinizing the Navy's major commands. Even though a substantial part of the business-efficiency side of a major command has to do with logistics, I was chosen to put together the brief due to my familiarity with what Clark was after.

Somehow we made it through Clark's visit, and after a year in my first flag officer job, it was time to move on to serve as Commander, Carrier Strike Group 2, otherwise known as the Theodore Roosevelt Carrier Strike Group due to the name of its flagship. Like any good Sailor, I looked forward to getting back to sea with more experience, a clearer understanding of how things get done in the Navy, and an even stronger motivation to make things better.

Anchor #3:
Lead Organizations

"Bureaucracy will generate enough internal work to keep itself busy and so justify its continued existence without commensurate output."

Cyril Northcote Parkinson

Firmly Establish Culture

"The culture of any organization is simply the collective behavior of its leaders."

Franklin Covey

"The truth is generally seen, rarely heard."

Baltasar Gracián

Think Strategically

"The attention you give to any action should be in proportion to its worth."

Marcus Aurelius

"Strategy wears a dollar sign."

Bernard Brodie

Understand Power

"Nearly all men can stand adversity, but if you want to test a man's character, give him power."

Abraham Lincoln

"The measure of a man is what he does with power."

Plato

Communicate!

"An order that can be misunderstood, will be misunderstood."

Napoleon

"Writing is refined thinking."

Stephen King

"Of all the powers bestowed on men, none is so precious as the gift of oratory."

Winston Churchill

ANCHOR 3
Lead Organizations

FIRMLY ESTABLISH CULTURE

TopGun was founded on two pillars: the instructors ran the squadron, and its excellence fed off positive peer pressure. Enterprise Rent-a-Car's culture was firmly established by the company's founder, Jack Taylor, as "Take care of your customers and your employees, and the bottom line will take care of itself." What do these highly successful teams have in common? A simply stated but deeply rooted culture.

The word "culture" derives from the Latin root "*culta*," which means preparing the ground for crops. Culture is indeed the ground—fertile or not—in which a team does its business. An organization growing in poor soil will struggle to succeed. Likewise, toxic workplace culture quickly drives people away.

Culture is revealed in how an organization behaves. It has a lot of ingredients: values, attitudes, work ethic, methods, trust, and a sense of responsibility to one another. Experts recognize several different types of culture, including star, bureaucratic, autocratic, and commitment. Coming up with your own culture demands good instincts for what works for you, for your mission, and for the many personalities that make up your organization. Whatever you adopt should be simple and powerful so every member of your team knows it and believes in it.

Like trust, good culture is hard to build and easy to destroy; its most important element is organizational integrity. It is far more than a set of slogans a leader puts on the wall; everyone has those, but not all organizations have a good culture. Driving good culture into an organization requires persistence. Moreover, as an organization grows—and especially if it grows quickly—good culture gets harder to maintain. One might call this "cultural dilution." It requires senior leaders to focus on keeping it intact.

THINK STRATEGICALLY

I've always subscribed to the notion that the art and science of strategy—in business, sports, or national security—is fundamentally about balancing four variables: the *operating environment* and an organization's *ends*, *ways*, and *means*. If a strategy does not somehow address these variables, then it cannot be effective. And if any of them should change, then one or more of the others must adjust, or the strategy can fall badly out of balance.

Leaders have to face reality in every aspect of their operating environment, or the rest of the strategy will be on shaky ground. For a business, the environment generally consists of competition and customers alongside technology and financial conditions. Ends are about what an organization is trying to accomplish. For a military force, it could be deterring or defeating a potential adversary. For a business, it is about generating revenue that falls to the bottom line as profit. It is helpful if ends are listed in a way that is prioritized, abstract, and enduring, which injects discipline into the process.

Ways are about how an organization goes about achieving its ends. For a business, it's about how to approach developing, producing, and marketing products and services with acceptable margins that will win in the marketplace. For a military it is about high-level concepts as well as tactics and procedures. Means are about the resources an organization needs to bring its chosen ways to life. For the military, it's about how borrowed or taxed money is spent on personnel, capability, capacity, and readiness. For a business, it's about human and capital resources, among other things.

Changing ways is the hardest element of strategy, as species and companies that have left the planet could attest. Indeed, too often when an organization's strategy falls out of equilibrium due to a change in the environment, it lunges for additional means rather than the intellectual effort and organizational courage required to formulate and transition to new ways.

UNDERSTAND POWER

There is nothing like closely observing the highest-level leaders in the land—in government, business, and athletics—to learn how power is exercised at that level. I've been fortunate enough to observe plenty of them, including two presidents, three Joint Chiefs of Staff chairmen, four secretaries of defense, many cabinet secretaries and legislators, countless senior flag and general officers, owners and CEOs of major corporations, and an NFL head coach.

Power translates into the ability to get things done. Some people simply aren't comfortable with the notion of power. Nonetheless, the most effective leaders (although not necessarily the most moral ones) use a combination of six commonly recognized types of power. *Positional* power is employed by virtue of one's position. *Reward* power is the ability to provide a benefit in the form of money, promotion, or recognition. *Coercion* power is exercised through the ability to punish, which can include the deterrent effect of such ability. *Expert* power is gained through recognized knowledge, experience, or privileged information. *Referent* power derives from personal charisma that results in the admiration of subordinates. *Persuasion* power is gained by virtue of one's ability to effectively articulate a convincing position through rhetoric or a well-crafted brief.

The more skilled the leader, the more adept he or she is at sensing which combination of types of power are needed and when, including the types with which one is least comfortable.

COMMUNICATE!

An organization will not respond unless its leader expresses his or her ideas, beliefs, and direction. Nobody outside the organization will respond to someone who cannot clearly articulate the organization's purpose and accomplishments. Hence, a leader cannot be effective without some level of mastery of the tools of communication.

This means mastering six interrelated factors that compose the tools of communication. The first is *messages*: good leaders pay a great deal of attention to crafting the right message and making it as clear as possible. Next comes *audiences*: good leaders are sensitive to the cultures, biases, expertise, seniority, and motivations of their audiences, including how a message might be misperceived. The third is *mediums*: leaders need to be aware of which mediums are and are not available to their target audiences, which will be most effective, and how the medium can distort the message. Next is *messengers*: often the leader is the key messenger, but this is not always the case, and it's important to choose wisely. It goes without saying that *timing* can make or break communication. Finally, simply transmitting a message does not mean it has been received and understood, so it is important to listen to the echoes provided by a *feedback* mechanism.

Learning to write and speak well are two of the most important—and perhaps the hardest—skills for a leader to develop. But it's well worth the time. Regarding the former, I've always found it possible for people to think well and not write well, but it is not possible to write well and not think well. Writing is a many-layered skill that starts with the most important thing: having something important to say. Next, you have to organize everything required to support your work. This is not easily done in one sitting; I used to carry a piece of paper around with me on which I wrote any thoughts that came to mind (now I can put them on my phone). Then you must organize those ideas into a logical flow, composing readable sentences and paragraphs that transition well, finding the hook that engages and delights the reader, and ultimately adhering to the basics of style, spelling, and grammar. It takes a lot of work. While you're never completely satisfied until your work achieves an acceptable level in your own mind, you must continue to revise it or abandon it.

Good speaking requires many of the same skills as good writing, with the additional layer of demeanor and delivery. Reading a speech or overusing PowerPoint is the quickest way to lose an audience. Recognize that a strategic pause is far more effective than the non-word "um"—work hard to eliminate it! Speaking well takes practice, feedback, learning to read an audience, and mastering intonation and gesture. I haven't perfected this and continue to work on it whenever I find myself in front of an audience.

TOP Because we were able to cobble together the Rover system on our F-14Ds, we flew mixed sections of Tomcats and Hornets over Iraq. *Photo by Daniel Sullivan*

MIDDLE While we supported our troops fighting ashore, our boarding teams were ready at sea. *Winnefeld collection*

BOTTOM After a seven-hour flight over Iraq with my RIO, Lt. Cdr. Dan Sullivan. *Photo by Daniel Sullivan*

Carry a Smarter Stick

My tour as the *Theodore Roosevelt* Strike Group commander may have been the most empowered job I've ever held. It was the perfect opportunity to bring my accumulated knowledge of naval warfare and my creative energy to bear on a large organization that would operate mostly over the horizon, free of bureaucratic intransigence.

The group consisted of the aircraft carrier USS *Theodore Roosevelt*— nicknamed the "Big Stick" in obvious reference to its namesake's famous saying—and its air wing as well as several guided-missile cruisers and destroyers and an attack submarine. In a familiar and welcome bit of timing, I took over at the beginning of the strike group's preparation for deployment, which would give me maximum influence over how we did business.

There was much to be done, beginning with the baby steps of how we went about planning for operations. As such, one of our first activities as a staff was to participate in a planning course conducted by the Navy's Atlantic Tactical Training Group. Unfortunately, I discovered a cumbersome method that encouraged slowly marching the team through a scripted, slow, serial process one topic at a time. I knew we had a problem when I entered a planning session and found my staff all huddled around a computer, agonizing over one step in the process and working on one briefing slide. This would not serve us well in a crisis.

We gradually developed a simple planning template and process that, using a shared drive and presentations linked to a single file, would allow people to work simultaneously on several aspects of a plan and then instantly bring it all together for periodic reviews. This way we could establish a horizon that enabled us to plan an operation in anywhere from six hours to sixty days using the same template. Because there's nothing worse than a perfectly assembled plan that perfectly violates a commander's intent, the process really benefits when the commander participates. This system allowed me to touch the cycle at just the right times without micromanaging it.

My next self-imposed task was to advance the art and science of how our naval forces understand what's happening on the surface of the ocean around them. During the Cold War, the advent of technically advanced systems such as the sexy SPY-1 phased array radar and AEGIS Weapon System was intended to counter the proliferation of advanced airborne threats. That led the most cherished operational specialty on board our ships to be antiair warfare and the datalinks that enable it. Absent a severe threat on the ocean's surface from a major competitor, the U.S. Navy lapsed into a strange apathy over the location, type, and identity of the many vessels plying the water within the range of its many sensors. These could include hostile ships within striking distance of a high-value asset such as the aircraft carrier or even ships smuggling contraband, including, during *Roosevelt*'s upcoming deployment, oil exports from Iraq. The surface picture was pushed into the back room. To care about anything on the surface was a dead end, especially for our highly technical enlisted warriors who wanted to operate complex systems.

This frustrated me years earlier when, as captain of *Enterprise*, I was appointed by our strike group commander, Rear Adm. Harry Ulrich, as the "Force Over-The-Horizon Track Coordinator," otherwise known as "FOTC." I wasn't sure I could spell FOTC, much less know what one did, but I was determined to be the best one I could be. I quickly discovered that Maritime Domain Awareness, or MDA, was on life support. There was an abundance of data available, but it was not being adequately used to generate information or knowledge, mostly due to the obstacles of old technology, a lack of emphasis and creativity, and poor training. While we made some progress on board *Enterprise*, I was determined that if the opportunity ever presented itself, I would try to do more. Now empowerment as an actual strike group commander reignited my determination to fix our surface awareness. I started by obtaining some first-rate outside assistance.

Each carrier strike group is provided a civilian representative from the Center for Naval Analyses (or CNA) during its predeployment training and deployment. This is a rite of passage for a young analyst to gain knowledge of how the Navy really works in order to improve understanding of what problems the Navy needs to solve. Often these promising and ambitious people are left to fend for themselves, trying to find something useful to do. While they were all good, I wanted the best because I knew exactly what I wanted this person to do.

Christine Fox, who I had met at Miramar during my tour at TopGun, was the best CNA rep I'd seen. Fortunately for me, she was now the head of the CNA organization. When she was asked for only her very best analyst, and perhaps delighted that a strike group commander would care enough to call, she responded in kind. When Dr. Susanne Wirwille arrived in the spring of 2005, ready to go to work, I challenged her to help solve the MDA problem.

We immediately set to work raising the profile of what it meant to understand one's surroundings on the surface of the ocean. My surface ship captains may have been annoyed by how I incessantly pestered them to provide better reporting. But that wasn't enough—they needed to be empowered by better technology and procedures.

One glaring deficiency was the almost complete lack of use of an important new asset in the MDA world—namely, the automated identification system, or AIS. This is a transponder that a merchant ship of a certain size is required to carry that automatically transmits its name, location, course, speed, and other important information to anyone within radio range to ingest it. This new signal dramatically enhanced safety at sea by enabling ships to understand their surroundings better and avoid approaching traffic. The airwaves at sea were flooded with this information. It was bad enough that Navy ships didn't have AIS automatically inculcated into their tactical displays. I found that most of our captains weren't even aware of it and certainly didn't have the most basic equipment to use the signal.

We quickly provided our ships with handheld AIS systems, and I demanded that their captains now append information gleaned from AIS onto the information tied to radar contacts automatically reported into a situational awareness system known as the Global Command and Control System, or GCCS. Unfortunately, because this system lives on a classified network, this had to be done manually because there was no way to automatically dump the information from an unclassified AIS receiver on the bridge of a ship into a classified network. The people who would have to do the work would much rather be involved in the more glamorous work of managing the air picture's high technology radars and data links. It required continual reinforcement and a few short and exciting conversations for the Theodore Roosevelt Strike Group to begin reporting what it saw.

Eventually, through some careful maneuvering within the bureaucratic rules governing electronic systems, some (shall we say) "artful acquisition" of key technology, and sheer determination to overcome technical obstacles, Susanne was able to get the AIS data dumped automatically into the GCCS consoles on board *Theodore Roosevelt*. This was first accomplished through what we called the "sneaker net," in which the information from a previous period (fifteen minutes to an hour) would be placed onto an unclassified disk that was then inserted into the classified GCCS system. The disk was then destroyed to avoid reverse flow from a classified network onto an unclassified network. While inefficient, we finally had near-real-time AIS information in GCCS to correlate to radar contacts or other information.

Eventually we appropriated a system known as Radiant Mercury that enabled one-way electronic transmission of unclassified data, which enabled us to "auto-dump" the information into the system. We exported this capability as best we could to all of our ships, which dramatically accelerated our ability to identify what our radars were seeing. And we did it on the cheap—it only cost around $1,200 to obtain the computer required to at least process the tracks and another $800 to buy the AIS receiver. We were even able to put an AIS receiver on board our E-2C aircraft, which had been equipped with a test system to be able to transmit information to the ship via our standard secret Internet protocol network, or SIPRNet. This enabled a huge increase in the area we covered with the system when one of these aircraft was airborne.

The next step was to inculcate into the strike group's operators the restless, perseverant mindset of challenging every piece of information, including radar tracks, AIS tracks, intercepts of other ship's radar signals, visual sightings, and the large database of merchant ships around the world available on the Internet—and to correlate it all into a high-quality surface picture. We then produced a color code for our displays that enabled our operators to discern quickly among friends, neutrals, unknowns, and hostiles. We also painstakingly convinced our embarked aircrews to report what they saw on the surface when not otherwise busy during routine flight operations. To do so, we established an air wing watch officer in our combat direction center we called "REMAX," since this person served as a broker of information coming in from the air wing.

This true revolution in MDA culminated with dramatically improved knowledge, quickly understandable by the consumer, of the many hundreds of tracks in the Arabian Gulf. When it all came together, it was an amazing picture.

All of this eventually corresponded with a visit by Adm. Mike Mullen, then the chief of naval operations, to *Theodore Roosevelt* while we were under way in the Arabian Gulf. Mullen was a familiar face, having worked for my father as his executive assistant when he was the commandant of midshipmen at the U.S. Naval Academy. My dad saw something important in then-lieutenant commander Mullen, who had managed to hit a buoy when in command of a small refueling ship, jeopardizing his career. While far too young as a midshipman at Georgia Tech to have any idea whether this officer had a future, he certainly impressed me then with his work ethic and willingness to think outside the box. We kept in touch over the years.

Admiral Mullen was concerned by the war in Iraq and wanted to see for himself that his Navy was doing everything possible to support our troops ashore. He also wanted to see what we were up to out at sea. He knew that too often the Washington establishment hunkered down in its own problems and overlooked the possibility that people in the fleet were advancing key innovations driven by real-time necessity. I give him immense credit for "getting out there." It is a vital trait for the leader of any large organization.

Mullen arrived after an exhausting couple of days in Iraq, and one of the first things I wanted him to see was our improved surface picture. I was worried when he appeared to be nodding off in the darkness of my command center; it looked as though our window of opportunity for showing the state of the art of MDA was closing fast. But I was relieved a week later to discover that he told his first meeting of senior officers back in Washington that he wanted all U.S. Navy warships to have the same surface picture as *Theodore Roosevelt*. It seemed like a real win for all of our hard work.

But that's when the Navy's technical bureaucracy took over. At first the phenomenon of "the CNO has spoken" took effect, and people wanted to know what we had just done. Unfortunately, it didn't take long for the systems command responsible for this type of system to step in. This vast bureaucracy imposed a long development time, testing requirements, and onerous rules—much of which appeared intended to preserve jobs—that threw sand in the machinery. "Not-invented-here-itis" and risk aversion were on full display. Too bad—but it offered valuable lessons about how organizations resist change, including the inescapable fact that practice often leads theory at the leading edge of innovation.

During my tour as a strike group commander, I was blessed to have the Spanish ship *Alvaro de Bazán* join our group for the last three months of our workup period and the first half of our deployment. The Spanish built a beautiful and capable ship, the first in its class, with the same SPY-1 radar and AEGIS Weapon System carried by our cruisers and guided-missile destroyers. They wanted to know how to operate the ship and deepen the bonds between our two navies.

It was a joy working with the Spanish. I traveled to Spain to meet the chief of their navy, Admiral Zaragosa, and we bonded immediately. Unfortunately, my luggage was lost on the way to Spain, so I called on the admiral in my traveling clothes, which fortunately were somewhat presentable. I reminded him that many words in Spanish sound like and have similar meanings as words in English, but others sound the same and have different meanings. I then joked that I would not tell him I was embarrassed but not *"embarazada"* (which means pregnant in Spanish) about not being appropriately dressed for our meeting.

Zaragosa got the joke, and we became friends. In fact, he flew to the carrier on our way through the Mediterranean, and we sat at my table and worked out the rules of engagement to which the *Alvaro de Bazán* would adhere after joining us on the rest of our deployment. I wasn't entirely sure I was empowered to do that, but didn't want to offer it to the bureaucracy, knowing it would likely take months to get a response.

We had great fun with our Spanish crew, which had pulled Sailors from other ships to adequately man the frigate. They were eager, cooperative, and friendly. When we hosted two different parties for their crew at our home, they cooked paella, a wonderful rice dish with seafood and meat native to Southern Spain. When we said our goodbyes halfway through the deployment, their Sailors gave me a beautiful paella pan, and that dish remains one of my favorite things to cook for family and friends. I learned a great deal about close coalition operations through our time together, which would come in handy later.

My staff and I got to know each other well as we progressed through our workup cycle and started our deployment. And the common theme of benefiting from spectacularly talented enlisted personnel during my command tours repeated itself during this tour. However, one person stands out: then-yeoman senior chief Nancy Hollingsworth. She was a "full-time support" Sailor, or FTS, who is an active-duty person serving in support of the reserve component. I hired her into a non-FTS job as my scheduler and administrative assistant during my previous tour at Fleet Forces Command when my original chief transferred to a more senior position.

Nancy—who overflowed with talent and optimism and also happened to be a gazelle of a runner—wanted a sea tour to round out her career. Even though she was still only a senior chief, I wanted to bring her on board as my staff master chief. But the FTS community assignment officers, or "dctailers," said she had been out of the reserve community too long due to her current job.

However, this occurred when the Navy was trying to get more chief petty officers—particularly women—to volunteer for sea duty. So I played hardball with the head detailer, suggesting that it wouldn't look good for them to turn down a female chief petty officer who was volunteering for sea duty. They immediately relented—another good example of working hard to get the people you want on board. Even though she was not technically assigned as a staff master chief (she filled a different billet instead), my staff and the entire strike group benefited from the positive example she set. She eventually was promoted to master chief and served a successful tour as the command master chief on board a destroyer, again on sea duty away from the FTS community.

When the *Theodore Roosevelt* Strike Group arrived in the Arabian Gulf in the fall of 2005, the second Iraq war was reaching its highest intensity in the wake of the Iraqi constitutional vote and in advance of its first real elections. U.S. and coalition forces were waging counterinsurgency warfare, gradually winning at the tactical and operational level but at high cost in terms of U.S. casualties. We were having a tough time fighting Sunni insurgents while under constant attack from Shia militias. Support from the air was critical, and under the leadership of a succession of Air Force air component commanders, it was a well-run operation. Many outdated procedures for close-air support and forward air control were rapidly jettisoned in favor of fresh ones enabled by new technologies.

I was determined to fly in this environment while serving as a strike group commander for three reasons. First and foremost, I wanted to uncover and rapidly correct any issues frustrating our aircrews that I might be able to help fix. I was not sure these issues would bubble up to my level and wanted to have the credibility of having "been there" when I fought for whatever we needed either from the Navy system or from the air component commander. Second, I wanted to see if we might capitalize on any innovation opportunities. Finally, and without taking excessive flight time from our junior pilots, I wanted to demonstrate to them that admirals can have fun too.

I would be flying the F-14D, which was much more advanced than the older F-14A Tomcats I previously flew. It possessed far more powerful engines, a new radar, and an infrared LANTIRN pod with a laser that gave the aircraft a quantum leap in air-to-ground capability, far more capable than what I pushed for years before in VF-211. Fortunately, I was allowed back into the cockpit, and the fleet replacement squadron and the two air wing Tomcat squadrons with which I flew did a superb job getting me back up to speed. I believe it paid dividends for the strike group and our troopers on the ground.

I began flying over the beach nearly immediately after arriving in the Arabian Gulf. These were tiring missions that involved a long flight from the Arabian Gulf into the heart of Iraq and two periods working with a Joint Tactical Air Controller (or JTAC, which were previously called Forward Air Controllers). In addition, the flight required three trips to an Air Force tanker—one on the way in, one with a tanker orbiting high over the battlefield, and one during the long flight home. These seven-hour-plus flights culminated with a landing back on the ship. I was glad to only fly during the daytime, but I almost always returned at sunset, landing in the surreal haze of the Gulf. I was exhausted after my first flight in-country but quickly grew into a routine of flying over Iraq about twice per week.

The traditional and cumbersome procedures for working with JTACs were completely altered by the battlefield in Iraq. Previously, pilots were given a scripted "nine-line brief" by a controller that included details of the safest run-in to the target, the location of friendly forces, and a description of the actual target itself. It was a difficult way to attack a target that required a lot of practice due to the need to juggle a lot of information while avoiding potential surface-to-air fire around a target area.

With no such threat in Iraq, and the more sustained nature of a counterinsurgency fight, the country was broken into ten-mile square "kill boxes," each with a phone-like "keypad" the JTACs could use to direct pilots to smaller areas. Most of the time we orbited and assisted the JTAC in monitoring activity in his assigned area. But things got exciting when the voice crackled over the radio saying there were "troops in contact" who needed air support.

On my first flight we were asked by our JTAC when we checked in: "Are you Rover equipped?" I had no idea what Rover was, but I quickly learned it was a system that enabled an aircraft to transmit its infrared video picture down to the controller on the ground. It was carried by Air Force F-16s and F-15Es, but not Navy FA-18s or F-14s. It was hugely beneficial in giving ground controllers a bird's eye view of the battlefield wherever they wanted an aircrew to point their sensor. Imagine a controller asking for a weapons delivery in a particular location, then quickly detecting that an aircrew is locked on the wrong target and correcting it on the spot. I'm sure a great deal of collateral damage was prevented simply by using this system.

This was something I probably wouldn't have heard about had I not been in the air with our aircrews over Iraq. They probably would have accepted that they didn't have it, and it would never have filtered to my level. But having personally experienced the limitations of not having this system, I desperately wanted it for my aircrews. We asked about obtaining it and were told it would be too hard to install on short notice in the FA-18 Hornet. This aircraft was reasonably new and had a configuration management system very much tied into the manufacturer, so bureaucratic obstacles similar to those that plagued my MDA effort would come into play. The Hornet would eventually get it, but nowhere near fast enough for our deployment.

However, the Tomcat was on its last deployment and was burdened by no such obstacles. We strongly expressed our need to the Naval Air Systems Command, which responded quickly, put together a solution, and sent a team out to the ship to hard-wire a system into our aircraft that would work. In fact, it worked superbly because the distance between the transmitter and the antenna in their jury-rigged installation was so short that there were few line losses, which extended the range we could communicate with a JTAC. We had Rover working on our first jet in around five weeks. I was elated!

Our jury-rigged Rover caused us to spend more time in what we called "mixed section," in which we would send a Tomcat and a Hornet out together. This was not optimal due to the different fuel consumption characteristics of the two airplanes, but each brought unique advantages to the battlefield. The Hornet carried a wider variety of weapons than the Tomcat as well as night vision goggle capability. The Tomcat now had Rover, carried a lot of weapons, and had a RIO on board to help manage communications.

Meanwhile, I also wanted to fly into Iraq to speak to the people we were actually supporting on the ground to ensure we were leaving no stone unturned on their behalf. I spent a lot of time with then–Air Force colonel Steve Shepro in Baghdad. Steve was a uniquely intelligent officer who spoke six languages and with whom I would work later when he was a two-star general. Shep was the officer in charge of all the JTACs in-country. We bonded immediately, and I found myself one eerie night in an *Apocalypse Now* setting, hitting golf balls off the roof of Saddam Hussein's former concubine's house into a lake, smoking cigars and drinking nonalcoholic beer, with helicopters flying all around.

We ended up with a few useful ideas, including that my aircrews would personally make a phone call to any JTAC we would be supporting on a given day. This would give my crews a much better feel for the type of operation they were supporting, allow us to preestablish ground landmarks with our JTAC, and form a bond with the unit on the ground. By all accounts, the Army units loved it, and I received several messages back from happy generals.

The question of whether we were doing the best we could for our embattled troops—who were contending with improvised explosive devices and ambushes—was constantly on my mind. I was troubled that we were only expected to fly sorties over Iraq five out of seven days—a traditional operational tempo for an aircraft carrier conducting sustained flight operations. I knew from my days on board *Enterprise* that we could do much better and could fly every day in a pinch. And *Roosevelt*'s superb captain and air wing commander, J. R. Haley and Bill Sizemore, respectively, had teams capable of flying this kind of schedule.

Just as I was contemplating how I would propose this tempo to them, they came into my cabin together and proposed the exact same thing. I somehow managed to contain my delight—I wanted this to be their idea. It was exactly the kind of teamwork and forward-thinking I relished. Both Haley and Sizemore leaped up a notch in my view both for what they were proposing and for proposing it together, avoiding the temptation to steal the credit. I asked a few questions but immediately approved their request. Not to my surprise, both officers were later selected for flag rank.

Another potential interruption in our ability to support our troops was the standard port visit an aircraft carrier makes every six weeks or so for both ship and aircraft maintenance and rest for the crew. This type of pause was necessary, but it was troubling to think that our crew would be enjoying beer ashore in Dubai while our troops were struggling so much in Iraq. There had to be a way to achieve continuity, and it occurred to me that, while we pulled *Roosevelt* into port, we could deploy a few Hornets ashore to Al Asad Airbase in Iraq, where the U.S. Marines based a few of their Hornets.

As so often occurs with something new, the obstacles were daunting. I could envision the reaction of our FA-18 maintenance personnel: "He wants to do what?" But because the fundamental idea was sound and important, it was worth the fight. I flew a Tomcat to Al Asad Airbase and conspired with the Marine wing commander ashore, Maj. Gen. Boomer Milstead, with whom I had two things in common. First, I discovered that he was a fellow longboard surfer. Second, he liked to challenge the system. I've always believed the two are related. We got along famously.

On my end, we managed to gather the right kind of equipment to support our aircraft (which differed in subtle ways from the Marine Hornets) away from the ship and provide force protection for the Sailors we would send to Al Asad Airbase to maintain them. We would have to train those Sailors to operate in the hostile operating environment of western Iraq, which included heat and ever-present dust that would impact aircraft maintenance.

On Boomer's end, he had to convince his people to support this idea and find the ramp space at Al Asad to park and maintain our aircraft. And we both had to navigate the land mines of those above us—especially in Washington, where roles and mission battles reign supreme—who might resist the idea.

Indeed, word of the idea filtered out of the theater as the detachment drew closer. Despite a distinguished history of Navy fighters operating ashore at Henderson Field on Guadalcanal during World War II, the antibodies appeared. The Navy folks in Washington, DC, asked what placing a detachment of Navy aircraft on the beach would say about the relevance of aircraft carriers. Their Marine counterparts—with the same programmatic concerns—asked what placing a detachment of Navy airplanes ashore would say about the relevance of Marine Corps aviation. It was amazing, but I was in no mood to be hindered in supporting our fabulous troops on the ground by parochial issues at the Pentagon.

Fortunately, we had built enough momentum that the detachment had to go forward. But Boomer and I were told by our respective chains of command in no uncertain terms to "never do that again." Meanwhile, the detachment was a huge success. Our pilots and maintainers operated safely. Our airplanes destroyed several improvised explosive devices that were threatening our troops, including at least one that was in the process of being emplaced by insurgents. It was a fantastic experience for our people, and we saved American lives. This was real vindication of our idea. Talk about a force multiplier! I came away believing that one squadron on board each deploying aircraft carrier should always be trained and equipped to move ashore, just in case.

As we prepared to leave the theater for our long transit home, we eagerly awaited the arrival of the carrier designated to relieve us: USS *Ronald Reagan*. Under normal rules, we were allowed to have a week or so of "underlap," in which no Navy carrier would be flying in support of operations in Iraq. This would permit our week-long transit (still in the Central Command area of responsibility) via the Red Sea to the Suez Canal, while also keeping carrier presence days among the affected combatant commander theaters balanced according to the global plan I helped develop so many years earlier. The Air Force would pick up the slack during the gap.

However, the commander of U.S. Pacific Command—Bill Fallon, my former boss—wanted to delay the arrival of *Reagan* to conduct an exercise with the Indian Navy that he deemed essential. The commander of U.S. European Command demanded no reduction in his scarce carrier presence. The commander of air forces in Central Command was unwilling to extend the gap in coverage, particularly at such a critical time for our troops on the ground in Iraq. The elephants were in a massive tug-of-war over USS *Theodore Roosevelt*, and we were stuck in the middle.

It would have been easy to duck under this and let the big guys in Washington somehow split the baby. From my experience on the Joint Staff, I knew how this would likely play out, including a potential extension of our deployment. So why not help find a win-win solution?

Of course, we had a simple answer we had already rehearsed: place a detachment of Hornets at Al Asad Airbase! What we were once scolded for now became an elegant idea that would get the elephants off each other's backs. We were ordered to put some of our airplanes in Iraq—this time, we sent six instead of four. Once again, our aircrews and maintainers operated successfully. We transited the Suez Canal on time, and when *Reagan* showed up in the Arabian Gulf, our Hornets flew to the Mediterranean Sea and recovered on board the Big Stick. The elephants went back to contentedly munching their hay.

During his visit to the ship while we were in the Arabian Gulf, I took Admiral Mullen to the open-air space aft of my flag bridge up on *Roosevelt's* island. This was a terrific spot for bonding after a long day. Nearly every night I would invite a group of my staff and other officers from the ship up to enjoy a cigar and relax a bit. It was a great way to pick up on issues I might otherwise not hear or to mull over career advice with my officers.

On this evening, Mullen and I spent the time alone. I was naturally curious where I was headed after the strike group tour but waited for him to raise it first. He said I'd be headed to Joint Forces Command to head up their concept development and experimentation directorate. It was flattering that my instinct for innovation might have been recognized, but because I had never heard of this organization, I didn't know what to think. Even though its name was appealing, I had in mind a more conventional Navy organization and didn't want to submerge out of sight and out of mind in Suffolk, Virginia.

A few months after returning to *Roosevelt's* homeport of Norfolk, I received a phone call from Rear Adm. Denby Starling, a good friend and fellow former *John C. Stennis* executive officer, who was in charge of naval aviation on the East Coast. He asked about an article someone wrote in the summer 2006 edition of naval aviation's *Tailhook* magazine that referred to the fact I flew over Iraq during my deployment. This revelation had apparently upset a senior flag officer in Washington, DC, even though I obtained permission to fly from my in-theater fleet commander—former Blue Angel Vice Adm. Pat Walsh. The article quoted me:

> I usually try to fly once or twice a week, conducting both training missions over the Gulf and patrols over Iraq. Such missions really help me to get a full understanding of what my crews are doing. Having flown these sorties for real, I have more credibility when I talk to my [Air Force] counterparts. Having seen Iraq from a pilot's perspective, I know what I'm talking about when I put forward ideas to the CAOC [Combined Air Operations Center] about things we want to try in order to better protect our troops on the ground. I can also [better] explain to them difficulties we might be having.

The upset senior flag asked what would have happened had I been shot down (by whom, I wondered?). Or if I crashed and was captured by insurgents. I replied that the Army didn't keep its general officers behind the barbed wire (in fact, I had been out and about on the ground a couple of times with several in Baghdad!). Moreover, flying with our air wing gave me valuable insights into how to support our troops better. I never heard another word but halfway suspect that Admiral Mullen, upon hearing of this tempest in a teapot, put an immediate end to it.

My final flight as a Navy fighter pilot occurred in 2006 when I left the strike group for my next job. I once again ensured a low-profile change of command by scheduling it at sea on board *Roosevelt* during a carrier qualification period. This time the system was on my side, as two-star officers (at least in the Navy) are not expected to have ostentatious changes of command. After an informal event in the empty hangar bay, I hopped into a Tomcat, launched off the ship, made two arrested landings, then flew on air wing commander Bill Sizemore's wing to Naval Station Oceana. In keeping with "final flight" traditions, I got out of the jet and was immediately soaked by a fire truck and a bottle of champagne, with my life vest inflated to add to the indignity. I was proud to have my two boys there, along with my mother-in-law, Bonna Werner (Mary was out of town that day). One of my favorite photos of my boys is from that event.

The opportunity to do, for such a long time, something I wanted to do from the day I was a freshman in college—living the ultimate in motor sports—was a pretty good run after all. I was about to begin a different kind of run by reentering the defense bureaucracy at an entirely new level.

TOP USS *Mount Whitney* (LCC 20), flagship of the U.S. Sixth Fleet, home to my Joint Task Force and NATO Response Force certification exercises. *Official U.S. Navy photo by PH2 Sarah Bir*

BOTTOM I toured the Russian cruiser *Moskva* in Lisbon, Portugal. It was later sunk by cruise missiles in the Russia-Ukraine war. *George Chernilevsky photo, public domain*

From the Danger Zone to the Gray Zone

When I walked in the door of the Joint Forces Command (or JFCOM for short) Joint Concept Development and Experimentation organization, otherwise known as the J9, I had no idea what I was getting into. The name was cool and implied I would have the freedom to spawn and nurture new ideas for the Joint force. It appealed to my creative instincts. But it turned out to be an immensely frustrating job, principally because of bureaucratic rivalries among civilian senior executive service leaders both inside and outside the organization.

I was only in the job for a year, but it took nearly that long to first get my arms around where the money was going and figure out whether we were making a difference for the Joint warrior. It seemed as though a substantial portion—although by no means all—of the people in the organization were working on ideas that interested them rather than ideas that would make the force better. And I did not feel we were well-connected to the warriors. Moreover, we were under constant pressure from those in Washington who did not believe in what we were doing—and I confess that sometimes they were right. It was a far cry from the rich problem set and innovative atmosphere we enjoyed on board *Theodore Roosevelt*.

I also had to keep a close eye out for the bureaucracy putting the "money machine" on automatic. For example, when I somewhat randomly asked why my information technology team was replacing hundreds of perfectly good computer monitors, the response was that the servicing distributor said they should be replaced every three years. Of course they said that. I filed this sort of tendency away for future use.

One bright spot for me was developing a solid relationship with retired Army general Gary Luck. Luck had served long and well and was passionate about getting Joint warfighting right. He was deeply involved in JFCOM's training effort, particularly in support of those who would command and control our troops in the middle of the fight in Iraq. I called him "Yoda," as he was not only full of sage advice, but he looked the part. I would often wander over to his office for coffee to test an idea on him or, more likely, to absorb any bits of wisdom I could.

The only thing the job really ended up doing was checking the block for holding a Joint flag officer billet, which was apparently a prerequisite to moving on to more senior jobs. Sure enough, within a year, I was nominated for my third star as the U.S. Sixth Fleet commander, based in Naples.

I quickly learned this job involved several other "hats" as well, including Commander, Striking and Support Forces NATO, also based in Naples, and Commander, Joint Command Lisbon, in Portugal. I was excited about the opportunity to rediscover the Italian language and culture I experienced as a young child in Naples many decades earlier. But I soon was informed that the nature of the Lisbon billet required me—and thus my family—to live in Portugal in the beautiful little tourist-and-fishing village of Cascais, on the coast just west of Lisbon. No problem! But I gave up on relearning Italian.

But before we could head overseas, I was once again called upon by Fox Fallon, who was now in charge of U.S. Central Command. This time he wanted me to come to Tampa to help him assess the situation in Iraq. It was the summer of 2007. Under the leadership of Gen. David Petraeus and Gen. Ray Odierno, U.S. troops were making progress in counterinsurgency operations and taking plenty of losses to improvised explosive devices, rockets, ambushes, and other attacks from both Sunni insurgents and Shia militiamen. Fallon was not sure whether the steep cost justified the slow progress toward a democratic and stable Iraq in blood and treasure. Fallon assigned me to work with a seasoned CNA analyst named Don Bowditch to dissect the issue.

I mainly worked from Tampa but also traveled extensively in Iraq. From the oil terminals in the Arabian Gulf and the port of Umm Qasr in the south to Baghdad in the center to Al Anbar Province in the west to Camp Speicher a bit further north, I was offered the opportunity to see firsthand how hard and smart our troopers were working. Our conventional forces were busy executing the now-classic "clear, hold, and build" operations introduced by Petraeus. Led by then-lieutenant general Stanley McChrystal, our special operations forces were slowly unraveling the insurgents' leadership network.

The latter was particularly eye-opening for me. I visited Stan at his head-quarters, spending an entire night with him as he patiently explained how his forces extensively linked intelligence and operations to create a cycle with which the enemy was having a hard time coping. They would run a series of special forces raids one night and bring any detainees and information from the site back to the headquarters. The next day was spent next day gaining information from those sources, melding it with all other available sources of intelligence, and then spinning it right back into the next night's raids. The enemy could not keep up with it, but it was exhausting for our people. I took the vital lesson of taking intelligence-operations cooperation to a new level for my future jobs. Stan deserves a lot of credit for both his inspiration and his perspiration—he was essentially continuously in theater for several years, personally executing his vision.

As the project wound down, I posed three important questions we should always ask when using force or, for that matter, any element of national power. First, what were the U.S. interests at stake that caused us to feel we needed to transform Iraq? It seemed as though the answer was that we had broken the country and that, in repairing it according to our vision, we might prevent Iran from exerting unwelcome influence. But I could not find the true abstract and enduring interests that were at stake—it felt like we were making it up as we went along.

The second question was whether the project was actually feasible. The institutional hubris of believing we could transform an utterly foreign culture with a thousand-year history into a fully functioning, enduring democracy seemed to be optimistic. There was no question whether our ground forces had mastered the art and science of counterinsurgency operations, so-called COIN. The skill and bravery of our troops was amazing from top to bottom. I admired our ability to adapt to a completely different type of warfare. I was even surprised by the Army's ability to bring battalions from separate brigades together on the ground into ad hoc brigades—I would never have guessed that Army culture could have handled this, but they did it magnificently.

I also admired our senior commanders on the ground, who were heavily invested in the mission—as one would expect—and who were determined not to leave before the job was done. However, it did not seem obvious that Iraq would remain stable, that Iraqi culture could handle the sudden imposition of a democratic system rather than being governed by a strong man, that they would accept the loss of their sovereignty long enough to make it work, or that Iran would ever accept this type of nation as a neighbor. It would take a herculean effort.

This led to the third question: was the price we were paying commensurate with the interest and feasibility of the project? We were losing a lot of people. I hated seeing our troops killed or grievously wounded when I wasn't sure their mission would ever be accomplished. Moreover, the American people were understandably not invested in this war enough to commit the resources required to make it happen. A small slice of the American people was fighting and sacrificing in a long war that had taken on a life of its own but was disconnected from the rest of our population. It seemed like the triumph of counterinsurgency tactics over strategy, and the ends, ways, and means did not seem to be in balance.

I found myself deeply sympathetic to both sides of this issue, perhaps a quality I gained from my uncle, Carl Builder. I agreed that leaving a destabilized Iraq lying at the heart of the Middle East was a recipe for instability. But I reflected on the daily toll in the grinding struggle for stability that had little chance for success absent total commitment to this war. I was constantly reminded of a saying attributed to Sun Tzu: "When the army engages in protracted campaigns, the resources of the state will fall short; we have not yet seen a clever operation that was prolonged."

In the end, my little team and I presented a plan that would allow us to gradually scale down our presence if—and only if—senior leadership were to determine that a balancing of interests and costs meant leading the effort in a different direction. It was not an entirely popular outcome, particularly with senior officers who were personally invested in the fight. Who could blame them?

The whole situation began to crystallize in my mind a concept I would later use that would balance clearly defined national security interests against risk and cost when using force. But that is for another chapter.

It was during this time that I met Lt. Gen. Marty Dempsey, who was the deputy commander of Central Command. As the deputy, he was given the task of making sure the command ran smoothly. I found in Marty a thoughtful, firm, thoroughgoing, and patient leader. Little did I know I would one day work closely with him when he served as chairman of the Joint Chiefs of Staff. Later in his tour, he served as acting Central Command commander, which I believe gave him important experience that few chairmen (most of whom are ex–service chiefs) have ever had.

After my thankfully brief stint in the summer heat of Iraq and Tampa, Florida, I was grateful to move on to Europe, where my attention shifted from active, hot conflicts in the Middle East to an entirely different form of competition and coordination. It was more akin to the so-called gray zone of warfare than the hot fights ongoing in Iraq and Afghanistan. Here I faced several new leadership challenges, including operating within the complex organism that is the North Atlantic Treaty Organization, and running three commands located in cities at opposite ends of the western half of the Mediterranean.

In those days, Sixth Fleet was the backwater of the Navy, principally because so many forces merely passed through the Mediterranean Sea on their way to the Suez Canal and Central Command. On the U.S. side, I was subordinate to a four-star U.S. Navy officer who was subordinate to the commander of European Command (EUCOM). Both of us commanded an operational NATO headquarters subordinate to the Supreme Allied

Commander, Europe, otherwise known as SACEUR, who was also the EUCOM commander. Yes, there are plenty of "dual hat" jobs in Europe, but somehow we kept it all straight.

The only Navy vessel permanently assigned to the Sixth Fleet was USS *Mount Whitney*, an old command ship based in Gaeta, Italy. There were ostensibly three reasons this ship still even existed. First, NATO felt it needed a command ship in case of a crisis (although it was fair to ask whether the need existed simply because the ship existed). Second, ripping the ship out of Gaeta on the heels of already having removed a submarine tender from a different Italian port would have been costly politically. And finally, having a command ship meant that if Naples-based Sixth Fleet needed to run an operation with which the Italian government disagreed, we could always get under way on board *Mount Whitney* and run it from there.

EUCOM maintained a joint task force that could be quickly assembled to conduct joint operations in the theater or elsewhere if necessary. Given the low frequency of crises in Europe, it was impractical to maintain a separate headquarters for this force. So command rotated among the Navy, Army, and Air Force component commands in Europe. As luck would have it, my year in Europe was the Navy component command's turn, and navigating through the qualification process required conducting a major exercise. This was an exciting opportunity to employ my ideas on joint command and control as well as what I learned from "Yoda" back at Joint Forces Command in Norfolk. It was also an opportunity to bring to bear what I learned from Stan McChrystal about the integration of intelligence and operations, which is something that at the time did not come naturally to Navy people. I literally had to pry intelligence officers out from behind the "green door" in my Sixth Fleet command center to sit alongside those monitoring and controlling operations. Once they were together, though, the whole enterprise became more effective.

At the other end of the Mediterranean, I was still in charge of Joint Command Lisbon. At the time, NATO maintained three active, full-time operational command headquarters, including one each in Naples, Italy; Brunssum, Germany; and Lisbon, Portugal. Two of these headquarters were run by four-star officers and were groomed to lead major operations.

In fact, the Brunssum headquarters was technically in charge of the NATO operation in Afghanistan. My three-star headquarters was a nod to Portugal and provided a third, full-time, rapidly deployable leadership team that could focus on smaller operations.

Meanwhile, NATO maintained a small coalition force in readiness centered on a brigade-sized unit and all the joint capability that needed to support it. This was known as the NATO Response Force, or NRF, and, like the EUCOM joint task force, it rotated among the three commands. Once again, as luck would have it, it was our turn in Lisbon to take over the rotation and become NRF qualified, in much the same way my joint task force was tested on the U.S. side. Both qualification periods occurred sequentially and successfully on board *Mount Whitney*, with the EUCOM Austere Challenge exercise held at sea and the NATO Steadfast Juncture exercise held at the pier in Stavanger, Norway.

These events were wonderful opportunities for the teams to learn from each other and for experimentation on the margins, with techniques intended to raise the bar on how staffs operate and inculcate them into an organization's fabric of process.

The first experiment involved creating a matrix organization that would better use my limited staff in Naples at Sixth Fleet. One dimension of the matrix focused on the softer skills of building expertise and partner engagement with the regions of Europe and Africa. The other focused on the standard functional areas into which operational military staffs are normally arranged, including planning, operations, communications, intelligence, and logistics. The intent was for the former dimension to dominate during day-to-day operations and the latter to dominate during a crisis.

Matrix organizations are challenging to operate. But I did not want to focus on the day-to-day at the expense of being able to handle a crisis, which I would later directly observe occur at U.S. Southern Command Headquarters during the aftermath of the Haiti earthquake in 2010. A matrix seemed the only way to get all the daily work done across our two primary areas of responsibility—Europe and Africa—yet still be able to focus the entire staff on a crisis, should one emerge. We experimented with this during our joint task force qualification exercise, and after a few hiccups it seemed to work quite well.

I also experimented with a different matrix during both the NATO and U.S. qualification periods. It is instinctive for a military staff to organize its information flow and efforts around the dominant dimension of how it is organized (e.g., its staff structure) rather than what it is trying to accomplish. This normally comes to light in a morning brief organized around the staff functions. The intelligence function speaks first to provide a situation update; then the operations function describes what has been done over the last period and what is happening now. The strategic planning function explains what is coming in the next phase, followed by the logistics, communications, and other functions. It's natural to do this, but these subordinate organizations generally speak out of their own "stovepipes," and the leader at the end of the table is left to make sense of the whole picture, not knowing how well the staff functions are coordinating their efforts.

We turned this on its head during both of our qualification exercises. Once we identified the four or five overall objectives for the operation we were conducting, we would organize our briefings around those objectives rather than around the staff organization. Thus, all the functions I listed earlier had to collaborate to assess progress and prospects for accomplishing the first objective, then the second, and so on.

This required an information integrator, so I pulled the smartest person on my staff aside to make that happen. Although the organization resisted at first, after only a few days it became the routine. Now each function had a better feel for working together to accomplish common objectives, and we were much more aware of what the others were doing. I used the technique to even greater effect during a subsequent tour.

With my NATO command, we also accelerated the use of secure chat rooms, which the United States had been using for years. NATO was on the cusp of bringing this technology forward, and I demanded that we be allowed to use it sooner than planned, arguing that we should be considered part of the test. So we introduced it on the eve of our NRF qualification exercise, which made my highly conservative, risk-averse, and suspicious European team members nervous. I had to reassure them this was easier than they might think and that they could rapidly adapt to the technology. I even went so far as to suggest that the "cool guys" were using chat rooms, so we should as well. I gave the team credit for taking the leap of faith from a crazy American and buying in.

These ideas are representative of only a few of the changes we brought to bear within the two commands, and they reinforced in my mind a framework I was nurturing in my head called "concentric circles of change." It refers to the stages of acceptance members an organization go through whenever a change agent is at work. My NATO command's initial resistance to using the chat room began with the circle I called "denial," progressed through "vicious compliance" and "well-intended misapplication," and ended up in our body of practice. Also, in seeking ways to measure the performance of my NATO and Sixth Fleet teams, I began to refine my thoughts about metrics because measuring the wrong thing in the wrong way can lead to undesirable results.

Leading a disparate NATO coalition toward common objectives constituted another set of valuable leadership lessons from my tour in Europe. Language and cultural differences, different rules of engagement mandated by different countries, differing proficiency levels, and even mistrust of the United States' motives were all potentially significant barriers to working together effectively. I had received a preview of this while hosting the Spanish ship *Alvaro de Bazán* in the Roosevelt Strike Group. Still, the JFC Lisbon tour treated me to a full dose of the challenges associated with working with a host of member states.

First, while representatives from these nations were sometimes resentful of the leadership role the United States played, they were even more distrustful of each other. Divides between northern and southern countries and between rivals like Greece and Turkey were only two of the gradients of which I needed to be aware.

Second, as much as our NATO allies admired the U.S. military's considerable capability and proficiency, I had to be particularly sensitive to their concerns about American expressions of superiority and that we would impose our procedures on them. At least once, I made it a point to deviate from U.S. joint command and control doctrine intentionally—and made sure they knew about it—to reassure them I was a committed "every nation is equal" player.

Third, even though most NATO operations are conducted in English (although, per NATO agreement, the French insist on using their language as well), and even though member nations' personnel serving on NATO staffs are expected to be proficient in English, I had to constantly be conscious of the potential for misunderstanding. Napoleon once said, "An order that can be misunderstood will be misunderstood," but he never managed a twenty-eight member-plus coalition! When making an important point, I would express it two different ways and then listen carefully for the echoes to ensure it was heard correctly. This is valuable advice even for those working in a common language.

Language differences also came into play when I was invited to give a speech at a festival in the beautiful town of Grasse celebrating the French admiral François Joseph Paul de Grasse, otherwise known as the Compte de Grasse, who blockaded the British army at Yorktown, Virginia. Although I took four years of French in high school, I was nowhere near proficient in the language. But I knew I could pronounce it acceptably well, especially with a bit of practice.

So I wrote the speech in English, had it translated by two different French speakers to be on the safe side, and then delivered it in pretty decent French. I ended up the darling of the elderly ladies in the audience, even though I had a hard time conversing with them when the speech was over. It was further affirmation of my belief in the importance of Americans at least trying to communicate in a host nation's language. As an aside, there has almost always been a warship named the Compte de Grasse in the U.S. Navy fleet. Given our periodic political challenges with that nation, it wouldn't be a bad idea to resume the tradition.

Toward the end of my experience in Lisbon, I observed the flagship of the Russian Black Sea Fleet, the Russian Federation ship *Moskva*, sailing up the Tagus River to make a port call in Lisbon. I was eager to ensure the Russians were aware of NATO's presence in Portugal and intent on satisfying my curiosity, as I had never been on board a Russian ship, much less met a Russian fleet commander. So, in a bit of chutzpah, I sent word to the ship that I was coming for lunch. To my delight and surprise, the Russian admiral accepted my "self-invite."

I expected a nice sit-down lunch in the admiral's cabin, which is what I would have hosted. Instead, after arriving aboard, I was ushered into a small conference room with a table in the middle loaded with finger food and glass decanters of vodka. Clearly, this was intended to be a drinking session intended to loosen me up. I declared immediately that, out of respect, I would share one glass of vodka with the ten or so Russian officers who were present in their yellow uniforms. The officers shrugged, poured a round, and then proceeded to drink all the vodka themselves.

Halfway through this session, a few members of the singing troop who were accompanying the *Moskva* around the Mediterranean entered the room. The group included a tall, attractive blonde, who was positioned immediately at my side. I thought, "Really?" After the drinking session, the Russian admiral gave me a short tour of the ship. Even though Dmitry Medvedev was serving his tour as the president of the Russian Federation, it was clear from the various posters around the ship who was in charge: Vladimir Putin. I also noticed that none of the offices I looked into had a computer on the desk. But the fleet commander was proud of the video teleconference capability in his cabin.

When the tour arrived on the bridge, I was urged to look through a pair of binoculars that looked like a set found on any U.S. ship from World War II. But it was clear the Russians were proud of them and wanted me to handle them. I was a little concerned that I might be a victim of the old "shoe polish on the binoculars" trick. But it was not the case. I was tempted when I departed to send a pair of modern, stabilized binoculars to my Russian counterpart.

I was fairly unimpressed by the Russian ship, which wound up being struck by antiship cruise missiles and subsequently burned and sank during the Russia–Ukraine war. But that didn't mean the Russians weren't skilled information warriors. While I was assigned to Sixth Fleet, they deployed their lone aircraft carrier, the *Kuznetsov*, to the Mediterranean to disproportionate effect. This ship was an old, rusty, unreliable hulk and could only carry a few tactical aircraft and helicopters. The ship only flew a couple of sorties at a time and only during the daytime, in contrast to the high tempo operations conducted by one of our aircraft carriers. Sometimes it couldn't even get under way, and we even once helped them once clear a range for a firing exercise. But this didn't matter to the European news media, who fell for the whole thing and highlighted the presence of a Russian carrier against the absence of an American carrier.

I began hearing rumors almost as soon as I arrived in Europe that Admiral Mullen was bringing me back to Washington to serve his director for strategic plans and policy, otherwise known as the J5. The first round of rumors suggested I would leave the Mediterranean six months after I arrived. That date passed, and I breathed a sigh of relief. But it was not long before the unavoidable call came: only a year after arriving in Portugal, we would be moving back to Washington, DC. Always wanting to show my appreciation for a host nation by attempting to speak in the local language, the last words in my change of command speech in Lisbon were "Ja tenu saudad de Portugal," which roughly translates as "I already hold longing in my heart for Portugal."

Because the U.S. Senate was unable to get my confirmation vote done until the last minute before their August recess, we made a hasty trip back to find a place to live (and, fortunately for us, were able to find one that was vacant), and we scrambled to get our kids into school. Before I knew it, I was back in the Pentagon.

TOP Adm. Mike Mullen (*left*) and Gen. Sergei Makarov (*right*) forged a relationship that enabled final agreement on the New START Treaty. *Office of the Chairman of the Joint Chiefs of Staff, photo by MC1 Chad J. McNeeley*

BOTTOM The entire New START team huddling in the Russian Ministry of Defense building during the end game of the negotiations. Lead negotiator Rose Gottemoeller is seated third from the right. Mike Elliot is standing to my right. *Amb. John Beyrle personal photo collection*

At the Center

fter my all-too-brief tour in Europe, I reported to the Joint Staff late in August 2008 as the director of strategic plans and policy on the Joint Staff, working for chairman Adm. Mike Mullen and all the other chiefs. It was a big step to plunge back into the Washington, DC, arena during an agitated period of Middle East conflict and tensions with Russia—and to do so for the first time at a high level.

Serving as the J5 meant spending more time briefing the Joint Chiefs of Staff and the combatant commanders, each with cross-cutting interests and strongly held views. Moreover, I would be entering a new forum: representing the military in the interagency decision-making process in the White House. Finally, my first six months on the job would coincide with a presidential election season and the transition between two administrations. It promised to be interesting, and it was.

Although I had increasingly become interested in strategy over the course of my career, I always viewed myself as an operator. In my earlier days as an action officer in the J3 Operations Directorate, I drew satisfaction from being as close to the operational world as one could be inside the Beltway. Back then, as a young lieutenant commander, I looked down my nose a bit at strategists as people who never really made a difference. I would soon learn how wrong I was.

In one of my first days on the job, Admiral Mullen was called to testify with Secretary of Defense Bob Gates on some long-forgotten issue in front of the House Armed Services Committee. I had previously supported testimony from other officers during General Powell's confirmation hearing and when Adm. Fox Fallon testified on military readiness. But this time I was seated behind Mullen as his direct backup.

When Gates had to leave halfway through the hearing, Mullen left as well since the two maintained a policy that they would always testify together so the members could not "divide and conquer." This meant that Gates' undersecretary for policy, Eric Edelman, and I would have to shift forward and assume their seats at the table and continue the testimony. Sensing my discomfort from being only a couple of days into the job, Edelman whispered as we slid forward, "Don't worry, you'll do fine."

Edelman was a smart, calm, and experienced hand in the policy business. He did not strike me as a being on the neoconservative end of the Republican Party, and we got along well. We finished the testimony with no apparent stumbles that day, which probably had something to do with the tendency for questions in the second half of a hearing, from the less-experienced junior members of the House committee, to be facile. Indeed, I quickly discovered the members were less interested in the answers than they were in making a statement for the cameras. Nonetheless, because it was the height of a presidential campaign season, many questions were laced with political angles. On one of my first days in the job, it was amusing to be accused of being responsible for President Bush's policy decisions. I deferred the political questions to Edelman, which he handled deftly.

The next pressing challenge was to support Mullen in two interactions with the chief of the Russian General Staff, Nikolai Makarov. After all the attention focused on the Middle East, the world was still adjusting to the reality of Russia having invaded the Georgian enclaves of South Ossetia and Abkhazia in August 2008. After a long-simmering conflict with Georgia, Russia used the pretext of a forceful Georgian response to separatists who had shelled Georgian villages to execute a long-planned invasion. They employed ground, naval, and air forces, information warfare, and cyberattacks to quickly, although clumsily, gain the advantage over Georgian forces.

Despite almost universal condemnation from the rest of the world, Russian forces only left Georgian territory in early October. And in a sideswipe at Western recognition of the independence of Kosovo years earlier and more recent signals about bringing Georgia into the NATO alliance, Russia quickly recognized the independence of the two breakaway republics. The crisis provided a clear glimpse of the changing face of warfare in the twentieth century, sometimes called "hybrid warfare" or "gray zone warfare" that would repeat itself in Crimea and the Donbas in Ukraine years later, eventually leading to naked Russian aggression in Ukraine.

In the aftermath of the Russian invasion of Georgia, Mullen and Makarov maintained the only open line of communication between Washington, DC, and Moscow. All other contact between the U.S. and Russian governments was broken off. The two made several phone calls, all of which were extremely tense. The Russian general expressed a host of grievances, which Mullen patiently countered, urging him to find a way to end the conflict and restore stability. The two men finally agreed that a meeting between the two would be helpful. After obtaining interagency approval, Mullen and a small group of staff, including me, traveled to Helsinki to sit down with the Russians.

The meeting occurred in an elegant private home on the city's outskirts, which the Finns used to host such meetings. I found Makarov to be a short, bright, and passionate man. Although I didn't agree with his longwinded categorization of grievances, it was possible to understand some aspects of his position. Mullen, ever the diplomat, listened closely and countered with his own points. Maintaining the high ground of the need not to allow this conflict to escalate, Mullen opened the door for building a genuine friendship that might lead to productive interaction in the future. Makarov seemed genuinely relieved that the discussion had not descended into chaos and conflict. It ended with slightly warmer handshakes than it started, and we parted company. I watched Mullen grow from being a young lieutenant commander working for my father into being a poised and well-respected leader, and this was one of his finer moments.

As the Bush administration entered its last six months in office, the issue of piracy off the coast of Somalia became a persistent irritant, gaining significant media attention. Somali fishermen, impoverished by over-fishing of their coastal waters (mostly by Chinese fishermen) and the waste dumped by passing ships, discovered that the conga line of merchant ships sailing close offshore between the Red Sea and the Arabian Gulf were sitting ducks. All they needed to do was wait at sea for a victim to pass by, pull alongside, threaten to fire their weapons at the ship, and then board the compliant vessel. The merchants couldn't steam fast enough to escape the little high-speed boats used by the pirates. It didn't take long for a host of ships to end up at anchor off the Somali coast while their companies negotiated for their release. It was a lucrative business for the pirates, and the State Department didn't like it one bit.

The interagency turned to the Pentagon to solve the problem. They made the case that we possessed the strongest Navy in the world, that free commerce on the high seas was a vital interest of the United States, and that piracy off Somalia was an embarrassment. Wasn't there anything we could do to make this problem go away? Was the U.S. Navy going to admit defeat to a bunch of ragtag pirates in little skiffs?

The Navy was instructed to divert a few ships from operations in the Arabian Gulf to the Horn of Africa to join an international coalition attempting to address the problem. However, the sheer size of the ocean areas involved—which only grew when the merchant community moved its ships further offshore, which was in turn countered by the pirates moving further offshore using "mother ships"—defied our ability to patrol it. We could steam rapidly to the scene of a captured ship, but once the ship was in the hands of the pirates, there was little we could do without endangering the crew.

The State Department then demanded that we provide security forces on board merchant ships. There was varying support from the merchant community for this approach. The U.S. forces required to accomplish this would have to be drawn from our already-stretched forces conducting operations elsewhere in the region. Moving them on and off the many ships transiting the area would be an enormous headache.

It was uncomfortable for me, the warrior, to tell civilians in the White House Situation Room that this was not a mission for the military. It was telling that few of the ships were U.S.–owned or flagged, crewed by American merchant mariners, or even carried U.S. cargo. We made the case in the interagency that the military isn't a police force and "we don't guard banks or shopping malls." We would respond to ships in distress—like police forces responding to bank robberies—but wouldn't take on the task of guarding all of them.

Instead we encouraged the merchant fleet to provide their own security guards. The only obstacles were the money required to do it, worried insurance companies, and reluctance by the various ports of call used by these ships to allow heavily armed security teams to embark and disembark transiting ships. Eventually, a combination of the Puntland authorities taking greater action ashore, the continued presence of coalition ships, and the merchant fleet adopting their own security measures rapidly attenuated the piracy problem.

It was during this period the opportunity arose to help a promising officer and myself at the same time. Word came down to all the senior officers on the Joint Staff that the chairman was looking for a new executive assistant and to "send over your best names." Typical practice is for a three-star general or admiral reluctant to part with their own hand-selected top performing officer to send their second- or third-best names. Instead, I sent my best officer, Capt. Michael Gilday, who was working directly as my executive assistant, down for an interview. Why not help this excellent captain learn at an even higher level? And why not have a silent advocate down in the front office? As of this writing, Gilday is now chief of Naval Operations.

Based on my interactive role with the White House, I ended up in the same room as President Bush several times. This usually occurred in support of Mullen during a National Security Council meeting. But it once happened during a meeting with some foreign official in National Security Advisor Steve Hadley's office when the president dropped by unannounced. I was on the outs for a while when Mullen found out about the latter—he was understandably not wild about one of his three stars suddenly being in a meeting with the president without him present. But there was nothing I could do about it since the drop-in was not previously announced. Bush just showed up, as presidents often do in a "scripted-but-unscripted" way to make a point with a White House guest.

Over the course of the autumn of 2008, the presidential contest between senators Barack Obama and John McCain drew to a close, with the former winning the electoral vote. Admiral Mullen's challenge was to ensure the military supported the transition between administrations from a politically neutral standpoint without irritating the outgoing or incoming administrations.

The transition was handled well by both parties. Perhaps it was easier for the Bush team because they were at the end of a second term and weren't the team that lost the election. But I also give them credit for taking the principled view that the election was over, and their job was to set the next team up for success, even if they were from the opposing party. I personally witnessed one instance in which Bush shut down a high-ranking cabinet member who voiced that this was the perfect time to make life difficult for the incoming team. Bush would have none of it. How we wish this behavior were still customary today!

Shortly after the inauguration I was introduced to Michèle Flournoy, who was nominated by Obama to be Eric Edelman's replacement and was hunkered down in a Pentagon office awaiting Senate confirmation. Eric told me, "You'll get along with these guys for a couple of weeks, and then you'll be at each other's throats." It was one of the few predictions he made that didn't come true, as I found Flournoy to be an experienced, intelligent, and gracious interlocutor. We would spend a great deal of time together in the White House Situation Room, and we remain good friends.

Meanwhile, the wars in Iraq and Afghanistan raged on. I continued to hold the same beliefs I developed during the window in which I supported Admiral Fallon's critical look at our involvement in Iraq. I was asked by Mullen to conduct a study on Afghanistan, which was shortly followed by direction from the White House for an interagency team to do the same. The latter study was led by Bruce Riedel, a former CIA analyst and counterterrorism expert serving on the National Security Council staff.

This study involved several visits per week to the elegant Eisenhower Executive Office Building for long meetings that attempted to unpack the challenges in Afghanistan and explore ways to turn the tide in our favor. I quickly grasped the divergence of views in the interagency, which would be repeated in the early months of the Obama administration, which directed yet another study. This effort was led by Lt. Gen. Doug Lute, who was detailed to the White House (and eventually became U.S. ambassador to NATO).

After seven years of war, five of which included deep ground forces' involvement in two nations, our Army and Marine Corps ground troops were exhausted. At one point Secretary Gates reluctantly approved fifteen-month long tours for Army troops—a hellishly long time to be in the type of nonstop combat they were experiencing. There was immense discomfort in both administrations that we might be pouring good money—and people—into an insolvable problem. But we in the military kept asking for more: more time, more money, and more troops.

The sense among the Joint Chiefs at the turn of the year was that we should begin shifting the weight of our effort from Iraq to Afghanistan. The former seemed to be calming a bit based on the good work our troops were doing, including the "Anbar Awakening" that began in late 2006 and reduced violence somewhat in the Sunni areas of Iraq. Meanwhile, Afghanistan—which theoretically contained a more immediate threat to the United States in the form of al-Qaeda—seemed to be deteriorating. This shift was bitterly resisted initially by Gen. David Petraeus, who had invested a great deal of personal effort in successfully advancing the counterinsurgency battle in Iraq and assumed command of Central Command from Admiral Fallon. Nonetheless, after a host of briefs in "The Tank," the group eventually agreed to begin advocating an eastward shift in our counterterrorism effort.

An important side issue during my tenure as the J5 involved pushing the department's acquisition system to get more Mine-Resistant Ambush Protected vehicles (or MRAPs) to our coalition partners. It was well known that the principal threat to our troops in both Iraq and Afghanistan was improvised explosive devices. Particularly lethal were those with explosively formed penetrators, primarily supplied by Iran.

Realizing we were losing far too many people and that the acquisition system was producing these vehicles too slowly, Secretary of Defense Robert Gates overturned the bureaucracy and dramatically accelerated MRAP production and deployment. Unfortunately, the derivative problem was that we were getting them to our people at the expense of our coalition partners. This led to a quandary: we had a natural inclination to take care of our people first, but we also genuinely felt for our partners and needed to keep them in the game.

The only way to resolve this problem was to urge even faster production and to assign a certain number to our partners. This was not an easy, snap-your-fingers solution. It required a host of video teleconferences that relentlessly pushed the system to do the right thing. I was privately satisfied when Ash Carter, then the undersecretary of defense for acquisition technology, and logistics, gave me a model MRAP in recognition of this effort, which I keep to this day.

A major portion of my time during the latter half of my tour as the J5 was spent supporting the Strategic Arms Reduction Treaty negotiations with Russia, known as New START. The existing treaty was soon to expire, along with all its important verification mechanisms. The Obama administration was anxious to improve the country's relationship with Russia, which was badly damaged by their invasion of Georgia. The Russians, anxious to get off the hook from their pariah status, seemed willing to negotiate. Finally—and a driving factor throughout the process—the administration bore an earnest desire to reduce the world's dependence on nuclear weapons, with the stretch goal of eliminating them entirely. All this added up to the fact that considerable energy would be put into the negotiations.

The U.S. negotiating team was led by Rose Gottemoeller, who previously worked with my father at the RAND Corporation after he had retired from the Navy. Fluent in Russian and an experienced hand at arms control, Rose was an inspired choice for what would be, not unexpectedly, a long and arduous effort. Her Russian counterpart was an equally experienced pragmatist named Anatoly Antonov (a career diplomat who, as of this writing, is the Russian Federation's ambassador to the United States).

Among the people supporting Rose was senior civilian Mike Elliot from my staff. My predecessor, Gen. James "Hoss" Cartwright, wisely hired Mike away from U.S. Strategic Command to provide much-needed nuclear expertise to the Joint Staff. Although civilian experts on nuclear matters were plentiful, Mike was a former Air Force officer who knew more about the history and employment of nuclear weapons and the associated policies than anyone else associated with the military. He sacrificed greatly by serving in this billet as a geographical bachelor. Mike was indispensable to the negotiations, and I learned an immense amount about the subject from him.

The plan was for Rose's team to operate forward from Geneva, with a group of senior officials—including me—back in Washington as the reach-back team. The negotiations were unbelievably complex, encompassing three different types of delivery vehicles (intercontinental ballistic missiles, submarine-launched ballistic missiles, and bombers), the number of warheads each side would be able to deploy or hold in a reserve stockpile, verification measures, and other touchy subjects.

The negotiations began in April 2009 and ran through eight rounds of intense discussions. I quickly learned we were better organized than our counterparts and had a much faster turnaround cycle for consultations between our forward and reach-back teams than the Russian side. However, this had the potential to lead to the phenomenon of "negotiating with ourselves," in which one side makes a proposal, and when a reply doesn't appear relatively quickly, the temptation exists to offer a fresh, more conciliatory proposal. In our case, the delay on the Russian side was due to their slower bureaucratic pace more than to a savvy negotiating style, but we had to be careful that the eager beavers on our side didn't get too far in front of our team in Geneva.

As we formulated our positions regarding how low we could go, we had our own set of internal struggles. A number of forward-leaning people in the administration wanted to be bold in proposing cuts. From the Pentagon, we pushed the limits down as hard as possible but insisted that we maintain both geopolitical and technical "hedges." We also wanted to balance the reductions to maintain leverage with the Russians in future negotiations. This was not always a popular position with State Department or National Security Council staffers. Still, I give President Obama and his team considerable credit for listening and, over time, agreeing with most of our positions. I believe their support was fortified by the strong sense that we made the best possible effort to get the numbers as low as possible while still maintaining a safe, reliable, and credible deterrent.

As the negotiations headed toward their climax, it became apparent that the Russians were undergoing their own internal struggles. As a result, we needed one last push to get the Russian military over the top, and only one person could deliver: Admiral Mullen. His previous establishment of a trusted relationship with his counterpart, General Makarov, set the foundation for an intense trip to Moscow in early 2010.

We spent several days in the ornate Russian military headquarters agreeing to the final numbers, surrounded by old paintings and tapestries from Russian history and memorabilia from more recent Soviet times. It would not have been possible to conclude the agreement with the highly suspicious and paranoid Russian military culture had Mullen not built the rapport with Makarov a couple of years earlier. The New START Treaty was finally signed by the two presidents on April 8, 2010, in Prague. If I remember correctly, in a classic example of signaling, the Russians flew a couple of Bear bombers near our coast the same day the treaty was signed.

Little did I know that this type of event would matter to me even more in the near future. That August Admiral Mullen summoned me to his office to say I'd be nominated to serve as the fourth commander of U.S. Northern Command—otherwise known as NORTHCOM—and simultaneously the twenty-first commander of the North American Aerospace Defense Command—otherwise known as NORAD. It would take nine months in sclerotic Washington, DC, for the nomination and confirmation process to run its course.

Toward the end of my time as the J5, I had my own experience with Russian military leaders while holding Joint Staff talks with members of their General Staff. We held these talks amid the so-called reset with Russia, a mere sixteen months after their invasion of Georgia. As the U.S. director of strategic plans and policy, I did not have an exact counterpart in the Russian military, so I wasn't exactly sure who would show up. I had visions of holding a symbolic dinner underneath the Apollo-Soyuz display at the National Air and Space Museum but quickly discovered that even someone as lofty as a three-star officer didn't rate spending the exorbitant fee charged by the museum for this kind of event. So we held our dinner at a restaurant and met on the campus of the National Defense University in Washington.

The three-star general sent by the Russians to the meeting didn't have the slightest interest in strategy and policy. Rather, he wanted to know how our Army managed its all-volunteer force and how they produced brigade combat teams. The Russian army was trying to transform itself based on its imperfect performance in Georgia. I remained circumspect about what I knew, claiming (with a great deal of truth) that I knew little about this due to my being a Navy officer. We would find out years later during the Russian invasion of Ukraine how poorly the Russians performed, evidently because when Sergei Shoygu became Russian minister of defense, he shut down the transformation effort.

On January 12, 2010, a devastating earthquake of magnitude 7.0 struck Port-au-Prince, the capital of the desperately poor and disaster-prone Caribbean nation of Haiti. The initial quake was followed by numerous aftershocks that destroyed the city. I was to have a front-row seat to how we would respond to a disaster in our hemisphere in what is now known as Operation Unified Response.

We were fortunate that talented Lt. Gen. Ken Keen, the deputy commander of Southern Command, was by chance on the ground in Port-au-Prince when the earthquake struck. We were even more fortunate that he was a fluent Portuguese-language speaker since our main partner in the relief effort was Brazil.

Southern Command had largely reconfigured itself to support interagency peacetime capacity-building in the Southern Hemisphere and needed to shift quickly to executing a major real-world operation, including a huge earthquake relief effort. Thus, it took a while for Gen. Doug Fraser to get the command's feet on the ground for what turned into a major effort complicated by an already poor infrastructure wrecked by the quake. It was incredibly difficult to organize and move the right equipment and supplies to the island without oversaturating its one little airport, while everybody and their brother also wanted to land their own special relief airplane and take credit for participating. It was quite a challenge to bring discipline to the system—without Ken Keen on the ground, we would likely have failed.

I visited Haiti with Admiral Mullen a couple of weeks after the relief effort started, along with a few civilians from our government. It was heartbreaking to see the dysfunctional, corrupt Haitian government worried more about its own survival than the nation's people. On the other hand, it was encouraging to see the Joint force at work—all the services were involved. The effort included our East Coast hospital ship, USNS *Comfort*, which performed numerous heroic feats of surgery on incredibly injured Haitians.

We encountered at least two political problems during the operation. The first was to handle the relationship with Brazil, which commanded the military element of the long-running UN Stabilization Mission in Haiti (with the ponderous acronym MINUSTAH). The Brazilians were intensely suspicious of our motives in moving a large force to Haiti, which they considered a client state. We also experienced a great deal of difficulty extracting our own troops as the operation wound down due to internal U.S. government pressure to leave the force behind to stabilize the country, including policing refugee camps. We worked hard to manage both issues. I left with a book chock full of major lessons learned that I was determined not to relearn after I assumed command of Northern Command.

As a teenager, I dreamed of living in Colorado, including doing everything I could to find bootleg Coors beer, which in those days was only sold west of the Mississippi and thus in great demand on the East Coast. Because we had relatives in the state, Mary and I became fond of skiing in Colorado. It wasn't exactly a forward warfighting command. Still, as the offspring of the 9/11 attacks, it seemed like an important place, with a host of key issues including counterterrorism, air defense, missile defense, disaster relief, the Arctic, nuclear deterrence, and relations with our neighboring countries.

So we headed to the Rocky Mountains. But first I had to get confirmed by the U.S. Senate.

Anchor #4:
Lead Execution

"To an even greater degree than the sea, [aviation] is terribly unforgiving of any carelessness, incapacity, or neglect."

Alfred Gilmer Lamplugh

Leaders Are Deciders

"Nothing is more difficult, and therefore more precious, than to be able to decide."
Napoleon

"Move fast. If we make mistakes, let them be because we moved too fast rather than too slow."
Lou Gerstner

Drive Excellence

"Some people aren't used to an environment where excellence is expected."
Steve Jobs

"I wouldn't give a fig for simplicity on the near side of complexity, but I'd give my life for the simplicity on the other side of complexity."
Oliver Wendell Holmes

Embrace Risk and Adversity

"Belichick . . . takes a lot of risks, and some things that look quite risky to us may actually be him engaging in some risk management."
Carl Kester

"We could never learn to be brave and patient if there were only joy in the world."
Helen Keller

Measure Wisely

"First measure the right things, and then measure them right."
Pearl Zhu

"When a measure becomes a target, it stops being a good measure."
Goodhart's Law

ANCHOR 4
Lead Execution

LEADERS ARE DECIDERS

People and organizations have to make decisions all the time. But one of the behaviors I observed throughout my career is how terribly difficult it can be for leaders to actually do. Decision paralysis can stem from various factors: a lack of familiarity with an issue and its complexity, a lack of unanimity or information, or fear of unintended consequences or blame if a decision goes south.

Yet one of a leader's most important jobs is to produce a decision that opens the door to execution. There is seldom enough information to make a perfect answer to any complex problem. Colin Powell said you will only ever have about 60 percent of the information required for a decision, and once you reach that point, it's time to decide. Even in the rare cases that all of the information is available, there is seldom a perfect answer.

Making no decision is actually a decision, and deciding what not to do is as important as choosing what to do. In any case, leaders must do their best to drill into the principles that govern the answer, find the best way forward, and then articulate the decision in a way that is clearly understood. If a leader has inculcated his or her principles into subordinates, it becomes both easy and important to delegate decisions, which in turn provides the bandwidth needed for that leader to focus on other critical tasks and opportunities.

DRIVE EXCELLENCE

Depending on the context, operational excellence leads to victory, profit, and safety. It doesn't just happen; leaders have to personally drive it into their organizations, which is accomplished within a framework of clearly articulated principles. I drew the following six interrelated principles from the Navy's nuclear propulsion program and my own experience in other operational disciplines:

Integrity is the bedrock principle. We trust our people to do the right thing and to admit their mistakes quickly, not only because it's expected of them but because they feel secure doing so. A culture of integrity should be deeply internalized in an organization. *Level of knowledge* requires a fundamental understanding of how "the machine," its associated hazards, and its processes and procedures work. Knowing even more than they think they need to know empowers people to more quickly detect when things are going wrong and to take action before it's too late. *Procedural compliance* is a vital component of any technically complex system, and its violation can result in a great deal of lost money or, worse, blood. From nuclear plants to airline cockpits, *formality* requires establishing a professional atmosphere, even when the operators are close friends, while also eliminating costly miscommunication. In many cases, it requires verbatim repeat back of instructions. *Forceful backup* requires that whenever an especially dangerous operation is being performed, there is an experienced person on the scene with no active role in the procedure who can quietly ensure it is executed correctly. It also means that anyone, no matter how junior, can stop the machine when it appears to be heading in an unsafe direction. Finally, a *questioning attitude* means constant alertness to when something is out of the ordinary and then never stopping at the first thing found wrong (because there is usually more than one thing wrong).

Close calls and mishaps can usually be traced to violations of more than one of these principles. Debriefing such events using their framework strongly reinforces them. I've written elsewhere about how strongly I believe in these operational excellence principles, so you can imagine how pleased I was to see them posted on the wall of my daughter-in-law's training squadron!

EMBRACE RISK AND ADVERSITY

One of the many things that kept me in the Navy was the exhilaration of being nearly constantly immersed in risk: flying airplanes at sea and in combat, driving ships, operating a carrier strike group, or briefing the president. The need to understand how others approach risk is why I started *The Adrenaline Zone* podcast with retired astronaut Sandra Magnus.

Bureaucrats are trained and incentivized to avoid risks. But high-performing leaders actually relish risk, managing it by first identifying it, then mitigating it, and then either accepting or avoiding the residual risk. Businesses and military units alike divide risk into two dimensions, likelihood and severity, often depicted on a chart. We humans have a tendency to focus on risks falling into the high-probability, high-consequences corner of the chart (and often what we find there is something that just happened anyway). Many organizations underemphasize the impact of the low-probability and high-severity quadrant (otherwise known "gray rhinos," where disasters like pandemics are generally found). It's also important to consider the speed at which a risk could deteriorate and the degree to which an organization can actually control it. Because a failure of culture can lead to corporate or other organizational missteps, it should be incorporated into any risk discussion.

In addition to managing risk, the most effective leaders find a way to turn negative events to their advantage. We are almost constantly confronted by adversity, both personal and organizational. Overcoming it requires imposing calm, first upon oneself and then upon the team. Things are never as bad (or as good) as they seem.

MEASURE WISELY

Every leader wants to measure performance. Unfortunately, people often seize on the wrong metrics for doing so. Many confuse the difference between the easily measurable and the meaningful. Others confuse input and output metrics. Yet selecting the wrong metrics can easily drive performance in the wrong direction.

To me, metrics, like risk, exist in a two-dimensional space, with one side aligned to input and output measures and the other to those that are qualitative or quantitative. A classic military example is air campaign metrics. For the overall campaign, one's sortie completion rate is a quantitative input metric, while the more important metric is the impact the campaign is having on the enemy. Yet sortie completion rate is also an output metric for the aircraft maintenance process. So a metric can serve as both input and output for two different processes at once. Clearly, the killer metric is a quantitative output metric, but this is a lot harder than it sounds.

Some of the most effective measures are those aligned with an organization's culture to really drive performance, such as Enterprise Rent-a-Car's key metric linked to customer satisfaction, using a simple and direct measure taken by a third party. There are countless examples of how using something readily measurable can lead to mistakes. An "identity metric" of 355 total ships has caused Congress to force the U.S. Navy to retain ships long after they should be retired; to buy large numbers of smaller, less capable ships rather than going after just the right mix; and to overlook the fact that these ships have to be manned and maintained (which always costs more than people acknowledge).

Finally, be on the lookout for subordinate leaders who, in attempting to achieve a target metric (such as quarterly revenue recognition in a business), corrupt themselves and those around them, then conduct reprisals against a whistleblower. This is a cultural slippery slope for any organization; a leader must ruthlessly eliminate it.

TOP Defense Secretary Robert Gates (*left*) promoting me before I assumed command of NORTHCOM and NORAD. His impressive combination of wisdom, wit, and experience was a gift to the Department of Defense. *U.S. Northern Command photo*

BOTTOM Robert Gates' successor, Leon Panetta (*right*), visiting NORTHCOM. A caring leader, he possessed an uncanny sense for the political dimension of a problem. *U.S. Northern Command photo*

High and Dry

The U.S. Northern Command is a four-star regional combatant command created after the terrorist attacks of 9/11. NORTHCOM is paired with the North American Aerospace Defense Command, also known as NORAD, a partnership with Canada started in 1957. Its main headquarters occupies a modern building at Peterson Air Force Base in Colorado Springs at the junction of the prairie and the Rocky Mountains. Its backup headquarters is only a few miles away, buried deep inside Cheyenne Mountain in the shadow of Pike's Peak.

Hurricane Katrina, which devastated New Orleans and the Gulf Coast in 2005, was an early test of the command. The storm revealed enormous cracks in our nation's ability to respond coherently to natural disasters, and a great deal of residual cross-institutional resentment between the National Guard and the active military components reverberated in the wake of the storm.

In 2010 Defense Secretary Bob Gates took the unusual step of nominating me—a naval officer—to lead both commands. Some members of the Guard bitterly complained because they believed Secretary Gates had promised to nominate one of their own as the next commander. That feeling was only amplified by the traditional rivalry—some would say animosity—between the Guard and the active-duty Army and Air Force. A dose of this hostility was aimed at me: what could a Navy fighter pilot possibly know about homeland security and the policy ins and outs of disaster relief, to say nothing about how the Guard operates? Little did the Guard know that this negative would turn into a positive for them because of the unbiased role I brought to bear due to the simple fact that I was not an Army or Air Force officer.

With this as a backdrop, I had to get confirmed by the U.S. Senate. At and below the rank of two-star general or admiral, promotions are determined by a selection board, approved by the relevant service's military and civilian chain of command, submitted by the president to the Senate as large lists, voted out of the Armed Services Committee, and then approved as a group by the Senate. Only rarely are these promotions controversial. At the next level, officers are only promoted to three or four stars when nominated and confirmed for a specific job carrying that rank. They can subsequently retire at that rank if they serve honorably therein for at least three years. Even further up the chain, the chairman and vice chairman of the Joint Chiefs of Staff, the service chiefs, and the combatant commanders are always asked to appear at a confirmation hearing in front of the Senate Armed Services Committee.

With the Senate in the hands of a Democratic majority, my nomination came before the committee when Sen. Carl Levin of Michigan chaired it. Levin was old school, steeped in the now long-gone collegiality our founders intended for the body. He asked tough but insightful questions and was curious, polite, and supportive. One could only hope that his cluttered office, with stacks of books and papers on every horizontal surface, was indicative of a neat mind. He often looked tired and rumpled, but he was a fantastic committee chairman and an empathetic and charming gentleman. Sadly, he was one of the last of a quickly vanishing breed of politically collegial members of Congress.

The committee's ranking member was Sen. John McCain from Arizona. I always held McCain in high regard for his immense sacrifice as a prisoner of war during the Vietnam conflict as well as for his deep patriotism. He was grumpy and irascible, but I hoped to build a solid relationship with him, as he served a border state that was important to NORTHCOM and was a fellow naval aviator.

I was fortunate to have two allies during my confirmation process. One was Lt. Gen. Craig McKinley. I had already developed a good relationship with Craig, an affable Air National Guard Officer hailing from Florida and serving as the chief of the National Guard Bureau. He would eventually be promoted to four stars when the Guard chief formally became a member of the Joint Chiefs of Staff. I really liked Craig and his spouse, Cheryl, who were friendly and cooperative.

My other ally was retired Marine major general Arnold Punaro, who previously served as the Senate Armed Services Committee's staff director and who often served as a consultant to prepare officers for confirmation hearings. He was not only a superb mentor for the tortuous process, but he was also an expert on the National Guard and provided many "important safety tips" about the relationship and Congress's interest in the institution.

Luckily for me, my hearing was conducted in tandem with Army general Keith Alexander, who was serving as director of the National Security Agency. He was nominated to head the newly established U.S. Cyber Command and thus required a new hearing. Cyber was such a hot topic that he received most of the questions. My only real takeaway was a promise to visit the Mexican border with Senator McCain as soon as possible after confirmation.

I arrived in Colorado Springs to take command of NORTHCOM and NORAD in May 2010. Based on my tour in Europe, I was already used to wearing at least two hats and looked forward to serving as a dual-hatted combatant commander.

Like the Department of Homeland Security at the time, NORTHCOM was a relatively new institution trying hard to fit into an existing system, with understandable resistance from the organizations that were either displaced or co-opted. As such, I inherited an organization that had survived an ugly birth and was now progressing through a difficult, insecure adolescence. I was determined to bring it into young adulthood.

One of the great things about being assigned to NORTHCOM and NORAD was the broad diversity of mission sets for which the two commands were responsible. If a natural or man-made disaster occurred in the United States, ranging from a hurricane or earthquake to detonation of a nuclear or chemical device, NORTHCOM would have a key role in assisting civil authorities in the recovery. If someone hijacked an airliner, I would be responsible for determining whether to bring it down before it could conduct another 9/11-like attack. We were also specifically charged with responsibility for defending the U.S. National Capital Region from air attacks.

I was also responsible for ballistic missile defense of the United States, and my headquarters was also a backup capability to advise the president in the event of a nuclear response to an attack on the nation. If the Russians attacked, NORAD was responsible for air defense. We were in charge of military operations in the Arctic and for nurturing our relationship with the Mexican army and navy. We assisted civil authorities on counterdrug operations. It was a busy place with diverse activity at my headquarters at Peterson Air Force Base, inside Cheyenne Mountain, and in our component commands around the nation.

I brought to NORTHCOM and NORAD a habit I learned from my father's brother, Carl Builder who, before he passed away, was a well-respected defense analyst with the RAND Corporation. Carl was absolutely brilliant—the clearest thinker I've ever known—a polymath who combined the skills of both rocket scientist and policy virtuoso. He was brilliant at dissecting a complex issue and courageous in challenging long-held assumptions. He was a master at understanding organizational DNA; his book *The Masks of War* explains the culture of the four services better than any other work I've read. Carl predicted in the early 1980s that transnational terrorism would become a major factor in our nation's security. I've always tried to emulate his analytical mindset, which begins with viewing the problem from a completely neutral viewpoint, striving to empathize with both sides of an issue.

I would quickly find the opportunity to exercise my uncle's approach. Other than simple internecine jealousy, the most significant source of friction between the National Guard and the active component was which one would have command of federal military forces during a disaster response.

The Guard believed that only an officer steeped in knowledge of the affected state could effectively lead the response. Moreover, each governor has strong political equities in ensuring not only that the response within his or her state is effective but that the state itself receives the credit for it. The active forces, on the other hand, felt there was something terribly wrong about yielding control of federal forces to a governor or state military officer. Moreover, the active component tended to question the ability of Guard forces to competently lead federal troops in the first place.

I felt that both sides, to a limited extent, were both right and wrong. Organizational ego had a great deal to do with it. But I also felt there were reasonable people—who I happened to like personally—on both sides of the issue. One of these was Craig McKinley. We pledged to work closely and open-mindedly together to heal the rift between the Guard and NORTHCOM, and here was our opportunity.

Fortunately, there was a mechanism, which had previously been rejected as impractical, for solving this seemingly intractable command and control challenge. It was legally possible for a Guard officer to serve as a "dual status commander," meaning he or she could work simultaneously for a governor and the secretary of defense. State forces would work for this commander in a chain that led to the governor, and federal forces would work for the same individual in a chain that led to the secretary of defense. Unity of command would be achieved.

If both sides could accept this, then the problem would be solved. For the federal side—including me—this meant sending nominated Guard officers through a specific training course that would qualify them to serve in this role. For the state side, this meant setting aside their inherent suspicion that this was only another way of seizing control of disaster response from the governors. But the adjutant generals (who are the lead National Guard officers in each state, otherwise known as "TAGs") were intrigued that a NORTHCOM commander would actually propose this as a solution.

So, with beautiful snow-covered Pikes Peak rising in the distance outside the window of my NORTHCOM headquarters office, Craig and I gathered a few respected National Guard leaders around the table. I was reminded while we were doing this of William Butler Yeats saying, "Talent perceives differences; genius unity." None of us were geniuses, as far as I could tell, but we found a way to overcome the differences between the two cultures in a way that worked for both. We hammered out a solid training program the Guard could live with that would prepare a few officers in each state for the role of dual status commander and that would soothe the concerns of the active force. With the help of Deputy Assistant Secretary for Homeland Security Paul Stockton, we sold this program to the Defense Department's leadership and the governors and put it in motion.

Several states were reluctant at first, but a few courageous and forward-leaning Guard leaders embraced the program, and we soon completed our first class. It quickly became a badge of honor for the fifty-four states and territories with National Guard forces to have a qualified dual status commander. We couldn't get officers through the training program fast enough. I was very proud of this effort, which better prepared our nation to respond to disasters and narrowed the cultural gap between the active and Guard forces (although tension will always exist between them, mostly over money). Several senior federal officials were relieved to have this problem off their plate, including Secretary Gates.

I am convinced that, had Gates nominated an Army or Air Force officer to command NORTHCOM at this moment in time, we would never have solved the dual status commander issue. There was simply too much organizational baggage. Even though the Guard was angry that one of their own had not been appointed, I think it worked out well for them in the end.

One of the initiatives I previously described from my tour as commander of Sixth Fleet and JC Lisbon was organizing operational briefs around objectives rather than staff functions. At my first once-per-week update brief, I quickly discovered that, like those organizations, NORTHCOM organized its thinking around its staff structure. Moreover, whenever I asked on the sidelines about a given issue, the experts from the most closely related staff function would appear in my office, with a senior leader in tow, to attempt to answer my question. But I wondered whether other elements of the organization enjoyed a common understanding with the team in front of me, and even more so whether any guidance I gave would propagate beyond that team.

So we adopted the same technique that worked at my previous commands, organizing our efforts around five pillars: air defense, missile defense, our relationship with Mexico, the Arctic, and support to civil authorities. In keeping with my experiment in Europe, I insisted that our weekly update be organized around these pillars. It was quite an adjustment for the staff, but, as before, they responded immediately. This extended beyond mere briefings; it permeated the command. When I had an off-cycle question or received a brief in my office, I insisted that a cross-functional group with expertise in the pillar being discussed walk to my office to address the issue. I believe that, although it was a difficult adjustment at first, this approach challenged the organization in a refreshing way and made for a more thoroughgoing approach to the many issues we confronted.

I also discovered that when a senior officer has a question, the system wants to schedule a meeting a few days later to answer it. This would give the staff time to work up the answer and make sure their boss could attend the meeting. I made it clear early on that I didn't want to wait for bureaucratically generated answers. I also wanted senior officers to be personally secure enough to allow their subordinates to visit and brief me. Millennial officers loved this, and it was an early education for me regarding how to work with this generation.

Nearly everything we did required a combination of speed and wisdom. If an airliner is hijacked, you have to get to it quickly, but you also have to make a perfect decision. If a hurricane or earthquake strikes, there is no time to argue over who will respond and how to do it. I was so intent on accelerating NORTHCOM's ability to get things done that I coined a Latin motto for the command: *Velocitas cum Prudentia*, or "speed with wisdom." I'm not sure it survived my tenure, but it sure was useful when the system gummed up.

Another challenge I faced on the NORTHCOM side of the command was the fractious relationship between the Mexican and U.S. militaries. It made no sense that we maintained a close relationship with our Canadian neighbors, but we were barely on speaking terms with our neighbors to the south. This breakdown was hindering our efforts to control the flow of drugs into the United States and was contributing to unprecedented and tragic violence in Mexico. But the Mexican military held a long-standing distrust of the

United States based on the problematic history between our two nations. Understanding that this was a steep hill to climb, I set about changing the relationship, which first and foremost meant forging a personal bond with my Mexican military counterparts.

The Mexican military is structured entirely differently from the U.S. military, which required careful navigation on my part. The United States has one civilian secretary of defense, a single chairman of the Joint Chiefs of Staff, and six service chiefs (including the new Space Force and the U.S. Coast Guard, which is part of the Department of Homeland Security but functions as a military branch). Mexico has a secretary of defense, who is a military officer and the chief of their army and air force, and a secretary of the navy, who is the chief of their navy and marine corps. So I not only had to interact with two different officers, but they were also technically peers of our secretary of defense while I was only a combatant commander. When I arrived, I could tell they both felt slighted by having the NORTHCOM commander as their daily counterpart.

This was all about understanding and managing the cultural context of the relationship. If I approached these two leaders acting as a superior military, it would not advance. Failing to acknowledge their equivalency to our secretary of defense would present a similar problem. With that in mind, I reached out to ask if I could visit them in Mexico City as soon as possible, to which they graciously agreed.

I first met with the chief of the Mexican navy, Admiral Mariano Francisco Saynez Mendoza. He was sixteen years my senior and a native of Veracruz. I hit it off immediately with this friendly and gracious officer. Of course, it probably helped that I was a naval officer myself. We played golf together several times in Florida, Colorado, and on the coast of Mexico. He also hosted me several times in Mexico City in the most gracious possible style. We used to joke that his forces apprehended a major drug figure whenever I visited him, so I should visit more often.

I also met several times with the chief of the Mexican army, General Guillermo Galván Galván. My first meeting with this officer was a little cooler and understandably so since the Mexican army was so deeply suspicious of the U.S. military. I never really knew for sure, but I was told that the graduation exercise from the Mexican War College involved repelling an invasion from the United States. That was an important signal to me that, even though we had no such intention, I would need to tread tactfully and carefully to build a relationship. I didn't sense that the door was closed, though. I discovered that Galván was a passionate New York Yankees fan, so I invited him to visit the Yankees' spring training camp in Tampa, Florida. He was introduced to Joe Girardi and several Hispanic baseball players and sat in the Steinbrenners' box. Later I took him to a Yankees playoff game in Minneapolis, Minnesota. I called it baseball diplomacy, but it worked in getting my counterpart to visit the United States to build a relationship.

I quickly discovered how careful we needed to be with the language used around our sensitive Mexican partners. This was an easy lesson based on my experience running a NATO headquarters. For example, even though the tactics were the same, it was insulting to refer to their struggle as a counter-insurgency as they were not fighting against a group trying to overthrow the government. They were also understandably highly sensitive to any potential presence of U.S. forces on their territory.

I tried to impress on both of these officers that we were willing to quietly assist in any way in helping them take down the drug cartels that were such a corrosive influence in both Mexico and the United States. I explained that we did not view our forces as inherently superior but that we had learned a great deal about the vital importance of integrating intelligence and operations during nine years of continuous fighting in Iraq and Afghanistan. The fusion centers that did this work maintained a tight cycle of night raids followed by sensitive site exploitation, interrogation, and intelligence analysis that fed the next night's raids. It was almost impossible for a targeted network to keep up, and they gradually began to unravel. I frequently offered to my Mexican counterparts that we were willing to pass along what we learned about running an interagency an operations center in a constructive way.

Our relationship with our Mexican allies eventually reached a point where we could agree on establishing a combined coordination center. This was a breakthrough: that the several different Mexican agencies with a dog in the fight of the counter-cartel effort would come together in a single effort was unprecedented. In a meeting with several Mexican officials, I agreed in principle to their request but would need to seek permission and guidance from my own government. I knew there would be major questions over how this would be run and who would be in charge. In the meantime, I took the opportunity to present my Mexican counterparts with Native American peace pipes to symbolize our impending cooperation.

Sure enough, the idea quickly escalated to the Deputies Committee of the National Security Council. I was fortunate that many of the members knew me from my work on the Joint Staff J5; otherwise, the idea might have perished on the rocks of interagency jealousy. The Drug Enforcement Agency (DEA) was concerned that the military would ruin potential legal cases. Others were concerned that we would be unintentionally complicit in a human rights violation or step into areas where they were already cooperating with Mexico. These were legitimate concerns, but we felt we had the right safeguards in place—we just wanted to help our partners help themselves. Our ambassador to Mexico at the time, Carlos Pascual, was a supportive partner and became a good friend.

In the end, DEA was designated to be in charge of the effort, with NORTHCOM providing most of the expertise. While this guidance stemmed as much from a major turf battle as anything else, it was actually a smart move, as long as DEA cooperated and didn't slow roll the effort. We did not want to indicate that the U.S. military would have responsibility for what was technically a law enforcement problem.

The Mexican military rapidly put together the supporting infrastructure, and the coordination center stood up. We were totally committed to supporting the Mexicans. Early in the process, the bureaucracy told us that no active-duty U.S. military personnel would be allowed in the center—they would all have to be civilians. So a then-serving Army colonel on my staff, a highly dedicated officer, actually retired and returned as a civilian so he could lead the effort. It was an amazing demonstration of dedication to an important mission.

We worked feverishly to establish a center in Colorado Springs to control unmanned aerial vehicles if we were allowed to provide that kind of support to the Mexicans. This required an enormous amount of missionary work with U.S. Customs and Border Protection, which was growing its own use of drones along the border. They were suspicious that the Department of

Defense would try to take over the mission. I was fortunate that Alan Bersin was then the agency leader, and we slowly won over the members of his aviation team involved in the effort.

As the center in Mexico came together, the different Mexican military branches and civilian agencies gradually lowered their barriers and began to trust one another. However, the showstopper was that we were not permitted by several of our interagency partners, including DEA, to conduct the close coordination with Mexico required to make these operations work. Moreover, there were not adequate numbers of unmanned aerial vehicles available to support the operation—most were operating overseas, even though far more Americans were being killed by illegal narcotics than by terrorists. Eventually, through a combination of frustration and the fact that they probably felt they learned everything they could, the Mexicans closed the center and stood it up elsewhere in Mexico. I felt it was a squandered opportunity.

At some point during this process I became frustrated with the way senior American officials talked about the Mexican counterdrug efforts. These well-meaning officials were not aware of Mexican sensitivities and often unknowingly said things that infuriated my counterparts. So I drafted an op-ed intended to point out how hard the Mexicans were trying and that their militaries were not only getting much better, they were improving their approach to human rights as well. As I was trying to figure out to which U.S. newspaper I would submit the piece, an American official made yet another unintentional but offensive set of remarks. So I published the piece in my blog on the NORTHCOM website.

I knew there were around 20,000 people following my blog, but I didn't realize how many were actually in Mexico. Fortunately, I was complimentary of the Mexican armed forces, and the piece was positively covered in a story above the fold the next day in the major Mexico City newspaper. I relearned a good lesson: communicating to and about our allies and partners in the right way can pay big dividends.

NORTHCOM and NORAD had two other major responsibilities. One involved missile defense of the United States, and the other involved preventing terrorist attacks, including the important role NORAD played in preventing another 9/11-style attack using airliners.

The former was complex enough. The Ground-Based Interceptor, or GBI, program had a troubled history. Due to the urgency of getting a defensive system into place, it was tested in parallel with its development. A few successes offset the inevitable failures—especially those occurring early in the program—from such an approach. Now there were theoretically enough interceptors in and out of the continental United States to at least defend against a limited attack or accidental launch. Fortunately, because of the limited pace of North Korean and Iranian missile development, the threat of such an attack remained fairly low during my tenure at NORTHCOM. The Missile Defense Agency (created because Department of Defense leaders knew the effort would die on the vine if given to one of the service branches) did an excellent job of tracking down the root causes of failures and fixing them. Their perseverance paid off, and I continued to gain confidence in the system, although there is much left to do to provide "right of launch" capability to deter such an attack, including directed energy.

Shooting down an airliner or other aircraft that might be part of a terrorist attack was a different story. The nation was not prepared to do this on 9/11 because nobody anticipated that a terrorist would hijack an airliner—much less four or more—and fly it into a building. Instead, NORAD was far more focused on a potential attack from the Soviet Union and its successor, the Russian Federation. Despite the best efforts of several pilots and ground crews on that awful day, we didn't have armed aircraft positioned to counter a terrorist attack. Since then a major effort resulted in the generation of a far more ready and responsive—and expensive—ability to respond to such an event in both the United States and Canada.

The NORAD agreement with Canada was put in place during the Cold War to counter the ominous threat of a Soviet attack bomber over the north polar region. The agreement is a shining example of trusted nation-to-nation cooperation around the world. My second-in-command at NORAD was always a highly capable Royal Canadian Air Force officer, and my headquarters was generously supplied with exemplary people by Canada.

Despite the amusing differences between our two cultures, Canada has always been a fantastic partner for the United States. We shouldn't forget that, on 9/11, literally thousands of Canadian families took in Americans who were stranded when our airspace was closed and many inbound airliners had to land north of the border. They stood by us—and endured disproportionate losses—in Afghanistan. And they were a vital partner in our efforts to defend North American airspace from the new threat of terrorism.

Should it ever happen, shooting down a potentially hijacked airliner or other aircraft would be a tricky affair. We first would have to detect the hijacking itself, then scramble fighters from one or more of our alert air bases in the United States or Canada and vector them toward the aircraft in question, hoping to intercept the aircraft in time. Then our pilots would have to discern the intent of those on board, using direct communications, maneuvers, observation, or other means. And if hostile intent were confirmed, the decision to down the aircraft would have to be clearly communicated to the fighters, who would then position for and conduct the attack, hopefully over an unpopulated area.

I found it impossible to devise a strict mathematical formula for determining an aircraft's intent. Rather, we used a list of potential indicators that a decisionmaker could assess in real time to judge whether the aircraft posed a threat. Should such an event occur, it was quite likely the decision would have to be made very quickly. We knew we would always try to reach higher civilian authority to make the call if possible. But I was empowered by the president to make the decision myself and was allowed to further delegate this authority to certain other qualified officers on my staff.

We wanted to take no chances regarding whether someone would be available to make the call. So we constantly practiced the procedures associated with such an event. It was a chilling experience, and we learned something each time we simulated it. Even though we launched alert aircraft to rendezvous on real airliners several times during my time in command, I was relieved never to have to make this terrible call for real.

Despite a great deal of unfair criticism leveled at the Transportation Security Administration, they have taken us a long way toward greater airline security. Hardened cockpit doors and other measures have further increased our ability to prevent such an attack. We have a more aware population that, knowing full well the implications of allowing a hijacker to gain control of an airplane, will be unlikely to allow it to happen. And we have benefited from the diligent work undertaken by our many intelligence and law enforcement communities—which have dramatically lowered the internecine barriers among them that existed before 9/11—to protect us.

Speaking of defending our homeland, the responsibility I took most seriously was my role in the nation's nuclear command and control structure. U.S. Strategic Command rightfully was the keeper of the keys on this important function, but we played an indispensable backup role. NORTHCOM was subjected to extensive periodic testing to ensure we were ready to manage this system in the event other elements were compromised and it fell to us. In participating in these exercises, I came to strongly believe that the system was poorly designed to obtain a decision from the president. Without getting into classified processes, it seemed to be more akin to interrogating a teenager on what he or she did on a Friday night rather than clearly and accurately eliciting the most important decision a president might ever make. As with most processes, it had grown a lot of "hair" based on attempts to eliminate any possibility for mistakes. But I was concerned it would take too long and resolved to try to fix it if I ever had the chance, which later proved to be the case.

One of the joys of being the NORAD commander was the opportunity to build a relationship with my Canadian counterpart, Gen. Walt Natynczyk. This fine army officer was a warm, wise, and cooperative partner who possessed a classic Canadian sense of humor. He also supported the special relationship between Canada and the United States. Taking him up on his gracious invitation to visit the Calgary Stampede and travel to the far northern reaches of the Canadian Arctic only deepened our cooperation.

The Canadians didn't ask for much: they wanted to be recognized as the strong players they were, to be treated as equals, to be given a voice, and to have their fair share of tough jobs. They stood out at NORAD as having integrity and team spirit, including hosting a golf tournament in which, on one hole, players hit their drive wearing hockey gloves and putted using a hockey stick. Like any small military, they were somewhat burdened by internal politics, but I treasured the opportunity to work with these fine men and women.

Life at the foot of the Rocky Mountains was pretty good. Although our two boys were enduring their fourth school district in five years, we enjoyed

Colorado Springs and frequently skied or otherwise enjoyed the mountains. The responsibility I carried at NORTHCOM and NORAD was highly rewarding. And who wouldn't enjoy leading "NORAD Tracks Santa"?

It was also great being out of Washington, DC. On the many trips my immediate staff and I would take to the Pentagon, we would joke about a portable toilet precariously perched on the roof of the building in support of some renovation work. "Yep, crap still runs downhill at the Pentagon." It was easy to speak disparagingly of the place, as I had every reason to believe I was in my last hurrah in the military. I fully expected to spend three full years in Colorado and retire to the home we were building in the beautiful little town of Breckenridge.

But, once again, "the system" had other plans.

TOP The Joint Chiefs of Staff *U.S. Army photo by Monica King*

BOTTOM The Vice Squad at the end of my service as vice chairman *Joint Staff photo*

The Vice Squad

L ess than a year into the job at NORTHCOM and NORAD, I addressed a formal dinner on a Friday evening before a group of Guardsmen in Louisville, Kentucky. This was part and parcel of reinforcing our more positive relationship with the National Guard. I was proud to help honor several heroic Guardsmen who served in Iraq and Afghanistan. It was a terrific evening and yet another reminder of the importance of the American heartland and of the citizen-soldier.

Not long before I was scheduled to present my speech, an aide "crouch-walked" behind our elevated head table to not attract attention and whispered in my ear that someone from the White House needed to speak with me urgently on the phone. What on earth could this be on a Friday night? I scavenged my mind for something imminently dangerous or controversial going on in North America, or even something I might have recently said that could offend the White House, and I came up blank. I excused myself from the table and walked outside onto a broad, empty veranda to make the call; I was informed that I needed to be in the Oval Office for an interview with President Obama at nine o'clock the next morning.

Based on a vague hint that Joint Chiefs chairman Admiral Mullen previously dropped while we were riding in a car together in Mexico City some months before, it dawned on me that I might be nominated by the president to serve as the next vice chairman of the Joint Chiefs of Staff. But I had no idea whether I was simply one of many being considered for the role or whether this was an opportunity for the president to look me in the eye before taking a recommendation from Secretary Gates and the chairman.

I'd been around two different presidents before—both Mr. Bush and Mr. Obama—but only as part of larger meetings. Then I was a bit player; this was different. I had never before been in the Oval Office, much less attended a meeting with a serving president that was actually about me.

I delivered my speech and informed my staff we'd be flying to Andrews Air Force Base outside Washington, DC, that night instead of Colorado Springs, that I needed to be in the White House in the morning, and that the whole thing was close hold.

I wasn't sure what to expect, but soon after arriving at a blessedly quiet Saturday morning West Wing, I was quickly ushered into the Oval Office. I was surprised to find myself suddenly alone with President Obama. It was a bit surreal to be sitting in the chair I had seen on television occupied by so many foreign leaders, right next to the president, in front of the fireplace. I jokingly (and privately!) chalked it up to the Forrest Gump Effect.

The president was in khaki slacks and a white shirt. He was clearly looking forward to playing golf on what was a gorgeous spring morning in Washington, DC. Obama is adept at putting people at ease—he offered an apple out of a basket on the table in front of us. I recall demurring, thinking, "Yep, like I'm actually going to munch on an apple in front of the president during a job interview." I also told myself to relax and be myself; the worst thing that could happen was a lasting memory.

We talked for twenty or thirty minutes—I have no idea how long it actually was. However, I principally remember two things from what turned out to be an enjoyable discussion, in which I think I learned more about him than he learned about me. First, I recall the president describing his thought process on intervening in Libya, which included a train of thought that matched my personal beliefs regarding the importance of allowing prioritized national security interests, rather than emotion, to guide decisions on the use of force.

Second, I recall him asking what I felt was the greatest threat to our nation's security at the time. He may have been expecting a senior military officer to point out shortages in the defense budget or something topical like al-Qaeda. Instead, I told him we were actually reasonably safe, and the national security imperative of deficit reduction was our most pressing security problem since no strong nation ever had a weak economy. While we could manage the immediate daily security problems we faced, we needed to ensure the long-term health of the nation.

Perhaps having a serving military officer say something like this was a "man bites dog" moment for Obama. In any case, he must have been satisfied enough by our conversation to tell Tom Donilon, his national security advisor, to approve my nomination. It was not long afterward that I found out that I would be the ninth vice chairman of the Joint Chiefs of Staff, pending confirmation by the U.S. Senate.

Gen. Marty Dempsey and I were publicly announced as the president's nominees for chairman and vice chairman in a Rose Garden ceremony. Gen. Ray Odierno, who would take Marty's place as chief of staff of the Army, was announced alongside us. As is customary for these events, it was a special moment to take my family into the Oval Office to meet the president in advance of the ceremony. It was a blistering hot day, and I was relieved to be relatively comfortable in my short-sleeved white uniform, and sympathetic to Marty and Ray perspiring in their dark black Army dress uniforms in the baking sunshine in the garden. As I stood there, I chuckled to myself that the "Never let 'em see you sweat" rule my old boss Colin Powell used to put out for leaders was really meant for those under pressure, but it seemed apropos at the time.

The teleprompter used by the president was not the glass plates mounted closely on either side of him that one typically sees. Instead, he read his remarks—ad-libbing from time to time—from a set of large television screens placed behind the audience. I thought, "How cool is this? I get to read the president's speech along with him." That is, until I saw the beginning of his remarks about me, which repeated the folklore about me gallantly turning

USS *Enterprise* around without orders after the 9/11 attacks to head north toward Pakistan.

I had briefed my aides never to allow anyone introducing me to use that story, as it could offend those who were closer to the decision. But nobody from the White House had asked for information or shared the points they intended to use for my introduction. Who were we to dictate how the president should introduce me? Shortly after the ceremony I called several people to explain that we had nothing to do with the story the president had just told on national TV.

And then the confirmation process began.

The billet of vice chairman, or VCJCS, was created—only barely—when the Goldwater–Nichols Act was passed in 1987. There were some on the Senate Armed Services Committee at the time who objected to there being a vice chairman at all ("What, another four-star?"). That the chairman and VCJCS would be subject to a two-year term—with reconfirmation required after each term—was apparently the compromise that broke free the position.

Only eight other people held this job before me, each with his own style. I recalled gaining a great deal of respect for Adm. David Jeremiah while serving as the "Vice" with General Powell while I was the latter's aide, never having a clue that I would fill his big shoes many years later. I also admired several other previous VCJCS, including two I knew personally: Adm. Edmund Giambastiani and Gen. Peter Pace.

As with other positions, including my first confirmation process on the way to Colorado Springs, the first hearing for a chairman or vice chairman is generally a friendly affair. It was rare at the time for a member to beat up on someone in uniform. Spouses are welcomed by the committee chairman who, for my hearing, was once again Sen. Carl Levin of Michigan. The chairman and ranking member make an opening statement. The prospective officeholder then makes a brief statement, and the committee members are then given time to ask questions. There are normally only a few senators in the room, as their staffers, who are managing their busy daily schedules, summon them at just the right moment.

Because the nominee doesn't have full knowledge of all the issues associated with the upcoming job, he or she is not normally expected to be fluent in the issues during a first confirmation hearing. This is true even though the nominee must answer a thicket of written questions prior to the hearing, from which staffers can glean "stump the stars" questions for their members. The best advice is to over-prepare and be judicious with one's answers, promising to work closely with the committee and to look into any matters of concern they express. Then get out the door with no self-inflicted wounds. A good bit of what a senator says or asks is for the cameras anyway, and a wise nominee keeps the answers short to not foreclose a legislator's hard-earned moment on TV.

Because the party out of power in the White House wants to use a nominee as an anvil on which to beat the president, a certain amount of skill is required to maneuver around questions intended to score political hits. And it is always entertaining to be questioned by an experienced prosecutor such as Sen. Lindsey Graham, who will try to pin a witness down with impossible-to-answer "yes or no" questions designed to box in the nominee, embarrass the opposite party, and get television exposure. But solid preparation capped by a murder board normally gets the nominee through the process.

While the preparation was challenging, I had been through it all before with Northern Command and was relieved when it was over. Not long afterward my nomination was forwarded by the committee, and I was confirmed on the Senate floor on August 4, 2011, by, if I remember correctly, a unanimous vote. It happened to be the day the infamous Budget Control Act was passed by Congress. It was also the last day my predecessor, Gen. James Cartwright, would be able to remain in office due to the statutory expiration of his term, so I would take over immediately.

The following morning, and in yet another low-key change of command, I passed the reins of NORTHCOM and NORAD to Army general Chuck Jacoby in a brief video teleconference. Once again I was able to evade a costly and self-aggrandizing change of command ceremony, better preserved for younger officers.

Mary packed up our family and moved back to Washington, DC, first living in temporary housing at Bolling Air Force Base in Anacostia, Maryland, and then finally moving into Quarters Eight at Fort Myer, adjacent to Arlington National Cemetery. The house was used by Col. George Patton in the late 1930s while he gloomily contemplated being sidelined during what appeared to be an impending war. The house was across the street from a grassy hill sloping down toward the Marine Corps Memorial and the Potomac River and enjoyed what we called "the House of Cards view" (drawn, of course, from the TV series of the same name) of downtown Washington, DC.

After confirmation I took several steps to impose my own style on the VCJCS position. The first thing I did was open the door that was previously sealed between the outer offices that separated chairman Mike Mullen's and vice chairman "Hoss" Cartwright's personal outer offices. There had appeared to be some tension between the two officers, and I wanted to clarify that if that was indeed the case, it no longer existed. I also removed a barrier that hid my office desk from anyone else in the room. Finally, I swapped out the long rectangular conference table for a circular table. I intended these changes to signal an air of transparency and warmth to the office.

The symbolism was not lost on visitors, particularly staff members. The work on the Joint Staff, elsewhere in the Pentagon, and anywhere else in Washington for that matter, is hard enough without having to contend with intimidating superiors. I wanted to leave no doubt that we were open for business in a collegial, precise, and responsive way.

Thus "the Vice Squad" was born. I was surprised no one else—at least to my knowledge—previously used the name, but it conveyed the tight-knit and welcoming culture I wanted among my team. I carefully retained or hired several key team players for my front office staff, including able administrative assistant Mary Turner. I also brought in several incredibly talented enlisted personnel to help manage the house and support my official role.

The job of the VCJCS rests on three key pillars: policy and strategy, investment, and people. While all three intersect with the actual members of the Joint Chiefs of Staff, each pillar generally involves relationships with completely separate bodies of people, most of whom have that single pillar as their only focus. Because the VCJCS has to focus on all three, the job requires agility, depth, and superb staff support. In that regard, it was remarkably similar to being the captain of *Enterprise*.

There were several tenets of my position to which I adhered during my time as VCJCS. One of the most important was maintaining a low profile with the news media. I didn't want to contribute to any willful "overmisinterpretation" by members of the media that could lead to a perception of daylight between my position and other senior leaders. There is enough media noise in Washington, DC, and I didn't need to add to it. Moreover, I bore no urge or instinct for personal notoriety and, unlike several other senior officers before me, no particular ambition that required developing a cult of personality in the public domain. I preferred life behind the scenes as a workhorse, not a show horse.

Finally, I didn't want there to be any doubt whatsoever regarding whether I was a "leaker." Perhaps the White House trusted me because they either sensed this or they had the FBI working leaks and never found anything on me since I simply never did it. In fact, I was thoroughly disgusted by those who did leak information, believing them to be either weak or unpatriotic or both.

Why do people leak information? Perhaps they develop an overly personal relationship with a journalist and feel obliged to provide information. Or they are upset over the direction a policy decision is headed and try to circumvent the decision by informing the media, hoping for a reversal. Maybe they simply gain satisfaction or exhilaration from having that kind of power. Or, in the case of investigative journalists' books, perhaps they want to make sure their side of the story gets told. None of them are paid or coerced by the media—that's not how journalism normally works in our country.

Meanwhile, the media are clever at getting people to talk. A favorite tactic is to present a trial story to someone hoping that person, believing the reporter is actually on to something, will shrug their shoulders and confirm, clarify, or even embellish it. In some cases, people respond to correct whatever inaccurate and potentially damaging information a reporter has uncovered. In any case, I spoke to only a few reporters, and then only to those whom I really trusted, and I always did so with a public affairs professional in the room, never privately.

The media would sometimes contact people in government trying to verify a story leaked to them and tended to hold back publishing something only if it could be proven to them that lives or other truly grave national security consequences were at stake. This was particularly true of special operations. I know of no instance when someone in the White House or elsewhere in the interagency leaked details of an operation to the media *before* an operation was conducted. But look out afterward, especially if the operation was successful. People either wanted to rush to give credit to the president for taking bold action, or they wanted to report the cool thing to a curious journalist to enhance their own credibility, or they simply didn't know better. Either way, we've lost a lot of vital tactics, techniques, and procedures due to post-operation leaks to the media.

I had many opportunities as VCJCS to take on the bureaucracy. However, there is no end to how a large institution like the Pentagon, with its many different organizations and career civilians, can resist action or change. Bureaucrats are driven by two things: (1) the power they have been granted, usually because someone once made a mistake that must never be made again, and (2) the fear they will be held accountable less for failure to act than for action they might take. I viewed it as a challenge to overcome these obstacles and speed up otherwise moribund processes. I wasn't always successful but did manage to find a few ways around recalcitrant bureaucrats.

The Pentagon has a long-held process of routing decision "packages" through what is known as a "chop chain," with a "suspense" or due date assigned by the originator. This is rightly intended to ensure each organization with interest in the matter at hand is given a voice in the analysis and recommended solution. The various organizations to which the package is "shot-gunned" in parallel can submit critical and noncritical comments, and every attempt is made to adjudicate them. To the degree that comments cannot be resolved, the rules suggest that the differences be pointed out to the final decision-maker. The suspense dates are normally overly generous, and organizations often either start late on the project or fail to anticipate the complexity of the issue and end up late anyway. Or, worse, if they are opposed to the proposed action, they will slow-roll it. Frustrated action officers are prone to fussing about this, but there isn't much they can do. As a result, this system produces all-things-to-all-people solutions that often lead to mediocrity.

I took on this problem two ways. First, for an issue that really mattered to me, I would always give a short suspense. This was not intended to bull-rush anyone into folding their position; rather, it was intended to get the many organizations working on the matter to start on it sooner rather than later. Second, I used the NATO "silence" procedure I learned while in command of JC Lisbon. Under this procedure, if an answer is not received by a suspense date, then concurrence is assumed. Perfect! You had to answer the paper on time or lose the opportunity to have a voice. So much for bureaucratic delay—it almost always worked.

Another technique was to create special organizations specifically designed to circumvent bureaucracy. I did this for special classified programs I didn't want held hostage to the bureaucracy, particularly those that might make an immediate difference for our troops.

I didn't always win. In fact, I often joked that, in retirement, I would become a cartoonist, not due to any particular skill or wit, but because I already had a mental draft of my first cartoon. It would portray a bureaucrat sitting at a desk with a full in-box and an empty out-box and a sign on the desk saying: "My job was created because someone once made a mistake."

One of the key tools in slaying bureaucracy and getting things done is to hire talented personal staff. I was blessed with executive assistants, deputy executive assistants, and aides who arrived at the office before me and stayed long after I departed. People from all the services like Navy captain Ross Myers, Air Force colonel Bruce "Sheriff" McClintock, Marine lieutenant colonel Kyle Ellison, Army lieutenant colonel Janice Chen, and many others were instrumental in any success the Vice Squad achieved. I always tried to keep in mind my own prior indentured servitude in positions like theirs. I made it a point never to enter the office on a weekend unless there was an ongoing major crisis. Most of my work could be done on the classified systems I had in my office in my quarters. I wanted them to spend more time with their families.

At the end of the day, leveraging bureaucracy to do what it does well and avoid what it does poorly is accomplished through personal relationships—with leaders, action officers, or the administrative people who support them. I cannot emphasize enough the old adage that much more is accomplished with honey than vinegar, a lesson that took years for me to learn and served me well as the vice chairman.

Nowhere was this truer than in the White House Situation Room.

TOP Talking about Syria inside the Situation Room *Pete Souza/Obama Presidential Library*

BOTTOM Gen. Marty Dempsey (*right*) was a fantastic boss and partner, and we were interchangeable in the Situation Room. *Defense Department photo*

The Situation Room

I estimate that I attended around 1,200 meetings in the White House Situation Room during my four years as VCJCS. It demanded more time than any of my other roles, and understandably so.

The room is actually within a complex centered on a windowless room in the West Wing located not far from the entrance to the building and adjacent to the White House Mess. The Sit Room itself is compact but large enough to hold a long conference table with perhaps eight comfortable chairs on each side, additional smaller chairs packed against the wall for "plus ones," and of course a chair at the end of the table. There are a couple of large screens for video teleconferences at the opposite end, with a few more screens along the side walls. There are a couple of other smaller meeting rooms in the immediate vicinity, and the communications and information center for the White House is next door.

The complex hosts a variety of meeting types, including internal White House strategy sessions and higher-level meetings involving the interagency. The president chairs National Security Council (NSC) meetings. NSC

Principals Committee meetings have the same composition except for the president and are chaired by the national security advisor. NSC Deputies Committee meetings are chaired by a deputy national security advisor. Lower-level meetings known as Interagency Policy Committee meetings are held elsewhere, usually in the Eisenhower Executive Office Building. A capable staff manages the tight transitions between the many meetings that cycle in and out of the complex during the day.

Although it varies with each administration, the discussion of a particular issue generally starts with a brief introduction from the person running the meeting. It continues with an intelligence overview provided by someone from the Office of the Director of National Intelligence, backed up by someone from the Central Intelligence Agency. Then the issue at hand is discussed by the participants, which normally include representatives from the State Department, the Office of the Secretary of Defense, the Joint Chiefs of Staff, the Treasury Department, the Office of the Attorney General, our mission at the United Nations, the intelligence community, and any other departments, ambassadors, combatant commanders, or others as appropriate.

A member of the NSC legal team is always present to weigh in on the issue being discussed. The lawyers often remind whatever group is in attendance that there are only three legally authorized uses of force under the UN Charter: legitimate self-defense (including collective self-defense) of a nation against an imminent or ongoing attack; a UN Security Council resolution authorizing the use of force; and an invitation from a sovereign nation to help with an internal matter.

I emphasize this point because international and domestic law are seldom mentioned in the blogosphere or by the talking heads appearing on television news shows. This is mostly because few of them have ever spent any time in the Situation Room facing a real crisis. They thus have little appreciation for how profoundly various legal considerations can shape the contours of our action—or lack thereof—in response to crises and other world events.

In my experience, Sit Room meetings resulted in several possible outcomes. The group could make decisions appropriate to the level of the meeting or reach consensus on recommendations to be passed up to the next level. Often the issue was simply too complex to cover adequately in one meeting, or the discussion was not productive enough, or not enough of a consensus was achieved, which resulted either in another meeting on the same subject or the issue being kicked back down to the next lower level for more work. Many meetings were required for the most difficult issues we faced, such as troop drawdowns from Iraq or Afghanistan, operations in Syria, or potential use of force anywhere else in the world.

Caps on numbers of troops in the Iraq and Afghanistan theaters and specified troop drawdown ramps were a source of considerable frustration for the Department of Defense, especially for those in the field. I could find sympathy with the administration's close control over these numbers: they were wary of the unconstrained growth in demand into which the military has often fallen over history. Indeed, sometimes it seemed as though commanders in the field felt as though any request should be approved as an entitlement, no matter the cost or impact.

On the other hand, troop caps led to behaviors that would have been comical had they not been so inefficient and, in some cases, tragic. For example, to maintain the lid on numbers of troops in Iraq or Afghanistan, the Army would deploy combat aviation brigades without their helicopter maintenance personnel, substituting civilian maintenance personnel who didn't count toward the cap. This broke the integrity that is so important to a military unit while putting many people at risk and costing more money.

While I didn't always agree with my colleagues from either the Bush or Obama administrations, I was impressed by nearly all of them. Steve Hadley and Denis McDonough were expert—and highly collegial—in running the many complex meetings required to keep the security policy trains moving. Despite his sometimes-gruff countenance, John Brennan was one of the most moral and compassionate men I've ever met. Michael Morell was the most thoroughgoing and clearly spoken intelligence analyst I've encountered. Michèle Flournoy brought together grace, expertise, and toughness in a powerful combination. Eric Edelman was a seasoned and collegial professional. Jim Miller was a highly skilled and experienced collaborator on nuclear and missile defense issues. Lisa Monaco is the smartest law enforcement expert I've known. Avril Haines, who, as of this writing, is the director of national intelligence, was the instant authority in the room on any issue of international law. These and others were highly intelligent and patriotic men and women who drove themselves literally to exhaustion doing the best they could for our country. To a person, they kept the best interests of our nation closest to their hearts. Many are my enduring friends based on the collegiality we developed while tackling the difficult issues of our day.

Despite the philosophical differences between the Bush and Obama administrations, once these people were given a degree of separation away from political partisanship, it is surprising how closely their views lined up regarding security. Indeed, in either administration, I never once heard any reference to domestic political considerations or tactics in the Sit Room during a national security deliberation. I'm not naive about this, but to the extent those discussions occurred in either administration, they often happened out of the earshot of us nonpolitical interagency players.

That is not to say I have no critique to offer, for there are a number of unhelpful habits any administration tends to fall into in the process of national security decision-making, including the tendency for the NSC staff meeting agenda to be driven by the most immediate crisis or the president's next meeting or speech. Sadly, the press of events always left little time for long-term strategic discussions.

The different backgrounds of the attendees also made for interesting differences in point of view. Diplomats generally have faith in their ability to solve today's problem today in a meeting with a foreign counterpart, using their skill in influencing a competitor's intent and finding solutions acceptable to both sides. They believe Daniele Varè's adage that "diplomacy is the art of letting someone else have it your way." They *should* feel this way: they are our country's principal negotiators and the first line of defense for our interests. They take pride in the elegantly crafted memo. But they often end up pushing unrealistic ideas and have little understanding of campaign planning.

On the other hand, warriors want to solve problems in the context of a campaign (and not necessarily a military campaign). They view issues from the perspective of an opponent's capability (since his intent can change overnight). They *should* feel this way: the military carries the burden when things go wrong or all other methods have been exhausted. Diplomats maintain laudable faith in soft power versus the warrior's similar belief tempered by the realization there are rarely enough resources placed behind soft power to make it really work.

I lump all these phenomena together under the rubric of "diplomats are from Venus and warriors are from Mars." Neither side is wrong; they just have different approaches that can be extremely effective when woven together with the other elements of national power, including economic, informational, legal, intelligence, and civil society power.

One tendency common to both groups is for the first question in a crisis to be "what are our near-term options?" rather than asking "what is the deep history of this situation, and what are our long-term interests?" Moreover, the answer does not always include "what happens next?" especially when the use of force—which has a long tail—is being considered. We have an unfortunate history of people, usually those who have never experienced combat, not bothering to ask these important questions.

We spent a lot of time in these meetings on the theoretical, trying to have it both ways. Overly ambitious, all-encompassing, idealist end states clashed with an environment in which our adversaries had a vote, we were working with serious resource constraints, and there were cultural factors we did not always understand. This was particularly true of the assessments of the conflict in Afghanistan in which I participated in both administrations.

Other times we found ourselves taking counsel of our fears, worrying that strong deterrent actions might provoke the very thing we were trying to deter. Do you place more forces in Europe to deter malicious Russian action, or would such a deployment actually trigger Russian aggression? This tendency was sometimes influenced by what I dubbed negative intelligence community bias. After all, intelligence analysts are trained to find and reveal the worst things that can happen. They need to be able to do this, but this tendency can result in a bias toward discussing all the bad things that might happen if we *do* act and not the bad things that might happen if we *don't* act. In addition to a desire to only take unanimous recommendations to the president, this often led to paralysis by analysis.

There were times that, when we actually did decide, I grew frustrated by how we failed to explain our decisions, particularly when action was limited by adherence to international law. Moreover, we sometimes acted as though *notification* to an ally or friend constituted *consultation*, which was an act of hubris normally interpreted as arrogance by our partners.

Yet, despite all these criticisms of the interagency process, I left the job with a real appreciation for the vast gulf between those actually making policy under terribly complex and time-constrained circumstances and those on the outside criticizing the outcomes. Americans need to understand that when one settles into a seat at the Sit Room table—including the one occupied by the commander-in-chief—the world suddenly looks completely different from the way it did on the campaign trail or within the blogosphere.

Everything changes from this vantage point, which is where real adults with global responsibility are charged with protecting our security, prosperity, and values in an extraordinarily complex world. Decisions in that room are enabled by the finest intelligence on the planet, the most comprehensive view of cross-cutting resource limitations, a global view of the other problems competing for attention, accountability for the lives of men and women exposed to danger, and a deep responsibility to uphold American values. This group must also account for the rules-based international order we created, including all of the legal restraints on use of force we put into place—and that we violate at peril of inviting others to do the same. When our adversaries are unconstrained by international law or the truth, we do the opposite because people across the globe count on the United States to do the right thing. It is why we have more allies today than any nation in history.

Unlike the op-ed writer or talking head on cable television complaining loudly from within one issue's stovepipe, the president's team has to look at the entire surface of the problem and employ all instruments of national power. As such, it is deeply frustrating to see how most Americans' information stream on national security issues is corrupted because so much of it is either politically motivated, misinformed, overreactive, or simplistic—or all four.

Among the most effective meetings we held were tabletop exercises. The first one we conducted with the NSC staff at the deputies' level was based on what would happen if Israel preemptively struck Iran's nuclear program. I instigated this exercise over my concern that few of my colleagues had *really* thought through the strategic, operational, tactical, and messaging implications if such a major event happened. So we deputies gathered in the Sit Room on one Saturday morning with doughnuts and coffee in hand, working through a scenario developed by the Joint Staff in the Pentagon.

The exercise raised previously unconsidered questions and brought new insights into the interagency process, which led to far greater understanding of this issue. Because it would be very difficult to convene a deputies or principals meeting late at night to determine the immediate U.S. reaction, the exercise left us much better prepared to handle such an event.

We did several other similar exercises—again, normally on a weekend morning—covering a variety of important subjects that shed a lot of light on what they might feel like in real life. Each one went a long way toward better informing policy decisions. They are a precious use of interagency time.

These events caused me to put together a "break glass" book for each of several potential crises with the latest disposition of our forces and other essential information for each one since I thought such an event would always happen at the worst possible time, and Dempsey or I would quickly find ourselves at the Sit Room table expected to have all the answers. These books were frequently updated and kept locked in my safe at home, at the ready for a no-notice Sunday morning meeting in the wake of a major crisis-precipitating event. Fortunately, I never had to use one.

Most principals or deputies had little knowledge of military matters, including our capabilities and limitations, command-and-control protocols, rules of engagement, and tactics for executing operations—especially our unique lingo. Thus, one of my roles was to explain courses of action in a readily understandable way to the attendees. The worst thing I could do was to appear to be slipping something past them using a complex explanation that people would be too embarrassed to admit they didn't completely understand. These people may not have known much about the military, but they were excellent bullshit detectors.

Getting this done required putting myself in my colleagues' shoes, avoiding jargon, and putting a lot of effort into simplifying the concepts without being pedantic. I impressed on my staff the need to distill whatever information we were trying to get across into the clearest possible, yet still meaningful, explanations for civilians. I'm proud that we succeeded most of the time. Of all the kind things Secretary of Defense Ash Carter said about me at my retirement ceremony, one of the most meaningful was "Sandy is able to explain things without condescension or oversimplification."

We deputies spent so much time together addressing fairly difficult and often depressing issues that we tried hard to keep a sense of humor. We often joked that the principals—the heads of the various government departments involved in security matters—should attend our meetings as back-benchers so we could actually get something accomplished. One of the many practices tolerated at these meetings was note-passing, which allowed people to consult independently and discretely. Of course, etiquette indicated that one must never look at the content of a note someone else was passing. But I have to admit that a few I both wrote and received could be pretty funny at times.

Serving in the interagency decision space was a sobering experience that provided a much better appreciation for how hard it is to formulate truly effective policy answers. And, as I experienced as VCJCS, the questions have only become more difficult in a security environment that grows more complex every day.

Anchor #5:
Lead Change

*"The people who think they're crazy enough
to change the world are the ones who do."*

Steve Jobs

Challenge the Assumptions

"All progress depends on the unreasonable man."
George Bernard Shaw

"Equilibrium is the precursor to death."
Richard Pascale

Lead the Creative Process

"Talent perceives differences; genius unity."
William Butler Yeats

"Innovation occurs at the intersection of creativity and courage."
Chris Darby

Overcome Resistance

*"The only thing harder than getting a new idea into the military
mind is getting an old idea out."*
Liddell Hart

"If you don't like change, you will like irrelevance even less."
Gen. Erick Shinseki

Sail Upwind!

*"If the highest aim of a captain were to preserve his ship, he
would keep it in port forever."*
Thomas Aquinas

"He who doesn't risk doesn't drink champagne."
Slavic proverb

ANCHOR 5
Lead Change

CHALLENGE THE ASSUMPTIONS

There's an old saying that "progress begins when you deny the current concept." Change leaders challenge the fundamental reasons that a concept or process is broken or that the prevailing environment is stable. They embrace disruption and restlessly look around the corner trying to spot something they can improve. It usually means overcoming one's anchor bias (in which one relies on the first piece of information presented) or confirmation bias (the tendency to selectively interpret new evidence as confirmation of one's preexisting beliefs) about an existing topic.

This can be incredibly hard because so many organizations grow into habits based on assumptions within seemingly settled circumstances. In *Surfing the Edge of Chaos*, Richard Pascale and his coauthors point out that when a living system evolves into a state of equilibrium, it's less responsive to potential disruptive change, which places it at great risk. IBM nearly failed in this regard in retaining its bias for mainframe computers even as its engineers foresaw the emergence of the personal computer. Kodak, Polaroid,

Blockbuster, and the dodo bird all failed because they missed imminent disruptive change. I experienced this tendency surprisingly frequently during my career. Examples are sprinkled throughout earlier sections of this book.

Innovation lives at three horizons of how technology and concept interact (many people interpret the three horizons as temporal; rather, they are conceptual). The first involves incremental technical improvements to an existing concept. This is the easiest and most common type of innovation: make the radar see a little further. The second horizon is out-of-the-box technical improvements yet still in service of an existing concept. Think stealth or precision-guided weapons. The third horizon is by far the hardest yet holds the highest leverage: rethinking an entire concept. The first two horizons are where American scientists, engineers, and the military excel. But it takes a special type of mind—like a Steve Jobs, or a set of large minds in a small group—to rethink the concepts that technology empowers.

LEAD THE CREATIVE PROCESS

Leaders must enable the creativity that drives change by leveraging their lifelong learning and relentless curiosity, both inside and outside their field, to either personally lead or directly enable the creative process. A restless mind is constantly making connections: most creative acts involve a synergy between two disparate ideas or technologies. A concept meets a technology. A technology spawns a concept. Technologies meet other technologies. Art meets engineering. Of how good ideas are born, novelist Stephen King says they "seem to come quite literally from nowhere . . . two previously unrelated ideas come together and make something new under the sun." Finding or enabling these synergies is leaders' business.

One of the greatest thinkers of all time, Albert Einstein, used "gedankenexperiment," or thought experiments, to help him understand knotty physical issues and think through the answers. This technique is about minds drifting "aimfully," working away both consciously and subconsciously at a problem. Meanwhile, creativity starves unless it's endowed with an almost flippant frivolity that can unlock the kind of intellectual risk-taking that yields truly new ideas. Innovation also demands spontaneity, which tends to wane with maturity—as leaders grow older, they need to resist this behavior.

I am frequently reminded of something the great American novelist Paul Horgan wrote: "You know the great secret? . . . It is to keep alive the child inside, alongside the man growing up."[1]

Innovation also depends on the hard work of getting to the simplicity on the far side of complexity. As Steve Jobs said, "Simplicity involves digging through the depth of complexity. To be truly simple, you have to go really deep."

Leading truly creative people can be challenging, for it demands a blend of empathy, failure tolerance, personality tolerance, ego stroking, and firmness. "Creatives" need to be enveloped in a safety net that enables their work. It's all about giving limited guidance and then letting people go crazy in a box. Innovative leaders relish the thought of others improving their ideas and give people the room to do so.

OVERCOME RESISTANCE

Change almost always meets resistance, and it takes a unique leader to push through it. As someone with a lifelong passion for leading change, I gradually understood why and how organizations resist it.

Change is hard. It demands that people suspend their disbelief. It requires extra work from people accustomed to a comfortable routine. Personal jealousy toward the person who has the new idea can be poisonous. People can oppose it out of fear they won't understand it and will be diminished in the organization or might even lose their job. Perhaps the change threatens an existing structure or a franchise. Change can also arrive at an inconvenient time for an organization, such as during a period of high activity on other fronts. Resistance can even come from how the change is announced.

One useful method for navigating barriers is what I label the "concentric circles of change." The innermost circle is *ignorance*: some people have not yet been exposed to the idea and simply need to be educated. *Denial* is about being in the initial stages of resistance to a new idea. In the circle known as *vicious compliance*, people realize they have no choice but to implement the idea but are determined to show it won't work. When people begin to understand the idea's value but unintentionally make mistakes or misrepresent it,

---

[1] Horgan, *Everything to Live For* (New York: Farrar, Straus, and Giroux, 1968), 90.

they are in the circle of *well-intended misapplication*. Finally, the outermost circle is populated by people who understand and accept the idea and serve as *culture-carrying advocates*.

When speaking with subordinates involved in a change effort, I've found it necessary to discern in which circle they reside because different circles require different treatment. Someone who is unaware of the idea requires a different approach from a denier, vicious complier, mis-applier, or accepter. Coaxing an organization through needed change usually requires a leader to leverage all elements of power appropriate to the task. Sometimes it's ugly, but it must be done.

SAIL UPWIND!

The best change leaders I've known have had a bias toward action rather than inaction. A leader can challenge all the assumptions and set the conditions for a new idea and still fail. Those I've known who stepped out and led real change—and there are precious few—understood that innovation without personal risk and the grinding work of transition is useless energy spent.

Leading change is not for the faint of heart. To succeed, a leader has to enlist every leadership characteristic I've described in the other anchors in this book. One must call on intense self-awareness, lead people and organizations effectively, push hard on quality execution, and create an atmosphere where creativity flourishes. It also requires a profoundly personal mixture of courage and determination. Thus, leading change comes full circle to leading yourself. Fear of failure will extinguish a change process every time. You have to be willing to completely buy into the risk associated with the change, whether it threatens your career or your financial or even physical health. Even though one should avoid uncalculated risk, having an almost flippant disregard for current career or financial well-being is a common characteristic of successful change leaders. As frightening as it seems, they know they can always do something else in life.

To quote novelist Stephen King, "The scariest moment is just before you start." Roy Disney said, "The way to get started is to stop talking and start doing." Indeed, getting started—kicking the system into motion, overcoming your natural procrastination, getting past admiring the new idea, and taking the first real step is the hardest part. Once the journey begins, everything begins to flow. But nobody will tear down the obstacles in your path for you. Only your spouse is likely to encourage you when the going gets rough. You have to be unwilling to accept "no" for an answer from both outside and inside your organization—and you might be surprised how resistance melts in front of that kind of determination. So go for it!

TOP President Obama informs Jessica Buchanan's family of her rescue from Somalia immediately after giving the State of the Union speech in 2012. *Pete Souza/Obama Presidential Library*

BOTTOM Frank Kendall and I brought together a group intended to improve our nation's infrastructure for nuclear command, control, and communications. *Department of Defense photo*

The Outside World
Inside the Beltway

I entered office as VCJCS only three months before Gen. Marty Dempsey became chairman, at the end of the first turbulent decade of a new century. We immediately forged a terrific partnership. I'm not throwing shade on any of our predecessors in believing we were closer in our beliefs and actions than any previous combination of our nation's two most senior military officers.

Together with our allies and other partners, our nation faced a legion of security challenges: an ambitious and aggressive China; a belligerent and resentful Russia; a recalcitrant North Korea; a deeply unstable Syria; a defiant and treacherous Iran; a destabilized Middle East and the extremism flowing from it; and increasingly pervasive transnational criminal activity, including drug and human smuggling as well as cybercrime. Each of these actors despises the global operating system—sometimes called the rules-based international order—our forebears created after World War II and are emboldened to attack it.

This system includes institutions; financial rules and norms; the dollar as the world's reserve currency; international laws; our many alliances, such as NATO and those in the Pacific; Internet standards; and a host of other processes established by the United States and its allies. Despite a constant undercurrent of conflict during its tenure, the system has maintained our freedom and prosperity, greatly benefiting the United States.

As Hal Brands and Charles Edel point out in their book *The Lessons of Tragedy*, this is not the first time such a system has emerged and ended up under attack. The Peace of Westphalia emerged after the Thirty Years' War. The Concert of Europe emerged from the Napoleonic Wars. Our current system grew out of the ashes of two world wars. Each time, generations gradually forgot the bloody wars that result when authoritarian nationalism rises and the glue holding the prevailing system together melts.

It is understandable that, during the confusion of the early twenty-first century, the nation's national security decision-making apparatus would struggle for a framework to enable it to focus coherently on all of these issues. Henry Kissinger's adage "No country can act wisely simultaneously in every part of the globe at every moment in time" was very much in play. When many thought we were experiencing "the end of history," the exact opposite occurred.

When we entered office, the United States possessed no cogent statement of "grand strategy." Things seemed so much simpler when "containment" of communism was the nation's one-word grand strategy. That strategy largely worked, with the notable exception of our intervention in Vietnam. The Bush administration's grand strategy seemed to focus principally on the spread of democracy as the key vector that would presumably usher in an era of global peace and stability. That strategy landed on the rocks in Iraq and Afghanistan because so much of the world is simply not culturally prepared for democracy's unique features.

The Obama administration's 2010 National Security Strategy was long on noble imperatives but lacked a simple organizing construct that would help us make sense of such a dynamic world. Early in my tenure as VCJCS, I decided to try to derive the grand strategy we were actually using based on my observations of the many discussions we had in the Situation Room. I came up with the following: "The grand strategy of the United States is to protect our national interests within a rules-based international order, using force as a last resort, avoiding entanglements or antagonizing major competitors, and advancing our prosperity and universal values wherever possible."

It was too long to be a classic grand strategy, but it was what we were actually doing. Each word was important. We would think of our own interests first. We would adhere to long-standing international laws and norms. We would use diplomacy before force. We would, if at all possible, avoid long and costly wars. We would avoid a dangerous major power confrontation. And we would hold ourselves and others accountable to what we believe are universal values. I found much to agree with in this strategic approach, and it was something the administration appeared to believe in and within which we could provide military advice.

Dempsey and I didn't want to make up that advice as we went along. We sought a bedrock framework for credible, consistent, and clear military advice regarding both the use of force and the Department of Defense's investment strategy. We settled on a set of abstract, enduring, and prioritized national security interests to guide our thinking. We tried to derive these interests loosely from expressions within the National Security Strategy so as to maintain alignment with the concept of civilian control of the military. They are actually consistent with Dwight D. Eisenhower's second campaign for the presidency under the theme "Peace, Prosperity, and Progress." We listed these interests as follows:

- *Survival of the nation.* Deterrence of a major nuclear attack on our country is the high end of the spectrum of this interest. However, an event unraveling the fabric of our society or our democracy, or fundamentally changing the character of our nation, lands here as well.
- *Prevention of catastrophic attacks on the nation.* This reflects any attack on the United States short of an existential attack. Threats to this interest could range from a limited nuclear attack from a nation such as Iran or North Korea to a major cyberattack on our infrastructure to a large-scale terrorist attack.

- *Protection of the global operating system.* This includes the global financial system, freedom of navigation, and the major institutions that are the framework for global stability, such as the United Nations, the World Bank, the International Monetary Fund, and Internet standards.
- *Secure, confident, and reliable allies and partners.* This includes the nations that depend on the United States to augment their security, including formal alliances in Europe and Asia as well as close partnerships with many friendly nations.
- *Protection of American citizens abroad.* This speaks to our ability to protect the people serving our country and private citizens who might be traveling overseas.
- *Protection and extension, where possible, of universal values.* This includes not only protection of human rights and democratic ideals but also many forms of humanitarian assistance.

Although we teased these interests out of the National Security Strategy, the interagency was a bit reluctant to use them explicitly. After all, interests should be explicitly determined and prioritized by senior civilians, not senior military officers. Some might state them another way or prioritize them differently, including placing universal values much higher on the list. Some might not want to be bound by something as clear and explicit, preferring instead a kind of useful ambiguity. But at least Marty and I had them, and they really clarified my thinking.

They were particularly valuable because they represented *risk to what* as a hierarchically superior idea to *risk from what*, which made more sense to me for formulating decisions and recommendations. In fact, we reconceived the chairman's annual risk assessment to Congress—which was previously organized by regions, which is more or less "risk from what"—around this framework. The new framework accounted for threats that are hard to describe as coming from a particular region, such as cyberattacks or terrorism. Perhaps most importantly, we used them as a guide to using force.

Recommendations on the use of force are tricky but terribly important—the blood of our precious women and men is at stake. All too often the term of art "vital interest" is invoked as the tripwire—blurted out in the Situation Room or by a talking head on television—for when we should or should not use force. But it's too easy to employ this term carelessly or as after-the-fact justification for a decision expediently made. Rather, our list of abstract, enduring, and prioritized interests gave us the discipline to get past those irritants to make fundamentally sound recommendations.

How did we do it? We would cast any given situation against our list of interests to uncover the intersections. The degree to which a situation intersected these interests regarding *how many* were affected, the *priority* of those interests, and the *degree* to which they were affected yielded their "correlation." Where correlation was high, we would recommend more national instruments of power brought to bear on the situation. With very high correlation and with no other option, we would be more likely to recommend the use of force, including willingness to do so unilaterally, with greater risk, greater financial cost, greater opportunity cost, and a harder push against the strictures of international law. The reverse would be true. Moreover, we would not recommend taking action simply to preserve the nation's "credibility" or to feel good that we had "done something, anything." Further, we would only recommend acting if there was a clear and achievable end state—something not always considered in the halls of power. We also had a corollary that, in protecting a low-level interest, we would use extra caution in recommending the use of force if it could result in an increased threat to a higher-level interest.

This approach largely explains Dempsey's and my assessment of the many crises we addressed during our tenure. In short, we were willing to send our people into harm's way for something that mattered a great deal, and now we had a way to answer that question. It allowed us to confidently resist poorly thought-through clarion calls for the use of force in several actual situations.

There is no better example of this than the most prominent situation during my tenure—namely, whether and how the United States might use its various instruments of power in the political, ethnic, tribal, and religious cauldron of Syria. This question had arisen before my tenure. Once President Obama stated that Bashar al-Assad must go, the matter took on greater urgency, as the interagency now needed to grapple with how to get that accomplished without violating the tenets of the grand strategy I articulated earlier, including adhering to international law.

Much of the discussion of providing support to the "moderate opposition" in Syria remains classified. But a major question we faced was whether and how to use overt military capability to place enough pressure on Assad that he would negotiate a change of government. We held a lot of Sit Room meetings to consider this question. In the process, the Department of Defense presented a host of different options, most of which centered on how we might arm and train the opposition.

There were several dimensions to this problem. Which groups would we support, and from which parts of Syria? What kind of weapons would we provide? Would we include man-portable surface-to-air missiles? Where would the opposition be trained? How long would that take? Would they be willing to leave their homes long enough to do it? Could we trust that the weapons we supplied would not fall into the wrong hands? How much would it all cost, and from where would the money come? To what degree would we support the opposition once we put them back into Syria? Where would we insert them? What would a follow-on governing arrangement look like? Could we trust the opposition to respect human rights?

We were also challenged to present options for establishing a no-fly zone. Many in the interagency retained comfortable memories of the Iraq no-fly zone during Operation Southern Watch. But there was a big difference. While Iraq kept one old surface-to-air missile battery in its southern no-fly zone, Russia helped Syria assemble a formidable integrated air defense system with a mixture of old and new missile systems in large numbers. And many of these systems were probably manned at least partially by Russians. Even the Israelis, when conducting strikes to protect their interests, struck from outside the envelope of these lethal systems. We could establish a no-fly zone, but it would cost a lot, demand a legion of assets that we might need in a pinch somewhere else, and potentially result in a lost or captured U.S. airman. Meanwhile, it would not create a safe zone, as it could not prevent Syrian artillery or other ground forces from taking action on the ground.

A few of the suggestions we received from Congress and other corners were unhelpful and distracting. One member thought we could simply place

Patriot missile batteries along the Turkish border to prevent Syrian aircraft from flying, not realizing the limitations on the range of those systems and that they could end up being attacked by artillery from within Syria. Another suggested using expensive Tomahawk missiles to crater Syrian runways, not realizing that Russian-supplied aircraft were built to operate from runways hastily repaired by bulldozers. We had better ideas, such as taking out Syrian pilots in their barracks. But none of them passed the essential tests of international law.

At the end of each meeting, after we presented new recommendations, the National Security Council legal team would present their view on the legality of the option. None of the three authorized uses of force seemed to apply in the case of Syria. Indeed, we were left with the uncomfortable notion that, as reprehensible as their actions were, Russia was actually acting within international law in its support for the Assad regime while we were considering actions at the edge of the law or beyond.

So we were left to consider whether stepping into the gray area of a "legitimacy" justification would be wise. Such a justification sits outside international law and would normally only be invoked if a coalition of nations was taking on a major issue such as genocide (which occurred when NATO overthrew the Milosevic dictatorship in Serbia). Care must be taken in doing this sort of thing. Acting outside of technical, customary international law, however justifiable, threatens our legitimacy as a major power and opens the door for other nations, including antagonists like Russia, to use the same arguments to justify actions with which we would disagree (although it does not seem to have prevented their aggression against Ukraine). It could even expose those executing such an approach to international criminal sanction. We left nearly every meeting tied in knots.

The entire national security team—Dempsey and I included—continued to resist the urge, coming at us sometimes from humanitarian quarters of the policy community, to send in a large ground force to deal with the problem once and for all. Such an intervention would be costly, push on the question of legality, and in any case fail to pass the test of correlation of interests. Yet the Syrian civil war ground on, with more and more civilians killed, eventually resulting in a new level of crisis: the Assad government's use of chemical weapons against its own population. This was a new outrage, and President Obama suggested to the media in August 2012 that "a red line for us is we start seeing a whole bunch of chemical weapons moving around or being utilized."

Time and time again, the intelligence community tried, in conjunction with a host of other entities, including nongovernmental organizations, to pin down without doubt that the Syrians had used these awful weapons. Slowly the evidence accumulated that Assad indeed was using chemical weapons, which was a gross violation of international norms but not international law. The question was: what do we do about it? We could conduct airstrikes on weapons or production facilities, but there was a great deal of concern over the potential release of a chemical plume that could do far more harm than good.

Working together with U.S. Central Command, we formulated a set of carefully tailored strikes that would send a clear message to Assad about chemical weapons usage and his military's vulnerability to additional attacks. There remained one question: would the American people—and, by extension, Congress—support such an action? This question intersected with the War Powers Resolution, passed in 1973 during the Nixon administration, which outlines the restrictions Congress placed on the president's use of force during a crisis.

By now it is well-known that, even after the interagency principals recommended that the strikes go forward, President Obama decided he would not do so without congressional approval. I believe he made this decision for several reasons. First, this was more than a small strike to remove a group of terrorists—it was potentially opening an entirely new theater of military operations. Second, as reprehensible as Assad's use of chemical weapons was, our action against a sovereign nation would be interpreted by many as violation of international law, and the president wanted the stronger case that would be supported by a congressional vote. He didn't want to let the members of what he viewed as a weak and divided Congress—many, if not most, of whom looked after their own interests before those of the nation—off the hook, especially if the strikes didn't accomplish their strategic objective. And there was also that always-looming question of "what comes next?"

After the president's decision, a number of deputies (including myself) and principals conducted group briefs to Congress, and it quickly became clear there was no unanimity for strikes. Members who previously urged action were now suddenly reluctant to own the responsibility by actually voting on it, perhaps due to having seen how they or others were held accountable for their Iraq War votes during previous elections. It's amazing how calls for action are quickly tempered when one suddenly assumes at least partial ownership of the action.

Candidly, I was not disappointed that the strikes did not go forward. To be sure, I spent a great deal of time with U.S. Central Command refining the target list. At first it was too small, and it didn't send the right messages. We spent a great deal of time trying to avoid harming any Syrians, including members of the military. We produced the best list we could, but I was concerned about what would happen after the initial strikes. Their intent was simple and limited: get Assad to quit using chemical weapons while sending a signal that we could do more if needed. Despite what many might think, the potential strikes were never intended to overthrow Syria's leader. I was concerned that people would never understand this in the sound-bite simplicity of media coverage and that, even if the strikes had the intended effect, they would have been deemed a failure if Assad did not disappear. I was further worried that mission creep would set in, especially if the strikes did not have their intended effect, and that pressure would grow for even stronger action. It was a quagmire waiting to happen, and simply didn't correlate strongly with our prioritized list of interests.

In the end, Congress never approved the action. However, the imminence of these strikes clearly energized Russia into increasing pressure on their client state Syria. What seemed like a flip comment from Secretary of State John Kerry that we wouldn't strike if Syria would agree to get rid of its chemical weapons suddenly got things moving. The timing was tight and fortuitous—had the Russians been paying attention, they would have seen that the United States was backing off its threat to strike before they applied intense pressure on Syria to give in on its weapons program.

In the end we were lucky rather than good. A comprehensive international effort, led by the Department of Defense's deputy secretary for acquisition, technology, and logistics, Frank Kendall, assembled a mobile chemical weapons destruction and movement capability. This effort removed most (although, as we later saw, not all) of these weapons and their production capability from Syria. Several of our allies took considerable risks in supporting the effort.

It was not long after the chemical weapons piece was resolved that the interagency began to sense that President Obama seemed to be more willing to move into the legal gray zone and take more overt action to help the moderate opposition. International pressure was mounting over the death toll and severe refugee crisis that was wracking Syria and its neighbors.

At precisely this moment, the situation in Syria entered its second major phase with the sudden rise of the Islamic State in Iraq and Syria, otherwise known as ISIS, and its rapid takeover of eastern Syria and western Iraq. Almost overnight, a major threat to our enormous investment in Iraq emerged from an entity that also promised to attack our allies in Europe and even the United States. This opened up an entirely new vista of international law. ISIS rapidly swept into Iraq, and, for a variety of reasons, the Iraqi Army melted in front of it. Some pointed fingers that the United States and its partners had done a poor job of training the Iraqi Army and then abandoned it when we pulled out at the end of 2011. Perhaps, but the cultural obstacles to overcome in manning, training, and equipping a competent army in a corrupt system, with three highly sectarian religious components and with no tradition of service or competence, were steep, a lesson we were to later learn in Afghanistan.

The pullout from Iraq was a pernicious issue that culminated through a frustrating series of meetings over the course of the summer and fall of 2011. Two powerful forces were at work. First, it was clear that the Obama administration, which took the reins vowing to end the war in Iraq, was not inclined to work diplomatic overtime to maintain a large force on the ground. Second, the only way the Iraqis would feel they had regained their sovereignty was for the U.S. presence to end.

The mechanism for the U.S. departure became the Iraqis' unwillingness to negotiate a status of forces agreement with the United States and its allies. The absence of such an agreement would expose U.S. forces to unwelcome legal risk. It was clear that if the Iraqis really wanted us to stay, it was a simple matter to reach an agreement that was good enough for both sides. But it was not to be.

The move toward pulling out was bitterly resisted by those on the ground in Iraq and in the Pentagon as well as by a number of angry members of Congress, all of whom felt the military's job in Iraq was not complete. We in the military were disappointed with what seemed to be the expedient nature of the policy decision. I felt the same sentiment as others that, regardless of one's beliefs of the wisdom of the invasion of Iraq in the first place, we had invested a lot of blood and treasure there and were leaving before the job was done.

But in all honesty, I can't help believe that many American soldiers are alive today who would have otherwise been lost to improvised explosive devices or rockets employed by Sunni insurgents or Shia militias, all in the service of what in the grand scheme was protecting a medium-level U.S. national interest correlation in the wake of a questionable decision to invade in the first place. Moreover, there is no guarantee whatsoever that the continued presence of U.S. forces would have prevented the collapse in western Iraq to ISIS. The deep sectarian divides among Sunnis, Shias, and Kurds in the Iraqi Army and poor leadership among most of its officers set the conditions for failure. The preferential leadership of Iraq's prime minister, Nouri al-Maliki, for the Shia majority—and particularly his suppression of the Sunni minority—was the catalyst for the country's disintegration. ISIS was simply the mechanism. It all harkened back to the study I conducted for Fallon in 2007 before I moved to the Sixth Fleet.

ISIS now controlled a large swath of Iraqi Sunni territory, including the Mosul Dam, which required near-constant maintenance lest it fail with catastrophic effects downstream. Moreover, ISIS was committing daily atrocities against non-Arab or non-Sunni Muslim segments of the population in the areas it conquered, including mass murders of the Yazidi people in northwestern Iraq.

Because the group attacked a sovereign nation asking for our assistance, military action against ISIS was now fully justifiable under international law, including against their bases in Syria. There was only one problem: Nouri al-Maliki. He had proven to be nearly impossible to work with, and Obama was unwilling to use force to protect Iraq unless he could find a different partner. In the meantime, the U.S. military was only permitted to use force to protect American citizens and prevent human rights abuses.

Eventually Maliki was replaced by Hydar al-Abadi, who seemed more willing to acknowledge and support a unified Iraq. Now we were permitted to open up the aperture of use of force, so we expanded the number of acceptable ISIS targets and eventually commenced strike operations in Syria.

The operation to recover the Mosul Dam foreshadowed that the Iraqis would eventually be able to defeat ISIS with our indirect support. Central Command commander Gen. Lloyd Austin, who felt badly burned by remarks the president had made in a meeting over the loss of the dam, made the wise choice to insist that the recovery operation include both Kurdish Peshmerga forces and the Iraqi Counter Terrorism Service. Because we were prohibited from having our forward air controllers (known as JTACs, for Joint Terminal Attack Controllers) colocated with these forces, our special operators adapted and provided close-air support using drones and phone communications. Watching the Mosul Dam being retaken on UAV video, it appeared as though it was possible to bring Iraqis back together—at least temporarily—to push ISIS out.

There were a host of other difficult issues the nation's security policymaking process faced during my tenure. The case of Bowe Bergdahl was a classic. This young soldier walked out of his forward operating base in Afghanistan and was captured by the Taliban. There were strong indications, but no concrete proof, that he did so voluntarily, with estimates ranging from the possibility that he had simply gotten lost to that he had willingly defected. Over several years occasional evidence surfaced regarding his situation, and our special operators worked hard to find and rescue him. In the meantime, sensitive discussions began, with the Qataris as interlocutors, for the beginning of potential peace talks that could end the war in Afghanistan.

One of the premises undergirding the administration's thinking was that a gesture of goodwill on each side could lead to more serious negotiations. There were a host of factions on all sides of this issue, ranging from those who believed the Taliban were terrorists who must be destroyed rather than negotiated with to those who understood that nearly all insurgencies ultimately end with a political settlement. Bergdahl was stuck in the middle: the Taliban insisted on release of five of their senior members who were being held in Guantanamo, and the only thing they had to give in return was a soldier who might be a deserter. It goes without saying that Secretary of Defense Leon Panetta was acutely uncomfortable with agreeing to this deal, from both political and ethical perspectives.

However, as the discussions both in Qatar and in Washington, DC, ebbed and flowed, we began to receive indications that Bergdahl's health was declining. We faced the prospect of having allowed a U.S. soldier to die in captivity when we had the means to save him, which might also have the beneficial effect of kicking off serious negotiations. In the end, the politically divisive decision was taken to transfer the "GITMO Five" to Qatar, which would hold them more or less in house arrest for one year, in return for Bergdahl.

I have mixed emotions to this day over how this all played out. I tended to view the deal more as a prisoner exchange than negotiating with terrorists. After all, al-Qaeda were the real terrorists, and we viewed the Taliban legally as combatants. But who knew what the GITMO Five would do after their one-year quarantine in Qatar was complete? As it turned out, Bergdahl was subjected to pretty rough treatment at the hands of the Taliban. It wasn't a wonderful deal, but it freed Bergdahl under the philosophy that we never leave a soldier on the battlefield, especially if his status as a deserter was in doubt. As usual, people who were not personally responsible for difficult decisions used the issue for political gain.

Among my most important roles as VCJCS was to be the grease in the machinery between our special operations forces (SOF) and the chain of command through the secretary of defense to the president. Thanks to the well-trained and disciplined operators within our SOF community, the Obama administration gradually gained faith in the SOF's ability to execute complex operations. The raid to capture or kill Osama bin Laden (which occurred while I was in command of Northern Command) was a huge confidence-builder.

It is not a matter of simply approving these types of operations. Senior decisionmakers want to understand risk to mission, risk to force, the confidence level in the associated intelligence, the way potential detainees will be handled, host nation basing and transit permissions, whether to inform the leadership of other nations that might have interests at stake, and how and when the operation will be disclosed and discussed in the event of success or failure. In the case of the raid on Osama bin Laden, the decision process was not overly time-critical, which was a good thing due to the raid's momentous implications. But in some cases in which a hostage might be moved at any moment or the location of a terrorist target might be fleeting, the process timing tightens up.

Getting a decision with complex implications could frustrate members of a force who had conducted rapid planning and wanted to get the operation under way. Worse, it always seemed like one of these operations "popped" on a Friday night, when most of Washington had gone home for the weekend. I was in the middle of it, and we made good progress in working with both warriors and decisionmakers in compressing this decision cycle as much as possible. We encouraged the operators to forward plans as they were developing them instead of waiting to forward a perfect plan. This would enable earlier contemplation by senior leaders as well as allowing processes in the interagency and White House to keep up with the operational urgency.

The bin Laden raid set a precedent that, when possible, we would allow the video from a SOF operation with major implications to be viewed from the White House Situation Room. It was useful for the senior staff who would observe the operation to be prepared to faithfully discuss the unclassified results and build additional confidence in our forces. My implicit agreement with the White House was that no real-time guidance or other interference would be provided by any National Security Council staffers. Questions were acceptable, but once the operation was approved, it was in our hands. I always attended these sessions to help explain what was going on as well as to ensure the agreement was honored.

The rescue in January 2012 of an American citizen named Jessica Buchanan and her Danish colleague Poul Thisted, who were being held by Somali pirates in a small encampment deep in the bush, are a good example of this process in motion. Hours before the operation began, a group of special operators set up shop in a small room off the Situation Room hallway, with access to communications and chat rooms used by the force. With our SOF representatives providing whatever narrative they could extract from their communications systems, the operation commenced. Without revealing any tradecraft, a group of Navy SEALs arrived at a position just outside the camp from which they commenced the assault. Maddeningly, clouds moved in just as the assault began. The staffers in the room just off the main Situation Room monitored quietly, offering only an occasional question. We knew the battle was joined, but we were literally in the dark. The SEALs on the ground had better things to do while they were engaged in the most intense portion of their operation than to convey the situation on the ground in real time.

However, within a few minutes, we were informed that the two hostages were rescued with no casualties among the SEALs. Later we found out that in the last few yards before reaching the camp, the SEALs lost the element of surprise and a firefight broke out. One SEAL rushed in and covered Jessica with his body. The fight was over quickly, with all hostage-takers killed and both hostages safe.

Many other such operations occurred during my tenure, including captures of terrorist suspects, other hostage rescues, and several raids in Yemen and Syria that are by now public knowledge. Most were successful. I give the Obama administration credit for investing the time to learn how these operations are conducted and maintaining confidence in the force. And I give our remarkable special operators, with whom I forged a close bond, all the credit for performing so professionally.

One particularly vexing issue during my tenure was the continual push by some members of the Obama administration to accede to the Ottawa Convention banning antipersonnel land mines. This was the most poorly understood issue of my entire tenure. I was as sympathetic as anyone to the horrible effects these weapons can have on innocents if they are not properly designed and employed. However, several factors mitigated against U.S. accession to the convention in the near term. First, unlike almost any other country that still uses them, U.S. antipersonnel landmines are all designed to disable themselves after a fairly short period of time—days or weeks. Even our antivehicle mines have these features, while most other nations' mines do not. Moreover, timely deployment of these weapons is absolutely vital in several close-in combat scenarios, such as in South Korea, where our troops could be rapidly overwhelmed by a huge North Korean army.

There were passionate people on both sides of this argument. UN Ambassador Samantha Power and Undersecretary of State for Political Affairs Wendy Sherman made logical and heartfelt arguments for acceding. Some felt that if we did so it would encourage others to as well. But I couldn't see it. I often asked what specific diplomatic leverage such an accession would give us, but it was never forthcoming. People just felt accession was the right thing to do without really understanding it.

One of my frustrations during this entire process was how hard it was to get my colleagues in the military to focus on the issue. They were simply and viscerally opposed to accession. They seemed not to realize I couldn't just make the issue go away from my perch on the Deputies Committee. I had to bring logical alternatives (which would cost money) to the table.

President Obama listened closely to both sides. While he challenged the Department of Defense to explore other means of accomplishing what antipersonnel mines do, he gave us some breathing room. His heart told him to get rid of them all, but his head told him doing so could have severe negative impacts in places like Korea. I believe he had the best interests of our troops in mind, and he didn't want to deal with the issue before Congress. The articulation of his decision does highlight, though, the importance of clear communications. In the NSC meeting that considered the issue, he said he wanted to have in hand by the end of 2016 a plan that would allow for eventual accession. Others heard him say he wanted a plan for accession by the end of 2016. There is a big difference. It took several meetings to untangle the real guidance.

Yet another issue that blossomed during my tenure was how the nation responds to cyberattacks. I had grown familiar with many of the complexities of cybersecurity during my tenure at Northern Command and resisted my team's desire to "own it" in favor of deferring to the National Security Agency commanded by Keith Alexander, located at Fort Meade in Maryland. They were the real experts, not NORTHCOM. But my education in the complexities, emotions, and suspicions associated with the topic really began in my new job.

The gradients were all over the place. Inside the government, the Department of Homeland Security jealously protected what it felt was its prerogative to lead the cyber defense of the homeland, even though they lacked any capability to do it. The FBI felt it was a law enforcement prerogative. Some in the Department of Defense felt it belonged within the department as a national defense issue. Outside the government, many in the business world were rightly concerned over how the potential for intrusive government efforts to improve security could negatively affect their companies' reputations, finances, and even legal positions. Congress wanted a full-throated say in how cybersecurity was conducted. Good points were made on all sides of the issue, but nothing was getting done.

During this, and in the aftermath of the criminal leakage of highly classified NSA information from Edward Snowden, the issue arose of whether the director of the National Security Agency, historically a military officer, should be dual-hatted as the commander of the military's new U.S. Cyber Command. On the one hand, some worried about combining the intelligence and operational aspects of each billet under one person. Others worried about too much span of control diluting the effectiveness of both entities. And it sure felt like a raft of civilians was eyeing the potential to be the next NSA director if the commands were bisected.

On the other hand, it would be enormously costly to duplicate the vast infrastructure shared by NSA and Cyber Command. And it made sense for one person to have oversight of actions the nation was taking in the maturing domain of cyberspace.

However, nearly every spy agency and the National Security Council staff recommended to President Obama that he split the two entities. I give him credit for recognizing that the Snowden affair was not caused by the command setup and that it made sense, at least for the near future, to keep the two organizations consolidated.

During this period, I did manage to contribute to the government's understanding of how to respond to cyberattacks through a small group on the Joint Staff that worked directly for me. Neither the director of NSA nor the commander of Cyber Command had the authority to respond comprehensively to a dynamic in-progress cyberattack on a civilian, government, or even military target. While permission to conduct purely defensive actions was not required, there was no authority in place for a U.S. government entity to respond offensively to cut off an ongoing attack at its source, much less act to prevent future attacks. There wasn't even a clearly understood process for getting that permission.

With this in mind, I asked my team to produce a flow chart to outline a notional decision process, including where situations might arise that someone would need immediate authority to take action to defend the nation. There were many potential decision points on the chart. Was the attack ongoing? Could we attribute it? Did we have a response already on the shelf? How serious was the attack? These were only a few of the potential variables. The chart grew more complex as additional factors were brought to bear, such as State Department concerns over defensive actions that might need to happen via a server located in another nation. We dubbed our chart, which grew to a fairly impressive size, "the pony blanket" and began socializing it with senior leaders, like Ash Carter and his cyber guru, Eric Rosenbach.

The chart—which was reminiscent of my effort many years earlier to codify a Navy fighter tactic using a computer program—eventually made it to even higher levels. It had the effect of clarifying senior leadership's understanding of our limitations in cyberspace as well as the contours of the authorities that either needed be or, in fact, did not need to be granted to senior government officials, including within the Department of Defense.

There are so many other security situations we dealt with during my tenure that it would take a separate volume to describe them all. However, it is worth mentioning the attacks in Benghazi, which cost the lives of four brave Americans, including U.S. Ambassador J. Christopher Stevens.

I was in the bowels of the Pentagon in classified meetings the day of the attacks. Because General Dempsey and our Africa Command commander coincidentally happened to be in meetings with the secretary of defense when the reports popped in, there was no need to pull me out.

An enormous amount of politically motivated disinformation, opportunism, and conspiracy theories surrounding this event linger to this day. Our country's deep political divides naturally led to immediate suspicion, finger-pointing, and attempts to capitalize politically on the tragedy. The suggestions often made regarding what the military could have done that night are utterly unrealistic and reflect gross ignorance of our actual posture and capabilities.

Just try to get F-16s based in Aviano, Italy, armed and fueled; their pilots satisfactorily briefed; permission obtained from the Italian government; aerial refueling support set up in other countries; fly the jets several hours to unknown territory under the supervision of a different combatant commander, in the middle of the night, with no real-time knowledge of events on the ground—much less having no qualified attack controller present on the ground and unlit radio towers everywhere preventing low altitude flight—and you get the picture. Yet many people think we can get an F-16 to any part of the world in minutes.

What I do know is that we learned from the attacks, as we always do. Candidly, the Obama administration could have done a better job communicating what had actually happened to the public and to Congress in the aftermath. In the Department of Defense, we worked even more closely with the State Department to beef up security at our more vulnerable embassies (which would not have helped in Benghazi because the attack was not on an embassy).

Perhaps the most significant effect was that the episode gave a greater sense of urgency to get our diplomats out of a country before a situation goes south. To a senior diplomat, an evacuation feels like an admission of failure, even when it's not the diplomat's fault, and they tend to be reluctant to leave when they need to. This lesson helpfully led to more expedited evacuations in both Libya and Yemen in the wake of the Benghazi attack.

Finally, in a previous chapter I described my angst over how our nuclear command and control functioned at the time. This was both a technical and a procedural problem. For the former, I forged an important partnership with Frank Kendall. We initiated and co-chaired the Council on Oversight of the National Leadership C3 System to thoroughly examine the prevailing technology and put steps in place to tighten it up. For the latter, I assembled a team that worked hard with U.S. Strategic Command and the White House to put more realistic procedures in place. I firmly believed the president needed more capability options and worked to recommend a more flexible mix using the available survivable triad resources that I believe ultimately enhanced our deterrent capability.

I hope this chapter gives the reader insight into the real sausage-making regarding security and foreign policy, including which instruments of national power to use and when. It is usually far more complex on the inside than simplistic campaign rhetoric or the daily buzz coming from media talking heads focused on a single issue.

My participation in this process probably consumed 60 percent of my time and was the most interesting part of the job. I spent the lion's share of the remainder helping shape the department's approach to investment, which required operating within a completely different culture from that of the policy world.

TOP It was always a joy to testify before Congress, here with my longtime colleague Christine Fox. *Joint Staff photo*

BOTTOM On the investment side of the Defense Department, I was blessed to be able to work with people like (*from left of author*) Undersecretary for Policy Jim Miller, Secretary Leon Panetta, Deputy Secretary Ash Carter, Comptroller Bob Hale, and Director of Program Analysis and Evaluation Christine Fox. *Department of Defense photo*

Into the
Bureaucratic Wind

The Senate vote confirming me to serve as VCJCS occurred on the day in 2011 the U.S. Congress passed the Budget Control Act, or BCA. The act was a desperate move intended to force both political parties to compromise between entitlements and discretionary spending—mostly defense—in a manner that would support deficit reduction. The budget carnage that ensued lasted my entire four years as VCJCS and beyond.

Stepping into this world was a daunting blend of process and posturing governed by the department's special culture. As the vice, I worked together with the deputy secretary of defense—first Ash Carter and then Bob Work—atop a complex, three-legged stool of requirements, budgeting, and acquisition. This system is supposed to convert the resources provided by the American people into military capability (how technically good our stuff is), capacity (how much stuff we have), and readiness (how prepared that stuff is to go to war).

It goes without saying that some kind of strategic vision is helpful in informing such a massive department's investment decision-making. A host of documents, each born for a different reason, purport to do this. The National

Security Strategy, which is largely a political document published by the White House, attempts to provide the overarching vision. The Quadrennial Defense Review is required by Congress every four years and has evolved into a massive effort torn in all directions by the various constituencies in the department. The National Defense Strategy, National Military Strategy, the Chairman's Risk Assessment, and other documents provide periodic strategic insight and guidance.

I had some experience with these processes before I entered the building as VCJCS, notably as the Joint Staff J5 wrestling with how to draw coherency from the multiple documents, which were too long and tended to say much the same thing in different ways. Thereafter, as the NORTHCOM commander, I participated in the periodic meetings Defense Secretary Bob Gates would hold with the department's senior leaders. At the last meeting I attended prior to handing over NORTHCOM in the late spring of 2011, Gates challenged the department to come up with $400 billion in savings over a five-year period. The BCA, which demanded even deeper cuts to the department's projected budget, was passed not long after that in early August.

In looking for a fundamental lens through which to view these processes, I drew from my belief that much of strategy consists of balancing four variables: the global security environment, the nation's security ends (what it is trying to protect or advance), its ways (how it goes about doing it), and its means (how it invests in the required tools through borrowing or taxation).

If one of these variable changes, the others must adjust to maintain equilibrium. If not, our national security enters a dangerous disequilibrium. Unfortunately, the department and the services that compose it often lunge for more means instead of new ways as the answer to a deteriorating environment (which is exactly what is happening regarding our current approach to China and its aggressive actions in the western Pacific). And it has a hard time handling the kind of decrease in those means represented by the BCA.

That is where I found the department after my installment as VCJCS in August 2011. I immediately expressed concern that there was no midcycle strategic guidance to accompany the impending cuts to the defense budget. We needed such a document to get the military element of national security into a new, rational equilibrium. While not ideal, at least it would be an equilibrium, and we would not be living a lie.

Unfortunately, none of the normal documents that could have accomplished this were due for revision in the near term. Left on automatic, the department would do what it always does: find ways to cut from the services' least popular, most vulnerable, or least politically empowered programs. It would then complain about the results using ambiguous adjective values of risk, such as "high" or "significant" measured against existing operational plans. Congress is not normally privy to these plans, which make them perfect ground to defend.

This approach was unacceptable, as it would result in living a lie. I felt we needed to do something quickly to have a strategy informed by the looming budgetary changes before submitting the president's budget in January 2012. The department's senior leadership agreed, and we set off on our task.

What followed was a fairly refreshing departure from the normal routine. We did not assemble a large group to conduct an enormous, months-long study in which "critical non-concurs" would result in a delayed document that is all things to all people. Rather, we started with relatively senior people, primarily in the office of the Undersecretary of Defense for Policy (led by Michèle Flournoy), the Cost Assessment and Program Evaluation Office (led by my former colleague at Miramar Christine Fox), and the Joint Staff. We worked closely with then-deputy secretary Ash Carter. To be sure, there was some horse-trading regarding strategic concepts and language. I wanted the department to explicitly include Chairman Dempsey's and my prioritized national security interests. Unfortunately, the idea was either too hard for many to understand or it was too difficult to incorporate into a secretarial-level document because it originated within the military. Nonetheless, the collective leadership of the department rapidly came to closure on what was labeled the Defense Strategic Guidance, or DSG.

One of the key elements the DSG needed to consider was the long-held Department of Defense (DoD) "force sizing construct" of being prepared to fight two simultaneous "major combat operations," or MCOs. This construct had long been considered sacrosanct in the department because it was a real resource driver. It was not only something people believed we might have to do one day, it was also an intellectual mechanism for the services to justify maintaining their force structure. Our operational plans—the high-level "ways" of the strategic balance—supported by the force planning construct were hidden behind a curtain of classification. So it was possible to declare with little opposition whether two MCOs were executable with acceptable risk using the current force structure. If they were not, then it was a good argument for more means.

There is a lot of wishful thinking in this business. I felt we would be severely challenged to honestly tell the American people we could fight two large simultaneous wars. And, despite the fervent hopes of many of my colleagues, there was no relief money waiting on the horizon to bring capability, capacity, and readiness back to the requisite level to do so. Alone, the BCA cuts were manageable. However, a funding horizon of a couple of years and continuing resolutions caused by congressional inaction threw too much sand into the machinery. Moreover, congressional red lines, such as a refusal to cut wasteful base infrastructure and unneeded programs, only made matters worse.

At an important point during our deliberations in the fall of 2011, Ash Carter and I convened a meeting in which we were to be briefed on this topic. The briefers pointed out that, based on the BCA cuts, the standard two MCOs would have to be moved even further apart in time than they already were. Ash and I looked at each other, each thinking the same thing: this construct was fatally broken. We clearly needed to face a new reality. The enemy has a vote, and we would not always be able to time conflicts the way we wanted to. Continuing this charade would not only risk having the civilian leadership of the country execute diplomacy based on a false assumption—and thus put them in a potentially untenable situation. It could also distort the shape of the force, as the services might configure themselves to fight two large wars poorly rather than fight a different construct well. Carter and I each clearly stated our mutual concern. You could have heard a pin drop.

This discussion drove DoD to settle on a new construct. We called it the "force planning construct" rather than the "force sizing construct" because we wanted to emphasize not only capacity, meaning size, but capability and readiness as well. We would be able to fight one large "defeat" conflict and one smaller "deny objectives" conflict simultaneously. This essentially constituted a new set of operational "ends" in the ends-ways-means balance, although it was not described in those terms. President Obama reinforced this when he pointed out to the Joint Chiefs and combatant commanders, assembled in the Roosevelt Room at the White House, that it was on him to keep the United States out of two major wars simultaneously.

The DSG process reinforced in my mind that the best work is done by large minds in small groups rather than the reverse. It also confirmed that, while an organization's most important tactical-level innovations surface from below, in many cases the most effective strategic-level guidance must originate from experienced, risk-tolerant, courageous senior leaders. Both of these principles seem to have occurred in every effective organization I've known.

Not everyone was happy with the "defeat/deny" construct. The services would probably rather have stuck with two MCOs, as they were now in uncharted territory for defending their force structure. Congressional defense hawks, facing defections from budget hawks, accused the department of having a "budget-driven strategy." Although we were using the term "budget-informed strategy," clearly these members missed Bernard Brodie's reminder that "strategy wears a dollar sign." It would have been grossly irresponsible to produce a pipe-dream strategy in order to provide a demand signal for resources that clearly weren't coming. It's interesting to note that other nations understand this. For instance, the 2016 Australian Defence White Paper makes note that "we have been careful . . . to match our strategy and capability plans with appropriate resources. This is the first Defence White Paper to be fully costed."

Several intellectual efforts followed the DSG work. First came the Strategic Capabilities and Management Review, otherwise known as the SCMR, in the spring of 2012. This was another out-of-cycle effort that made the department uncomfortable, but it was accomplished in a more conventional manner than the DSG.

The second was the standard Quadrennial Defense Review, conducted after the 2012 election cycle during the spring, summer, and fall of 2013. With rare exception, and despite all the efforts of a great number of talented and hard-working people, it suffered from the normal Pentagon bureaucratic process. None of these efforts were endowed with a particularly well-constructed organizing construct. For example, the QDR listed the three pillars of "defend the homeland, build security globally, and prevail in combat," which seemed like one "end" and two "ways" rather than a meaningful balance among the key strategic variables.

The remainder of my tour was spent within the new construct, trying to apply the balanced ends, ways, and means model to a cumbersome investment process, in a world that was changing rapidly.

The words "complex" and "dynamic" are frequently—and aptly—used to describe this world. While we were preoccupied with two fruitless counter-insurgency wars in the Middle East and South Asia, our potential adversaries were busy recovering from their shock at the precision-guided weapons and stealth capabilities we demonstrated during the first Gulf War. They also closely watched the systems and tactics we evolved afterward, such as unmanned aerial vehicles, special operations forces capabilities, networked command and control, stealthy vehicles, and missile defense.

So, anxious to find ways to counter U.S. advantages, these potential adversaries began evolving their own capabilities. They emulated or stole our tactics and technologies to hasten the development of their own. They also searched for asymmetric capabilities designed to counter our key strengths. This included developing, among other things, GPS jamming to negate our precision-guided weapons, sophisticated antiaircraft and antiship missiles, large quantities of cheap theater ballistic missiles to overwhelm our expensive missile defenses, and antisatellite capability to disrupt our communications, intelligence, and precision navigation and timing.

They also placed many of their key assets within hard and deeply buried facilities. Finally, the emerging field of cyber warfare emerged as a high-leverage, difficult-to-attribute method for adversaries to attack us in areas on which our society and military depend far more deeply than they do.

Bundled together, these advances spawned a method of warfare that has variously been labeled "anti-access/area denial warfare," "hybrid warfare," and "gray zone warfare," in which adversaries capitalize on the capabilities they have developed while circumventing ours. Antagonists have done this since the beginning of warfare. In the modern version, Russia and China have significantly eroded the capability advantages we have traditionally used to offset the twin tyrannies of initiative and distance. Moreover, they have successfully pushed against the limits of U.S. willingness to use force, gaining ground in the process.

Carl von Clausewitz said that statesmen and commanders must consider "the kind of war on which they are embarking; neither mistaking it for, nor trying to turn it into, something that is alien to its nature." Our adversaries are changing the nature of warfare, yet we are trying to keep it the same. The military branches have their eyes wide open to these changes. But they approach the problem from a deeply parochial point of view, struggling to embrace anything other than incremental improvements in how they already intended to fight rather than finding disruptive ways to present our adversaries with new dilemmas. It is like a company seeing disruptive change looming but unable to muster the will to change in anticipation.

The deck is stacked against changing this approach due to what I would call the nonvirtuous flywheel. It begins with combatant commanders who must be able to "fight tonight" and build their operational plans based on the forces that are available or that they hope will be available. When they come up short, they seldom have the staff resources or imagination to envision new "strategic ways" to present our adversaries with new dilemmas, leading them to demand more and better means.

This is music to the services, which maintain the flywheel's momentum by focusing on the way they want to fight rather than how the adversary might choose to fight. They also approach the problem from a deeply parochial point of view, with their dominant warfighting communities maintaining deeply held beliefs in the concepts and capabilities with which they grew up. As such, they focus on "identity metrics," which are too often politicized but by which the health of their branch is judged. These metrics include numbers of ships, soldiers, Marines, and fighter squadrons. While it is true that "quantity has a quality all its own," it's not worth much if it's in the wrong place, not modernized, and not relevant to the fight of the day.

Congress is the next willing accomplice in maintaining the fly-wheel's momentum. Members desperately want to maintain existing programs—whether bases or industry—within their constituencies rather than opening the aperture to disruptive capabilities that will present our adversaries with new dilemmas. Finally, industry, which desires to maintain its franchises in the DoD budget, is the final force that keeps the flywheel spinning.

Aggravating this problem is the constant battle among capability, capacity, and readiness for scarce dollars. At the beginning of the budget process, leaders will tend to say they will never allow the force to "go hollow," meaning they will not sacrifice readiness for force structure and modernization. But when it comes time to jump off that cliff, these leaders realize that as hard as it is to recover readiness, recovering force structure is even harder. Once again, Congress is a willing accomplice: a member often cares less about whether the squadron that is based in his or her district is flying than the base and the squadron staying put.

As a result, we are at risk of falling into what former Facebook CEO Sheryl Sandberg has described as "the innovator's dilemma: a company gets big and stops moving and stops staying ahead." A similar sentiment comes from author Richard Pascale in *Surfing the Edge of Chaos*: "Equilibrium is the precursor to death." Biologists call this "genetic drift," in which an organism continually refines its winning evolutionary formula until an environmental or other change occurs that destroys the species in one fell swoop. We are perilously close to that one fell swoop.

This tendency is further amplified in times of financial stress, when companies are less willing to invest in research and development in order to save the bottom line. As former IBM CEO Sam Palmisano said, "You spend more time arguing amongst yourselves over a shrinking pie than looking to the future, so you miss the big turn."

The forum in which a "big turn" becomes most starkly apparent is the actual execution of a contingency plan in combat, but waiting for that moment to begin changing is exceedingly dangerous. Hints of missing the big turn sometimes appear in war games or exercises, but bias often creeps into these forums either in the design or reporting of the results. Or results are simply ignored, such as the many wargames in which U.S. forces have lost to China.

The U.S. Army suffers from this tendency regarding our concept for ground wars in Europe and Korea. Despite Russia's poor performance in Ukraine, existing NATO forces will be challenged to overcome that nation's advantages of singularity of command, expertise in hybrid warfare, proximity of the bulk of their forces to the fight, initiative in starting the fight, internal lines of communication, effective electronic warfare, highly effective massed artillery fires, and the world's most capable tactical air defense systems. Moreover, it will be difficult if not impossible to move enough U.S. ground forces, as currently configured, across the Atlantic—even if their equipment were not destroyed along the way—in time to avoid a Russian fait accompli among our Eastern allies. And no adversary—especially Russia—will again make the mistake Saddam Hussein made in allowing U.S. forces to fully build up before a war.

Thus, under the current operational construct, NATO would find itself either attempting to retake lost alliance territory or, possessing little conventional ability to impose costs on Russia, having to escalate quickly to the use of nuclear forces. Or both. Those who believe we possess enough conventional superiority to avoid a "no-first-use" policy regarding nuclear weapons are simply out of touch with this problem. Our NATO allies are unlikely to pick up the slack, but it is important that Europe survive against an authoritarian, rapacious Russian regime. Simply stated, we do not want to have to rescue Europe again.

The answer to this dilemma would seem to be stationing a lot of additional troops in Europe, but that is politically infeasible—Congress will no more permit that than it will another base closure round. Rather, it will require establishing and maintaining highly ready, large, and heavy equipment sets in the most likely theaters, along with highly trained personnel that can be moved quickly to fall in on them. This will require shrinking the Army in order to free the resources required to procure the equipment needed to preposition in Europe and Korea and maintain enough gear to also train the force that will rapidly move forward. But a smaller force is anathema to most Army leaders, who, like all the services, have their own identity metric. Yet this concept of a smaller, deployable force would be able to cycle through the Army's training centers more frequently and would be less provocative to those—particularly the paranoid Russians—we are trying to deter. And it would present a real dilemma for Moscow.

The Army is not alone: the U.S. Navy suffers from a similar conceptual problem regarding China, where the strategic environment has dramatically changed. It is now exponentially more hazardous to operate ships on the surface of the ocean. Just look at what happened to the Russian ship *Moskva* in the Black Sea in 2022. Low altitude, weaving, supersonic cruise missiles using jamming, and even antiship ballistic missiles are causing an increased amount of space on ships to be dedicated to defending these ships—if they can be defended at all. There still remain important roles for aircraft carriers and surface ships in other theaters, but these assets would be at grave risk in a conventional fight against China—they will have to stand off a long way in order to survive.

One way to rethink deterring China is to rethink its center of gravity which, as with any totalitarian government, is their leadership. It is about what they wake up in the morning and fear the most—namely, control of their people. In China that has historically been known as the "Mandate from Heaven." We see this fear every day in China's government's behavior. Targeting that center of gravity under a new strategy is a whole-of-government problem, with our military working in close concert with diplomatic, economic, and information warfare on a rich escalation ladder. Our response to Russian aggression in Ukraine is an instructive example if we will only see it for what it is. While that doesn't mean radical and immediate change for our Navy, it does mean change. It means things like nonlethal ways of stopping ships, dramatically enhanced information warfare (not just cyber warfare) that can influence Chinese society, and a twenty-first-century technical approach to offensive mine warfare.

Our most advanced mines are no more capable than those used in World War II, except some can be delivered more accurately using precision-guided capability. They still have primitive fusing devices and are only effective in shallow water. We should bring these mines into the twenty-first century using technology that would enable them to be positively controlled, be frequently updated, act as a sensor, use machine learning for acoustic discrimination, and be lethal in deeper water. The ability to selectively seal off Chinese naval assets or commercial shipping from leaving or entering port would be truly disruptive, presenting a new dilemma to Chinese ambitions in its neighborhood. Sadly, this capability has no constituency.

The third example of how exposure of operational plans can reveal interesting angles on the balance among capability, capacity, and readiness has to do with the never-ending struggle over force presence versus for surge. The presence advocates—including and especially the combatant commanders, who use forces every day—make the point that preventing wars is the best approach and that requires maximum forward presence. The surge advocates counter that if one expends every bit of force liquidity on presence, there will not be enough left to fight the war should it actually happen. Both sides have a strong case in this "chicken-and-egg" debate.

Harkening all the way back to my global naval force presence policy days, it seemed to me that we needed to shift our operating concept to something a bit more flexible. Early in my tenure as VCJCS, we rapidly wore out the force due to Central Command's demand for a two-carrier presence during an extended period when it appeared as though Israel might strike Iran's nuclear program. I felt we could be more thoughtful about moving these assets around the globe, particularly due to their high strategic mobility attributable to their nuclear propulsion plants. Perhaps we didn't need a carrier off the coast of Iran all the time, and perhaps having one present at random and unpredictable intervals would be enough to deter the worst malign Iranian behavior.

So I originated a concept called "dynamic presence," in which a carrier (and other forces) could swing between, say, Central Command and Pacific Command on an unpredictable basis. If Iran was conducting an exercise, the carrier might be there for the duration. A few weeks later, if our forces on the Korean peninsula conducted an exercise, the same carrier might suddenly appear there, moving between the Pacific Command and Central Command theaters. The whole thing would be unpredictable and would make the most use of our assets while keeping potential adversaries on their toes. It could also reduce the overall number of these units that were deployed, give the force breathing room to recover overall readiness, and eventually generate a better surge posture.

This idea was bitterly resisted by the combatant commanders, who viewed their force presence as an entitlement rather than a request (or what I called a "desirement") and did not want to give it up. I took quiet satisfaction when, four or five years later, Secretary of Defense Jim Mattis (a former combatant commander) demanded a similar concept.

Meanwhile, the system crunched along. There are many forums in which the investment triad's processes occur, including variants of all three owned by the individual services and other DoD components. For the overall department, the VCJCS leads the Joint requirements process through the Joint Requirements Oversight Council, or JROC. The undersecretary of defense for acquisition, technology, and logistics leads the acquisition process through a number of forums, including the Defense Acquisition Board. And the director for cost assessment and program evaluation leads the budgeting process. Although its name often changes with the incumbent, at the top of the process was a meeting known during my tenure as the Deputy's Management Action Group, or in an acronym-rich department, the DMAG.

On paper this was a good and necessary system for investing the nation's resources in military capability. But, for various reasons, it is nowadays mired in bias and bureaucracy. The culprits are service parochialism, the unbelievable growth in complexity of the platforms and weapons systems the military buys, the natural growth of the department's bureaucracy as the services geared up over the years for budget battles, and increasingly intrusive congressional oversight.

The DoD has embarked on several efforts in an attempt to speed the process up. I tried to streamline the requirements process by vastly downsizing Joint Requirements Oversight Council meetings (it is nearly impossible to make decisions in a room full of people), improving on the accelerated processes my predecessor started, drastically shrinking requirements documents (reducing most from over three hundred pages to less than twenty), and shortening timelines (including using the "silence" procedure I adopted from NATO to eliminate "sand-bagging"). We also supported several small groups in the department charged with producing disruptive change quickly, such as the Strategic Capabilities Office and a small group who worked directly for me on highly classified programs.

Deputy Secretary of Defense Bob Work and I believed the department was set in its ways and needed to embark on change, so we took on this system using a mechanism we labeled the "Third Offset." Bob deserves full credit for the name and the perspective he brought to articulating it. I don't know where he gained it, but Bob possessed an exceptionally keen sense of the department's history. It was useful in providing much-needed perspective to the department's efforts to balance ends, ways, and means. Particularly effective was his description of the previous technological offsets the department enjoyed. The first offset was a near-monopoly on nuclear weapons and the concept of using them to prevent the Soviet Union from overrunning Western Europe. That offset was lost with advances in Soviet nuclear weapons and doctrine. The second offset was the development of precision-guided weapons and other technologies such as stealth.

It was this second offset that so shocked the rest of the world, particularly the Russians and Chinese, when it was demonstrated in the two Gulf Wars. But even those advantages were eroding, as I mentioned, and it was clear to Bob and me that we needed to seek the next offset. This fit well inside the "ways" portion of my ends-ways-means point of view of the department's investments.

Offsets could happen one of two ways. Perhaps we would find some major technological breakthrough that was either so hard that only we could produce it or that we could keep so secret no other nation would know about it. Or—in a fast-paced and transparent world of technical advances propagated by the commercial sector, in which the market capitalization of an Apple or a Google is larger than all defense contractors combined—we could set up a rolling offset program with which an adversary would have a hard time keeping up. I felt the latter was more likely the case in a world in which the ability of our adversaries to recover from an exposed advantage on our part—such as unmanned aerial vehicles or precision-guided weapons—shrank to as little as three years.

As such, I tried to help drive the department in the direction of industries that are not burdened by DoD rules—in places such as Silicon Valley—that might be able to produce high-leverage advances on quick timelines. I was looking for highly agile payloads to put on existing or future platforms, including "small smart things." These might include new types of mine-like munitions that would allow friendly troops to pass through but would prove lethal to enemy troops, which would help assuage the Obama administration's angst over land mines. It might include a constellation of small, synthetic aperture radar-equipped satellites that, unlike electro-optical birds, would be able to provide rapid warning of an impending enemy missile launch in all types of weather and at night.

The little team I assembled on the Joint Staff was full of good ideas, many of which remained classified. I cannot name the experienced special operations officer I brought in to run the program, or the remarkable PhD in electrical and nuclear engineering who served as our technical expert. I can only say that the group did remarkable, rapid, take-no-prisoners work—always within the legalities of the system—to bring new capabilities to bear.

Several existing organizations, such as the Defense Advanced Research Projects Agency (or DARPA), the Air Force Rapid Capabilities Office, and the department's own Strategic Capabilities Office (then led by a bright fellow Georgia Tech alumnus named Will Roper) continued good work on out-of-the-box projects.

I also made it a point to meet Chris Darby, the director of the intelligence community's venture capital firm, known as In-Q-Tel. This organization provides seed money to startups that have something the intelligence community can use but that are also scalable to a larger commercial market. Being careful not to compete with In-Q-Tel, I encouraged Bob Work to create what is now known as the Defense Innovation Unit-Experimental, or DIUX, initially in Silicon Valley. I promised Darby that we would not compete with his group.

But the key to our future competitiveness will be in new ideas created by visionaries, which are then courageously accepted by service chiefs, Congress, and industry, even when those ideas threaten identity metrics and the dominance of established communities. It will not be easy. As military historian Liddell Hart, who fought at the Battle of the Somme in World War I, said, "The only thing harder than getting a new idea into the military mind is getting an old one out."

May the best ideas fostered by the boldest leaders win.

TOP The Washington Nationals have always been incredibly supportive of our wounded warriors, including sponsoring an amazing softball team. *Joint Staff photo*

BOTTOM The Country Current is a talented group of musicians who allowed me to show real Americana to distinguished foreign visitors. I wrote a song with their lead, Kenny Ray Horton (*second from right*). *Joint Staff photo*

It's about the People

T he most rewarding and frustrating pillar of my job as VCJCS centered on people. It was rewarding because of the opportunity to lead—and grow the potential of—the finest men and women this country has to offer. It was frustrating because a small minority didn't always bring credit to the institution. Unfortunately, I was quickly treated to a major component of the latter.

In the autumn of 2011, not long after I took the helm, it was clear that the military was not making adequate progress on the subject of sexual assault. I have long been an advocate for women in the military, including not only their professional advancement but also countering this pernicious crime. Well before survey results appeared that showed an unacceptable trend in unwanted sexual contact, I used my convening authority as VCJCS to bring together the vice chiefs of the services to generate ideas, share best and worst practices, and instill a greater sense of urgency in addressing this problem. We held several meetings, agreed to share information, and even brought a few members of Congress over to the Pentagon to discuss the problem. This was not window dressing: we really wanted to hear their concerns and ideas and share a few of our own. We all felt the same way about the young men and women in uniform that we did about our own kids.

In the spring of 2012 a semiannual report on sexual assault in the military was published. It calculated, based on surveys and extrapolation, that around 6 percent of women in the military experienced some form of unwanted sexual contact. While much lower than the rest of society, and including all forms of contact, I grimaced over the unfortunate fact that nearly everyone in Congress and the media interpreted this to mean that 6 percent were the victims of aggravated sexual assault or rape—which was not true. Nonetheless, the numbers were disturbing and unacceptable. We needed to do much better.

The chiefs were emotional about this in "the Tank." Far from wishing away this corrosive problem, they felt a solemn obligation to the young men and women in their care. Secretaries of Defense Leon Panetta and Chuck Hagel felt the same way. The entire department redoubled its efforts with a host of initiatives ranging from training to producing special advocates for victims to altering the way assault accusations were handled by the chain of command. This included over fifty initiatives that fundamentally changed how the department tackled this challenge. Through the concerted efforts of civilian and military leaders, including commanders holding their people account-able, DoD managed to decrease incidences of unwanted sexual contact from 6.4 percent in 2012 to 4.4 percent in 2014. That may not sound like much, but it is almost a one-third drop. The rate found on college campuses was far higher—as I recall it was around 20 percent. But even 4 percent is too high.

The White House, which was initially and understandably suspicious that we didn't "get it," eventually provided strong support for our efforts. We invited them over to attend any meeting they desired. Once we convinced them how serious we were and that we actually had several good ideas, they backed us. They even asked the superintendents of the service academies, who had grappled with this problem for years, to help with an underappreciated problem on other college campuses.

The military has always led the nation in attempting to resolve social issues—including, during my time in service, attacking racial discrimination, drug abuse, and sunsetting "Don't Ask, Don't Tell." Once we've instilled the right sense of urgency, we are effective to the point of leading society. For this reason, I strongly resisted removing authority from military commanders for prosecuting this crime. I was also concerned because it is so hard to prove many of these crimes beyond a shadow of a doubt, and commanders have the tool of nonjudicial punishment at their disposal, which has a lower standard of proof. We all want the same thing, and it remains to be seen whether removing commanders' authority, which occurred in 2021, will make a difference. I honestly hope so.

Another dimension of the people pillar of the VCJCS job was the need to ensure the best possible care for our wounded warriors. Thanks to remarkable advances made by the military medical community in battlefield stabilization and care, many more of our brave young men and women who would have otherwise been mortally wounded in combat come home alive than in any previous conflict. The spectrum of care, from immediate response on the battlefield to getting a patient to an in-theater trauma center within the "golden hour," to the remarkable team working in our hospital in Landstuhl, Germany, and finally to our stateside hospitals—was unbelievably good. But the grievous injuries these men and women experienced, both seen and unseen, were something the system never had to manage on such a scale.

Mary and I were introduced to the wounded warrior community while living in Colorado Springs, where the U.S. Olympic Training Center hosted the Warrior Games each year. This Paralympic-style event pitted teams of wounded, ill, and injured warriors from each service and the special operations community against each other in a variety of events under the belief that "ability overcomes disability." Led by wonderful Charlie Huebner from the U.S. Olympic Committee, the games were a key contributor to recovery for these young men and women.

The opening for us to get more involved in this continuum arose when we were invited to an Aleethia Foundation "Friday Night Dinner" (Aleethia means "truth" in Greek) at the Italian Embassy in Washington, DC. These dinners, held in venues across the Washington, DC, area, were organized by a great American named Hal Koster, a Vietnam veteran and former restaurant owner. For many of the young men or women who attended, it was the first time they ventured out of the hospital after being hurt, which was a far more daunting prospect for them than I previously realized.

The evening we attended was our first exposure to the idea. In a touching display of generosity and outreach, the Italian embassy and Finmeccanica Corporation brought an orchestra and opera singers down from New York, who put on a wonderful show. They followed this with a sumptuous presentation of Italian food. Afterward we were able to meet the wounded, ill, and injured warriors who were the event's purpose.

As we moved down a line of warriors and their families, we encountered a bright young woman named Jessica Allen, with her two kids and her husband, Charles, who lost both legs in an IED explosion. We asked how things were going, and she responded that the medical care was fantastic but that more could be done for families and caregivers. This piqued Mary's interest, and Jessica invited her to Walter Reed Medical Center to see for herself. Mary responded that if she paid a visit, there would be a group waiting for her at the curb when she arrived and she would probably only see all the good work being accomplished at the center, not where things might be improved. Jessica then offered to take Mary incognito, as her Aunt Mary.

Mary took her up on the offer. Although she was generally impressed, she immediately sensed a need for advocacy for these families and took up the cause. She also became widely known as "Aunt Mary." It wasn't about finding "gotchas" for Walter Reed. Instead, it was about recognizing that a lot was actually going right at Reed, but there were a number of quality-of-life improvements that could easily be made to support the trying circumstances experienced by these families.

One example appeared immediately when they encountered a young Marine's mother at his bedside. Once again, they asked how it was going, and the woman replied that it was going as well as possible given her son's serious wounds but that she had to quit her job as an attorney because the ward did not have Wi-Fi capability. She could have been working on briefs and other papers while watching over her son if Wi-Fi had been available. This was stunning—we would never even have considered something like this. The ward had Wi-Fi within a couple of weeks. Among the many times my position helped get something done, this sort of thing was the most rewarding.

It would take volumes to describe how Mary's network and the broad span of issues she touched grew over the time "we" were in the job of VCJCS. Because she accompanied me on the USO tours we took overseas, she got to see firsthand the critical care facilities in Afghanistan and Germany. In fact, she and our USO performers experienced six rocket attacks in one night at one of our bases in Afghanistan. She demonstrated a lot of poise and calm during this event, even laughing when the phrase "Find the POO" came crackling over the radio. "POO" means "point of origin," and in this case referred to the base's security forces' efforts to find the location from where the rockets were fired.

Mary quickly became involved in the White House's "Joining Forces" initiative, recognizing that advocacy from First Lady Michelle Obama and Second Lady Jill Biden would be incredibly useful in advancing the cause of these families. She sensed that Joining Forces was more than just political expediency for the administration—their hearts were in it, which was refreshing. Mary also got deeply involved with the USO for the Washington and Baltimore Metropolitan areas, with the Elizabeth Dole Foundation, as a member of the grant committee for the Newman's Own Foundation's effort to provide funds to grassroots organizations helping wounded warriors and their families, and as an ambassador for the Tragedy Assistance Program for Survivors, or TAPS. The latter organization was founded by a military widow named Bonnie Carroll and is dedicated to providing immediate and comprehensive assistance to military families who lose a loved one, regardless of cause.

But Mary had even more direct impact in specific instances with individual families. There are too many examples to mention here, including helping a severely injured warrior obtain a special stand-up wheelchair, which was generously provided by the U.S. Chamber of Commerce. Secretary Ash Carter called her out in his remarks at my retirement ceremony when he said, referring to a different family, "I was at the Warrior Games a few weeks ago, and a service member came up in a wheelchair with his wife, and his wife pointed to the wheelchair and said, 'We have that because of Mary Winnefeld.'"

And you know there is something special in your spouse's heart when she gets a frantic phone call at two o'clock in the morning from someone who is traveling and their severely injured husband has disappeared from his VA residential treatment facility, and your spouse immediately gets dressed and drives to the scene to help return him safely to the facility.

If nothing else, the military is a family business. Mary walked the talk, and I'm immensely proud of and grateful to her for it. She was the best example I'd seen of selflessly taking great care of our great people. As recognition for her efforts, she was asked to throw out the first pitch at a Cincinnati Reds home game and is the sponsor of a Navy ship, the littoral combat ship USS *Sioux City*. But her real reward is her private knowledge that she lived up to the spirit of giving inculcated into her by her parents.

One of the fascinating dimensions of the people pillar was the opportunity to learn how to lead members of the millennial generation. To begin with, even though I am not a millennial, I started by thinking back to what mattered to me—and what frustrated me—as a young officer on the Joint Staff. I could remember sitting at my computer, knowing that guidance had to pass downward through several layers before reaching me, and thinking, "if only I had five minutes with the boss to get guidance on this project, I wouldn't waste so much effort." I also knew that face time with the boss really mattered—in my case, not so much to suck up and hope for recognition but to learn how they thought. I was determined to account for these factors in my dealings with the millennials who now worked for me.

I was also increasingly aware of how this generation likes to live and work. These factors are fairly well known: they want to do something bigger than themselves, they care less for bureaucracy than any previous generation, they like working collaboratively, and they want to work for a boss who "gets" how they think. So I made a point of bringing them into my office when working on a particular issue and encouraging them to debate me. It was why my table was round, not rectangular. I was willing to pass products back and forth with them, with my "fingers on the keyboard," even going so far as to ask them if I messed up their work while trying to collaboratively improve it together. I think they appreciated the approach.

Millennials are also members of the "everybody gets a trophy" generation, so I felt it was important to walk around to thank them whenever I could. My deputy executive assistants were diligent in reminding me to get out and around, and it was one of the more fun parts of the job.

Speaking of people, one of the great things about serving as VCJCS was the opportunity to interact with a lot of accomplished people. I was privileged to lead USO tours to provide a little relief and entertainment to our troops overseas. In the process Mary and I got to know talented people like quarterbacks Peyton Manning and Andrew Luck, former major league pitchers Randy Johnson and Curt Schilling, coaches Chuck Pagano and Clyde Christensen of the Indianapolis Colts, American Idol contestants Ace Young and Diana DeGarmo, entertainers Anthony Anderson and Dennis Haysbert, 2015 Miss America Kira Kazantsev, and singer-songwriter Phillip Phillips. Each of these remarkable Americans was willing to give up a week in which they could otherwise be making money in favor of an exhausting but rewarding trip overseas and into the unknown on an uncomfortable military aircraft.

These people could be incredibly giving. In 2012 when the Colts played an exhibition game in Washington, I invited Clyde Christensen and Andrew Luck over for dinner and attended the next day with a severely wounded Marine. I'll never forget taking this young Marine, who was quiet and withdrawn due to his injuries, into the Colts' locker room after the game. Despite their rush to get back home, nearly every Colts player spent a couple of minutes with him as he sat in his wheelchair. They were genuinely interested in his situation. Their sobering realization that they are privileged to play a professional sport while young men and women make sacrifices for our nation shone through clearly. On the way home, the young man was ecstatic, and I really do think the event contributed to his recovery process.

We also developed a close relationship with the Washington Nationals baseball club, owned by the Lerner family. It was obvious to Mary and me shortly after we took the job that this special organization consistently bends over backward to reach out to our military members and their families. They host wounded warriors at each home game, provide a hundred free tickets to military kids at Sunday games, honor each military service one day per season, put on a wounded warrior celebrity softball game, support veterans hiring events, and conduct a host of other activities that cost them millions of dollars in potential revenue. Yes, you do well by doing good, but the Nationals consistently go above and beyond the call.

Indeed, the Nationals really stood up as an organization for our military family on September 16, 2013. That day an active shooter at the Washington Navy Yard—right next door to Nationals Park—took the lives of twelve people and wounded three. The team immediately canceled that day's game, opened the ballpark, and gave away the already-prepared concession food to the families who flocked to the area. They also set aside a special spot in the stadium for those who tragically lost a loved one. The next day the Nationals took their batting practice in Navy hats. A few months later, the club erected a memorial to the victims in their center field gate area.

We hosted a Fourth of July party each year for the Nationals players at our house on Fort Meyer, largely due to the fantastic support and friendship they gave the military. It was a chance to give back to a team that gave so much to our military.

One of the perks of being VCJCS I mentioned earlier was living in a great house with a superb supporting staff. I felt it important to use this staff not only to entertain dignitaries outside our own government but to also thank senior civilian government officials I particularly respected when they left their jobs. We did the latter at our own expense, but it was welcome recognition for people we respected and who were never exposed to the military's way of taking care of people when they depart a job.

We tried to make this process special by choosing a memorable vibe for each event. Often it was an old TV show with a catchy theme song. I would rewrite the lyrics and ask our favorite military combo, the Navy's Country Current to play the song in addition to providing their normal entertainment. "The Bob Hale Hillbillies" (for the then-serving DoD comptroller), "Millergan's Island" (for Jim Miller, then-undersecretary of defense for policy), and "Vickers Acres" (for Mike Vickers, then-undersecretary of defense for intelligence) were fitting sendoffs for several of our friends. When Deputy Secretary Ash Carter left with only one month's notice, he was treated to

"High Pentagon Drifter," after the Clint Eastwood character who readies a town to repel returning outlaws only to depart just before their arrival. When we hosted a dinner for the deputy directors of the intelligence agencies, we had the menu cards written backward and upside down, and provided a mirror at each seat so people could read them. It was a way to lighten up an otherwise tough business. We were particularly honored to host the farewell dinner for Secretary of Defense Leon Panetta. For him, we butchered "When the Moon Hits Your Eye" and provided a menu card with some of Panetta's Yogi Berra-esque quotes, such as, "Chaos can get a little out of hand sometimes."

Toward the end of my tour, a Navy musician named Kenny Ray Horton, who was one of the members of the Country Current, told me he wanted to write a song about my career, offering to bring over a six-pack and sit together on our front porch to make it happen (which I trust may be how a lot of country music gets written!). The last thing I would ever want is a song written about me, especially if it was written by me. But I was touched, so I offered to sit with him to write a song and quickly suggested we shift to writing something about our wounded warriors and their medical and family caregivers. It's named "You're My Angels" and takes someone who has been injured in combat through battlefield care, a field hospital, and a reunion with his spouse. Here's how it goes:

God-awful, hot, tired, dirty days
We prayed up, manned up, and got on our way
Drove through the gates of hell, into the unknown
I can't remember what happened to me
But I'll never forget what you did for me
It's a special kind of love that brought me home

I woke up and looked up, the lights were so bright
Unfamiliar faces in their own kind of fight
Pulling me back from the gates of hell, I was slipping away
But that determined look in those angels' eyes
Right then and there made me realize
It's a special kind of love that would bring me home

(Chorus) War is hell—But you're my angels
Sent to me—From God above
War is hell—But you're my angels
I never would have made it home without your love

You walked in, I saw you, the fear on your face
I was broken and battered and feeling disgraced
Wondering if you'd stay with me through your own kind of hell
One kiss from my angel, I knew I was blessed
You took the weight of the world off my chest
Your special kind of love would bring me home

The song may never win any country music awards, but the experience was more personally meaningful than I expected. I have to confess to being a bit emotional when the Country Current performed the song for me in the Pentagon during my last week on the job.

Living in Washington, DC, meant we were only an hour's drive away from Annapolis. I was honored to have been asked by the Naval Academy to review a couple of parades, including the Color Parade at the end of the year, when the honors for being the best company are passed on from the incumbent to the winner by the Color Honoree (who used to be known as the Color Girl during male-only times). My father, who was the Color Company commander in 1951, was able to attend. Sadly, my mom, who was 1951's Color Girl, was slowly succumbing to Alzheimer's disease. It was deeply touching to review the same parade where, so many years earlier, my dad and mom kissed under all the flags. The Color Company commander that year was a woman who chose her mom as the honoree. Her resemblance to my mom was striking, all the way down to the white dress and classy southern hat she wore.

Nowadays when I'm asked if I miss anything about being in the military, I always respond, "yes, the people," even though I'm involved with many other wonderful folks now that I've transitioned to civilian life. I was privileged to have served for thirty-seven years with the finest men and women our nation produces. I watched them put their cultural differences aside and work as a team—a good example for the jaundiced, politically angry elders in our society who are doing our country so much harm. I saw them at work on the flight decks of aircraft carriers, and in some of the most challenging combat conditions our troops have ever experienced. I saw them in boot camps and at the service academies, where these amazing young people begin their service to our country. I saw them overcoming grievous wounds with courage and determination. And, of course, I saw them at Arlington Cemetery, where so many of the best we have are laid to rest.

Yes, indeed, people really are everything.

TOP Handing my father's sword to my son James during my retirement ceremony. *Joint Staff photo*

BOTTOM My great-grandfather's Prussian cavalry sword being delivered by the caisson horse Klinger, for my son Jonathan. *Joint Staff photo*

Going Ashore

With about eight months left in my job as VCJCS, it was time to contemplate the next step on the journey. There was a history of vice chairmen moving up to serve as chairman of the Joint Chiefs, and the timing would have been good since my term was up only three months before Marty Dempsey's term. However, and despite Mary's support, I decided it wasn't right—even if I were to be asked—for several reasons.

On the personal side, I always felt as a junior officer that waking up in the morning and thinking about what I needed to do that day to be a flag officer would induce the wrong behaviors and take a lot of fun out of the job. I felt the same way about this from the moment I took the job as vice. I would be less effective if I woke up thinking about positioning myself as the next chairman. I was young enough to try something new and eager to get out and learn new things. And while they would never say so, my family had been through a lot, and Mary deserved a break.

On the congressional side, I had already been through three confirmation processes, among many other opportunities to testify before Congress. My

317

second hearing as vice was nothing more than an anvil on which to hammer the president, something that politically neutral senior military officers detest. While I was on good terms with a few congressional leaders, I could sense the increasingly toxic political process on Capitol Hill, and I wanted nothing to do with it.

On the executive branch side, I spent six years, both as the J5 and as the vice, attending meetings in the White House Sit Room. As much as I admired the people from two different administrations I worked with, I wasn't wild about spending four more years in that environment. Finally, on the military side, I was not sure how well the service chiefs would support my inclination to challenge how we need to prepare differently for future battlefields, particularly the need to pursue new strategic ways rather than simply demanding more and better means in order to counter ambitious China and angry Russia. Changing this culture would mean pushing a heavy rock up a steep hill. I had already pushed hard enough, and it was time for someone else to try.

Whenever such transitions loom, there are a variety of ways people gauge the willingness of potential candidates to take the job. Without going into any detail, I simply made it clear to a couple of the right people who asked me this question that I would stay if asked, but my preference was to retire, and there were several capable successors available to fill Dempsey's job.

As always, there was a lot going on behind the scenes. Long after I retired, at the end of October 2016, at the climax of that year's presidential election. campaign, a series of e-mails from the account of John Podesta, who was a counselor to President Obama and was now running Hillary Clinton's presidential campaign, were made public via WikiLeaks. Among them were e-mails between Podesta and Chris Kirchhoff, a civilian friend who worked in both the Pentagon and the White House. Kirchhoff apparently was asked to weigh in on the choice for the next chairman. He wrote that "Winnefeld is seen as the clearest thinker . . . [but] . . . is often too abrasive to military and civilian leaders." In a different e-mail, he wrote, "Winnefeld is a lucid thinker in a crisis whose grasp of the substance of military options would best serve you and the president in a true emergency." Finally, one of the e-mails indicated that National Security Advisor Susan Rice was apparently "not opposed to but also not particularly excited by" my potential choice.

None of this offended me in the least—it is part and parcel of the discussions that always occur when senior leader nominations are considered. If anything, Kirchhoff's comments were mildly flattering. The only thing puzzling was the part about being abrasive, so I searched my memory for when I might have given that impression, as I always tried to be collegial with my colleagues, including juniors, peers, and seniors. The only thing I could conclude is that sometimes during investment discussions in the Deputy's Management Action Group meetings, I felt it necessary to be blunt and realistic about what the services were trying to do with their budgets, including perpetuating concepts I felt were behind the times.

During this period—in the spring of 2015—I was honored to be asked to fly with President Obama on Air Force One down to Atlanta when he gave a speech to the student body at Georgia Tech—my alma mater—on the importance of affordable college education. I met the president at the White House, and we flew together in his helicopter to Andrews Air Force Base, where we walked on the tarmac to the light blue and white Boeing 747. I have to admit that it was as surreal as my interview in the Oval Office four years prior. I was worried my presence would be misinterpreted by the media—who often dramatically overestimate the ambition of senior military officers—that I was a front-runner in the chairman sweepstakes.

Once we were airborne Obama invited me into his office on the plane. We talked about the trip, and he asked how I felt. Perhaps I'm misinterpreting his intent, but I believe that, in the way only a skilled politician can, he was offering the opportunity to say I wanted to stay on. My reply made it clear that I had been honored to serve our country and I was OK with moving on. I was grateful for his skill and tact.

In the end, I was sincerely delighted when the president nominated Gen. Joseph Dunford, then commandant of the Marine Corps, to be Marty Dempsey's relief. Joe is a Boston native and a superb leader who was a fantastic chairman under the difficult circumstances of a presidential transition and the unique challenges of serving in the Trump administration.

So the Vice Squad ran through the finish line. As Washington, DC, summer days go, the afternoon of July 31, 2015, was mercifully cool and dry. I had not wanted a retirement ceremony in keeping with my long-standing desire to not have events focused on me. I was delighted that my changes of command departing USS *Enterprise*, the Roosevelt Carrier Strike Group, and NORTHCOM and NORAD were low key. But my staff and others convinced me that a retirement ceremony was important for my staff and my family. So I agreed to do the event, but it had to be consistent with my style. There was no way I was going to have a conventional ceremony in the drab and dusty auditorium in the bowels of the Pentagon where, lacking a better alternative, so many people go to say farewell. The thought of trooping down all those stairs for a pro forma ceremony was deeply depressing.

There were many options, but each was problematic in one way or another, and I wanted something symbolic that met the twin needs of being special but not ostentatious and that highlighted other people rather than myself. It didn't take long to settle on using the broad, grassy hill across the street from our quarters on Fort Myer. Named Whipple Field after a Union general who died at the Battle of Chancellorsville, it enjoyed a stunning view of Washington, DC. While we were taking a chance with the hot summer weather, it seemed appropriate to have the audience facing our nation's capital, symbolic of the nation and constitution our military swears to protect.

I was delighted my dad was there because we lost this man, who was such an inspiration to me and others for his service and integrity, only four months later. I was deeply honored that Secretary of Defense Ash Carter and Chairman of the Joint Chiefs of Staff Marty Dempsey agreed to speak. They did a terrific job. But I was particularly proud to have my older son, then-midshipman third class James A. "LJ" Winnefeld III as the final keynote speaker. To be sure, I viewed this as a training opportunity and gave him the option of opting out. But I'm glad he agreed because he absolutely knocked it out of the park—one of the proudest moments of my life.

When my turn at the podium arrived, I asked LJ to join me, and I passed him my Navy sword, which I inherited from his grandfather. I could almost sense the angst among the attendees—a collective unspoken groan expressing, "what about his other son?" As LJ went to take his seat, however, an Army cavalryman charged the hill from his position out of sight at the bottom of the hill. The timing was perfect. The horse stopped right next to the podium, and the cavalryman graciously handed down the Prussian cavalry sword carried by my great-grandfather, who had immigrated to the United States in 1896. I called Jonathan forward to accept it, and all was right with the world. He was beaming because as the younger son, he always felt like second fiddle, and to be taken seriously in this way meant a lot to him. Sadly, we lost this kind and beautiful young warrior against addiction to an overdose of fentanyl-laced heroin two years later during his first week of college.

Jonathan's sword was delivered by a very special horse named Klinger. Klinger is a caisson horse used to pull the caskets of our fallen servicemen and women to their final resting places in Arlington National Cemetery. A wonderful group known as TAPs, which I mentioned in the previous chapter, provides military families who have lost a loved one with care and support. Years before, they had created a children's book about Klinger who, as a colt in Kentucky, grew up wanting to be a racehorse but instead was called to perform his role at Arlington. What better way to transition into honoring many of the groups who, during Mary's and my tenure, had done so much to support our wounded warriors, their caregivers, and Gold Star families?

And of course, I saved the final moments of the ceremony that closed my military career to honor Mary herself, this wonderful woman with a heart of gold, who was my soulmate and companion during most of my career. She brought her Midwestern values into a foreign world and raised a military family. In the process, she unselfishly developed an extensive network that linked people who could make a difference for those who needed help. That is why I dedicate this book to her. I fervently hope that the last sound I hear before passing to the other side of life, whatever it has to offer, is her sweet and gentle voice.

As I look back on my career through the lens of the many places I've been, the many things I've seen, and the ways I've tried to make sense of it, it seems worthwhile to reflect for a moment on where we're headed as a society and as a nation.

This century's turbulence in global economics, health, and security leaves us facing a murky future. Democracy and the global operating system are under attack from both the outside and the inside. From the outside, the principal competitors who wish to take down this system are Russia and China. While we were preoccupied with the fool's errands of counterinsurgency and nation building, they developed new, full-spectrum ways of waging war with which we are having a hard time coping. The long-held concepts we would use to counter these potential aggressors will soon no longer work.

That's why I have so often written and spoken about how important it is for our military to challenge all its assumptions, develop new concepts, and partner those new concepts with new technologies. We cannot afford a "Kodak moment" in a rapidly changing world where our competitors are on the offensive.

But our system is also under attack from the inside from our increasingly toxic political culture. What began as a post–World War II distribution of American political opinion inside a centrally aligned bell curve gradually divided into two disparate humps on either side of neutral that began to accelerate apart due to the advent of politically aligned twenty-four-hour news media. Now, largely due to social media, we see those individual humps themselves fracturing into pairs, with humps on the far left, center left, center right, and far right. These divisions reached a new peak amid the 2016 and 2020 election campaigns and the insurrection in January 2021. To be sure, there has always been a certain level of partisan rancor in our nation. But the deepening level of anger and dysfunction of our political class are causing the world's long-held admiration for the United States to fade.

The humps on either extreme are growing, which is sapping our competitiveness to the point that our leadership of the post–World War II international order is at risk of failing. I like to use a metaphor that resonates with the title of this book, which takes me back to my teenage years, when I raced sailboats competitively with my friend Eric Zoehrer. We were pretty good, even as kids. Once, at an East Coast championship event for the International 470 class, we were leading the field by a mile, which does not often happen. Then we young fools got into a fight. A real fight. I have no idea to this day what it was about. After a while, one of us looked up and said "we'd better stop this, or everyone is going to catch us." We barely won. That is the situation we are in today as a nation. Would that our political leaders had the same wisdom as we teenagers.

So whenever someone urges me to consider running for some political office, I remember the crisp wisdom of Winston Churchill: "It is always dangerous for soldiers, sailors or airmen to play at politics. They enter a sphere in which values are quite different from those to which they have hitherto been accustomed." I cherish the freedom of thinking for myself rather than tuning my beliefs to what someone else says I must believe or that I must falsely express in order to be elected. It is so disappointing when an officer who has reached a high level in the military—but usually not high enough to experience the political class in full—mistakenly steps forward into that arena.

Nonetheless, it is encouraging that we Americans, to whom so much of the world looks for inspiration and leadership, are bathed in blessings every day—often without fully appreciating them—that will carry us through perilous times.

We have spectacular geography that is the envy of other nations. Unlike many other industrialized nations, our demographics are healthy due to immigration, as long as political populism doesn't do away with it. We enjoy a rich bounty of natural resources, including self-sufficiency in petroleum and some of the finest farmland on the planet. We run the world's highest-quality economy and benefit from an unsurpassed culture of creative entrepreneurship. Descended from those who risked it all to come to this country, our people are the most creative nation on the planet. We are thus the standard-bearers for a host of technologies and processes, such as the Internet, on which global commerce depends. And although it has its challenges, we have the best higher education system of any nation.

We enjoy a culture of the rule of law that many of us take for granted—one only has to live in a nation lacking it to understand how important it is. We have the strongest military on earth, at least for now, and the largest number of quality allies any nation has ever had. We are a resilient and self-correcting society—recall how quickly the nation turned away from McCarthyism in the 1950s. Last, but not least, is a widely recognized moral authority that we will retain as long as our leaders are wise in their use of our nation's instruments of power.

Nothing is ever as bad or as good as it seems. The real question for our nation is who are the guardians of our future against the shrill and divisive politics of the present? Absent an existential national crisis, will our political leaders ever overcome their impulse to put job security over national security? Will they work together on compromise solutions to our nation's problems? Will they withdraw into populism and isolationism, or will they view the United States as having a special role that sometimes puts global interests ahead of narrow national interests? Will they do what it takes to keep our nation strong in all ways—not merely through its military but through all the other elements of power in the face of ambitious and confident global competitors? Will they approach the world with principled strength, which is what our allies respect and our adversaries fear?

Our children's future depends on the answers to these questions.

Index

Note: page numbers in italics refer to figures.

About the Author

ADMIRAL SANDY WINNEFELD graduated from the Georgia Institute of Technology with a degree in aerospace engineering and served for thirty-seven years in the U.S. Navy. He instructed at the Navy Fighter Weapons School, also known as TopGun, and served as senior aide-de-camp to Gen. Colin L. Powell. He commanded a fighter squadron, the amphibious ship USS *Cleveland*, and the aircraft carrier USS *Enterprise*. As a flag officer, he commanded a carrier strike group, two NATO commands, the U.S. Sixth Fleet, U.S. Northern Command, and the North American Aerospace Defense Command. He retired after serving as the ninth vice chairman of the Joint Chiefs of Staff. Admiral Winnefeld is a frequently published author and a director or advisory board member for several companies operating in a broad spectrum of business sectors. He is a distinguished professor at the Sam Nunn School of International Affairs at Georgia Tech, where he is also a member of the Engineering Hall of Fame. He is also a Senior Non-resident Fellow at the Belfer Center for Science and International Affairs, John F. Kennedy School of Government, Harvard University.